YOUR MOST COMPREHENSIVE AND REVEALING INDIVIDUAL FORECAST

SUPER HOROSCOPE

LIBRA 2000

September 23 – October 22

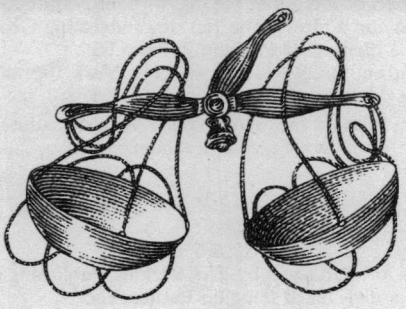

BERKLEY BOOKS, NEW YORK

The publishers regret that they cannot answer
individual letters requesting personal horoscope information.

2000 SUPER HOROSCOPE LIBRA

PRINTING HISTORY
Berkley Trade Edition / August 1999

All rights reserved.
Copyright © 1974, 1978, 1979, 1980, 1981, 1982
by Grosset & Dunlap, Inc.
Copyright © 1983, 1984 by Charter Communications, Inc.
Copyright © 1985, 1986, 1987, 1988, 1989, 1990, 1991, 1992, 1993, 1994, 1995,
1996, 1997, 1998, 1999
by The Berkley Publishing Group.
This book may not be reproduced in whole or in part, by
mimeograph or any other means, without permission.
For information address: The Berkley Publishing Group,
a division of Penguin Putnam Inc.,
375 Hudson Street, New York, New York 10014.

The Penguin Putnam Inc. World Wide Web site address is
http://www.penguinputnam.com

ISBN: 0-425-16884-0

BERKLEY®
Berkley Books are published by The Berkley Publishing Group,
a division of Penguin Putnam Inc.,
375 Hudson Street, New York, New York 10014.
"BERKLEY" and the "B" logo
are trademarks belonging to Penguin Putnam Inc.

PRINTED IN THE UNITED STATES OF AMERICA

10 9 8 7 6 5 4 3 2 1

CONTENTS

THE CUSP-BORN LIBRA	4
The Cusps of Libra	5
THE ASCENDANT: LIBRA RISING	6
Rising Signs for Libra	8
THE PLACE OF ASTROLOGY IN TODAY'S WORLD	10
Astrology and Relationships	10
The Challenge of Love	11
Astrology and Science	12
Know Thyself—Why?	14
WHAT IS A HOROSCOPE?	16
The Zodiac	16
The Sun Sign and the Cusp	17
The Rising Sign and the Zodiacal Houses	17
The Planets in the Houses	20
How To Use These Predictions	21
HISTORY OF ASTROLOGY	22
ASTROLOGICAL BRIDGE TO THE 21st CENTURY	28
THE SIGNS OF THE ZODIAC	31
Dominant Characteristics	31
Sun Sign Personalities	56
Key Words	58
The Elements and Qualities of the Signs	59
THE PLANETS OF THE SOLAR SYSTEM	67
The Planets and the Signs They Rule	67
Characteristics of the Planets	68
THE MOON IN EACH SIGN	78
MOON TABLES	85
Time Conversions	85
Moon Sign Dates for 2000	86
Moon Phases for 2000	90
Fishing Guide for 2000	90
Planting Guide for 2000	91
Moon's Influence Over Plants	91
Moon's Influence Over Health and Daily Affairs	92
LIBRA	93
Character Analysis	94
Love and Marriage	99
LIBRA LUCKY NUMBERS FOR 2000	128
LIBRA YEARLY FORECAST FOR 2000	129
LIBRA DAILY FORECAST FOR 2000	133
November and December Daily Forecasts for 1999	231

THE CUSP-BORN LIBRA

Are you *really* a Libra? If your birthday falls around the fourth week in September, at the very beginning of Libra, will you still retain the traits of Virgo, the sign of the Zodiac before Libra? And what if you were born late in October—are you more Scorpio than Libra? Many people born at the edge, or cusp, of a sign have great difficulty in determining exactly what sign they are. If you are one of these people, here's how you can figure it out, once and for all.

Consult the cusp table on the facing page, then locate the year of your birth. The table will tell you the precise days on which the Sun entered and left your sign for the year of your birth. In that way you can determine if you are a true Libra—or whether you are a Virgo or Scorpio—according to the variations in cusp dates from year to year (see also page 17).

If you were born at the beginning or end of Libra, yours is a lifetime reflecting a process of subtle transformation. Your life on Earth will symbolize a significant change in consciousness, for you are either about to enter a whole new way of living or are leaving one behind.

If you were born at the beginning of Libra, you may want to read the horoscope book for Virgo as well as Libra, for Virgo holds the keys to much of the complexity of your spirit. Virgo reflects certain hidden weaknesses, uncertainties, and your secret wishes. You are eager to get involved with another person, yet you are pulled back often from total involvement by your sense of propriety or your wish to be pure and unspoiled. You hover between poetic romanticism and stiff mental analyzing.

At best, your powers of criticism serve you to develop your potentials and enhance the life of your partner. In that way, you are helpful and loving, considerate and faithful—a pure marriage of mind and body, head and heart.

If you were born at the end of Libra, you may want to read the horoscope book for Scorpio as well as Libra. Scorpio dominates your finances, money, assets, potentials, and your values in general. Although your sexual expectancies can be naive, unrealistic, and even adolescent, you are passionate, excitable, and highly seductive.

You may vacillate between a desire to please another and a fanatical determination to maintain control and survive on your own. You can love with a fatal obsession, where you will blind your eyes to keep peace in a relationship—then suddenly declare war. Although you could prolong the agony of a situation in order to avoid a confrontation, you are the personification of awakening passion and a spirit that longs for the joys of companionship and the simple harmonies of life.

THE CUSPS OF LIBRA

DATES SUN ENTERS LIBRA (LEAVES VIRGO)

September 23 every year from 1900 to 2000, except for the following:

September 22				September 24
1948	1968	1981	1992	1903
52	72	84	93	07
56	76	85	96	
60	77	88	97	
64	80	89	2000	

DATES SUN LEAVES LIBRA (ENTERS SCORPIO)

October 23 every year from 1900 to 2000, except for the following:

October 22	October 24			
1992	1902	1911	1923	1943
96	03	14	27	47
2000	06	15	31	51
	07	18	35	55
	10	19	39	59

THE ASCENDANT: LIBRA RISING

Could you be a "double" Libra? That is, could you have Libra as your Rising sign as well as your Sun sign? The tables on pages 8–9 will tell you Libras what your Rising sign happens to be. Just find the hour of your birth, then find the day of your birth, and you will see which sign of the Zodiac is your Ascendant, as the Rising sign is called. The Ascendant is called that because it is the sign rising on the eastern horizon at the time of your birth. For a more detailed discussion of the Rising sign and the twelve houses of the Zodiac, see pages 17–20.

The Ascendant, or Rising sign, is placed on the 1st house in a horoscope, of which there are twelve houses. The 1st house represents your response to the environment—your unique response. Call it identity, personality, ego, self-image, facade, come-on, body-mind-spirit—whatever term best conveys to you the meaning of the you that acts and reacts in the world. It is a you that is always changing, discovering a new you. Your identity started with birth and early environment, over which you had little conscious control, and continues to experience, to adjust, to express itself. The 1st house also represents how others see you. Has anyone ever guessed your sign to be your Rising sign? People may respond to that personality, that facade, that body type governed by your Rising sign.

Your Ascendant, or Rising sign, modifies your basic Sun sign personality, and it affects the way you act out the daily predictions for your Sun sign. If your Rising sign indeed is Libra, what follows is a description of its effects on your horoscope. If your Rising sign is not Libra but some other sign of the Zodiac, you may wish to read the horoscope book for that sign as well.

With Libra on the Ascendant, Venus—the planet that rules Libra—is rising in your 1st house. Venus here gives you the kindest disposition, genial and likable, and an elegant bearing, always graceful with just a touch of showiness. Your mind is well disposed to learning all that is subtle and fine, artistic subjects in general, and your body is attuned to refined, symmetrical rhythms. You could unselfishly put yourself in the service of noble causes, or you could get carried away with a life of sensual pleasure. A vain pursuit of brilliant company or an endless search for the perfect lover could waste your talents.

Your need for partnership underscores most of your activities, not only your love experiences. You have a highly developed social consciousness which acts as a spur to other people. Your insistence on fairness and honesty maintains the standards of any group of which you are a member. You bring a well balanced sense of social values to bear on group activity. The group dynamic is reciprocal, as you benefit by being needed, feeling that people appreciate and admire you. Though satisfying, your social and cultural participation is not sufficient. You must find a love partner with whom you can share everyday living as well as more exalted purposes.

You are well adapted for a life in tandem with another person. Like the Scales, the zodiacal symbol of Libra, you need that sensitive presence of another to achieve balance, to come to rest, both sides of the scales poised in perfect agreement. Alone, you may at times be indecisive, even idle. Seeing all sides of a question and being loathe to choose one side may cause an inability to act. When partnered, you gain a sponsorship that frees you. You can then weigh matters, make decisions, exercise judgments. As arbiter, judge, lawyer, you have no peer.

You put your individual stamp of beauty and harmony on your environment. Style-conscious, with an eye for line, color, and movement, you express your artistic sensibilities in all your surroundings. A blend of loveliness and liveliness is what you seek. Sometimes you can be fickle, a faddist. You can bewilder your close circle by endless experimentation with what pleases you and feels right. This vacillation is equally true in your love life; you may exhaust a round of admirers before you choose to settle down.

More sensitive than most people to nuances, perhaps underneath the surface activity you sense something awry; you will shy away from any situation or suggestion of tastelessness and vulgarity. Ever seeking harmony, you may need to select and discard until you find the right blend. Through this selection process you never really lose your intensity. You are deeply imbued with the belief that you can and will find equilibrium; this belief constantly nourishes, renews your spirit. But you can lose other things, such as opportunities to utilize your talents or a chance to negotiate in a personal relationship.

The key words for you with Libra Rising are balance and harmony. You may need to settle for less than your idealized conceptions so that you can deeply experience, rather than merely visualize, what life and love have actually to offer.

RISING SIGNS FOR LIBRA

Hour of Birth*	Day of Birth		
	September 22–26	September 27–30	October 1–6
Midnight	Cancer	Cancer	Cancer
1 AM	Leo	Leo	Leo
2 AM	Leo	Leo	Leo
3 AM	Leo	Leo	Virgo
4 AM	Virgo	Virgo	Virgo
5 AM	Virgo	Virgo	Virgo
6 AM	Libra	Libra	Libra
7 AM	Libra	Libra	Libra
8 AM	Libra	Scorpio	Scorpio
9 AM	Scorpio	Scorpio	Scorpio
10 AM	Scorpio	Scorpio	Scorpio; Sagittarius 10/6
11 AM	Sagittarius	Sagittarius	Sagittarius
Noon	Sagittarius	Sagittarius	Sagittarius
1 PM	Sagittarius	Capricorn	Capricorn
2 PM	Capricorn	Capricorn	Capricorn
3 PM	Capricorn	Aquarius	Aquarius
4 PM	Aquarius	Aquarius	Aquarius; Pisces 10/3
5 PM	Pisces	Pisces	Pisces; Aries 10/6
6 PM	Aries	Aries	Aries
7 PM	Aries	Aries	Taurus
8 PM	Taurus	Taurus	Taurus; Gemini 10/2
9 PM	Gemini	Gemini	Gemini
10 PM	Gemini	Gemini	Gemini; Cancer 10/2
11 PM	Cancer	Cancer	Cancer

*Hour of birth given here is for Standard Time in any time zone. If your hour of birth was recorded in Daylight Saving Time, subtract one hour from it and consult that hour in the table above. For example, if you were born at 6 AM D.S.T., see 5 AM above.

YOUR RISING SIGN

Hour of Birth*	Day of Birth		
	October 7–12	October 13–18	October 19–24
Midnight	Leo	Leo	Leo
1 AM	Leo	Leo	Leo
2 AM	Leo	Leo; Virgo 10/15	Virgo
3 AM	Virgo	Virgo	Virgo
4 AM	Virgo	Virgo	Virgo; Libra 10/22
5 AM	Libra	Libra	Libra
6 AM	Libra	Libra	Libra
7 AM	Libra	Libra; Scorpio 10/15	Scorpio
8 AM	Scorpio	Scorpio	Scorpio
9 AM	Scorpio	Scorpio	Scorpio; Sagittarius 10/22
10 AM	Sagittarius	Sagittarius	Sagittarius
11 AM	Sagittarius	Sagittarius	Sagittarius
Noon	Sagittarius; Capricorn 10/11	Capricorn	Capricorn
1 PM	Capricorn	Capricorn	Capricorn
2 PM	Capricorn; Aquarius 10/11	Aquarius	Aquarius
3 PM	Aquarius	Aquarius; Pisces 10/17	Pisces
4 PM	Pisces	Pisces	Pisces; Aries 10/21
5 PM	Aries	Aries	Aries
6 PM	Aries; Taurus 10/10	Taurus	Taurus
7 PM	Taurus	Taurus; Gemini 10/18	Gemini
8 PM	Gemini	Gemini	Gemini
9 PM	Gemini	Gemini; Cancer 10/17	Cancer
10 PM	Cancer	Cancer	Cancer
11 PM	Cancer	Cancer	Cancer; Leo 10/22

*See note on facing page.

THE PLACE OF ASTROLOGY IN TODAY'S WORLD

Does astrology have a place in the fast-moving, ultra-scientific world we live in today? Can it be justified in a sophisticated society whose outriders are already preparing to step off the moon into the deep space of the planets themselves? Or is it just a hangover of ancient superstition, a psychological dummy for neurotics and dreamers of every historical age?

These are the kind of questions that any inquiring person can be expected to ask when they approach a subject like astrology which goes beyond, but never excludes, the materialistic side of life.

The simple, single answer is that astrology works. It works for many millions of people in the western world alone. In the United States there are 10 million followers and in Europe, an estimated 25 million. America has more than 4000 practicing astrologers, Europe nearly three times as many. Even down-under Australia has its hundreds of thousands of adherents. In the eastern countries, astrology has enormous followings, again, because it has been proved to work. In India, for example, brides and grooms for centuries have been chosen on the basis of their astrological compatibility.

Astrology today is more vital than ever before, more practicable because all over the world the media devotes much space and time to it, more valid because science itself is confirming the precepts of astrological knowledge with every new exciting step. The ordinary person who daily applies astrology intelligently does not have to wonder whether it is true nor believe in it blindly. He can see it working for himself. And, if he can use it—and this book is designed to help the reader to do just that—he can make living a far richer experience, and become a more developed personality and a better person.

Astrology and Relationships

Astrology is the science of relationships. It is not just a study of planetary influences on man and his environment. It is the study of man himself.

We are at the center of our personal universe, of all our relationships. And our happiness or sadness depends on how we act, how we relate to the people and things that surround us. The emotions that we generate have a distinct effect—for better or worse—on the world around us. Our friends and our enemies will confirm this. Just look in the mirror the next time you are angry. In other words, each of us is a kind of sun or planet or star radiating our feelings on the environment around us. Our influence on our personal universe, whether loving, helpful, or destructive, varies with our changing moods, expressed through our individual character.

Our personal "radiations" are potent in the way they affect our moods and our ability to control them. But we usually are able to throw off our emotion in some sort of action—we have a good cry, walk it off, or tell someone our troubles—before it can build up too far and make us physically ill. Astrology helps us to understand the universal forces working on us, and through this understanding, we can become more properly adjusted to our surroundings so that we find ourselves coping where others may flounder.

The Challenge of Love

The challenge of love lies in recognizing the difference between infatuation, emotion, sex, and, sometimes, the intentional deceit of the other person. Mankind, with its record of broken marriages, despair, and disillusionment, is obviously not very good at making these distinctions.

Can astrology help?

Yes. In the same way that advance knowledge can usually help in any human situation. And there is probably no situation as human, as poignant, as pathetic and universal, as the failure of man's love.

Love, of course, is not just between man and woman. It involves love of children, parents, home, and friends. But the big problems usually involve the choice of partner.

Astrology has established degrees of compatibility that exist between people born under the various signs of the Zodiac. Because people are individuals, there are numerous variations and modifications. So the astrologer, when approached on mate and marriage matters, makes allowances for them. But the fact remains that some groups of people are suited for each other and some are not, and astrology has expressed this in terms of characteristics we all can study and use as a personal guide.

No matter how much enjoyment and pleasure we find in the different aspects of each other's character, if it is not an overall compatibility, the chances of our finding fulfillment or enduring happiness in each other are pretty hopeless. And astrology can help us to find someone compatible.

Astrology and Science

Closely related to our emotions is the "other side" of our personal universe, our physical welfare. Our body, of course, is largely influenced by things around us over which we have very little control. The phone rings, we hear it. The train runs late. We snag our stocking or cut our face shaving. Our body is under a constant bombardment of events that influence our daily lives to varying degrees.

The question that arises from all this is, what makes each of us act so that we have to involve other people and keep the ball of activity and evolution rolling? This is the question that both science and astrology are involved with. The scientists have attacked it from different angles: anthropology, the study of human evolution as body, mind and response to environment; anatomy, the study of bodily structure; psychology, the science of the human mind; and so on. These studies have produced very impressive classifications and valuable information, but because the approach to the problem is fragmented, so is the result. They remain "branches" of science. Science generally studies effects. It keeps turning up wonderful answers but no lasting solutions. Astrology, on the other hand, approaches the question from the broader viewpoint. Astrology began its inquiry with the totality of human experience and saw it as an effect. It then looked to find the cause, or at least the prime movers, and during thousands of years of observation of man and his *universal* environment came up with the extraordinary principle of planetary influence—or astrology, which, from the Greek, means the science of the stars.

Modern science, as we shall see, has confirmed much of astrology's foundations—most of it unintentionally, some of it reluctantly, but still, indisputably.

It is not difficult to imagine that there must be a connection between outer space and Earth. Even today, scientists are not too sure how our Earth was created, but it is generally agreed that it is only a tiny part of the universe. And as a part of the universe, people on Earth see and feel the influence of heavenly bodies in almost every aspect of our existence. There is no doubt that the Sun has the greatest influence on life on this planet. Without it there would be no life, for without it there would be no warmth, no division into day and night, no cycles of time or season at all. This is clear and easy to see. The influence of the Moon, on the other hand, is more subtle, though no less definite.

There are many ways in which the influence of the Moon manifests itself here on Earth, both on human and animal life. It is a well-known fact, for instance, that the large movements of water on our planet—that is the ebb and flow of the tides—are caused by the Moon's gravitational pull. Since this is so, it follows that these water movements do not occur only in the oceans, but that all bodies of water are affected, even down to the tiniest puddle.

The human body, too, which consists of about 70 percent water, falls within the scope of this lunar influence. For example the menstrual cycle of most women corresponds to the 28-day lunar month; the period of pregnancy in humans is 273 days, or equal to nine lunar months. Similarly, many illnesses reach a crisis at the change of the Moon, and statistics in many countries have shown that the crime rate is highest at the time of the Full Moon. Even human sexual desire has been associated with the phases of the Moon. But it is in the movement of the tides that we get the clearest demonstration of planetary influence, which leads to the irresistible correspondence between the so-called metaphysical and the physical.

Tide tables are prepared years in advance by calculating the future positions of the Moon. Science has known for a long time that the Moon is the main cause of tidal action. But only in the last few years has it begun to realize the possible extent of this influence on mankind. To begin with, the ocean tides do not rise and fall as we might imagine from our personal observations of them. The Moon as it orbits around Earth sets up a circular wave of attraction which pulls the oceans of the world after it, broadly in an east to west direction. This influence is like a phantom wave crest, a loop of power stretching from pole to pole which passes over and around the Earth like an invisible shadow. It travels with equal effect across the land masses and, as scientists were recently amazed to observe, caused oysters placed in the dark in the middle of the United States where there is no sea to open their shells to receive the nonexistent tide. If the land-locked oysters react to this invisible signal, what effect does it have on us who not so long ago in evolutionary time came out of the sea and still have its salt in our blood and sweat?

Less well known is the fact that the Moon is also the primary force behind the circulation of blood in human beings and animals, and the movement of sap in trees and plants. Agriculturists have established that the Moon has a distinct influence on crops, which explains why for centuries people have planted according to Moon cycles. The habits of many animals, too, are directed by the movement of the Moon. Migratory birds, for instance, depart only at or near the time of the Full Moon. And certain sea creatures, eels in particular, move only in accordance with certain phases of the Moon.

Know Thyself—Why?

In today's fast-changing world, everyone still longs to know what the future holds. It is the one thing that everyone has in common: rich and poor, famous and infamous, all are deeply concerned about tomorrow.

But the key to the future, as every historian knows, lies in the past. This is as true of individual people as it is of nations. You cannot understand your future without first understanding your past, which is simply another way of saying that you must first of all know yourself.

The motto "know thyself" seems obvious enough nowadays, but it was originally put forward as the foundation of wisdom by the ancient Greek philosophers. It was then adopted by the "mystery religions" of the ancient Middle East, Greece, Rome, and is still used in all genuine schools of mind training or mystical discipline, both in those of the East, based on yoga, and those of the West. So it is universally accepted now, and has been through the ages.

But how do you go about discovering what sort of person you are? The first step is usually classification into some sort of system of types. Astrology did this long before the birth of Christ. Psychology has also done it. So has modern medicine, in its way.

One system classifies people according to the source of the impulses they respond to most readily: the muscles, leading to direct bodily action; the digestive organs, resulting in emotion; or the brain and nerves, giving rise to thinking. Another such system says that character is determined by the endocrine glands, and gives us such labels as "pituitary," "thyroid," and "hyperthyroid" types. These different systems are neither contradictory nor mutually exclusive. In fact, they are very often different ways of saying the same thing.

Very popular, useful classifications were devised by Carl Jung, the eminent disciple of Freud. Jung observed among the different faculties of the mind, four which have a predominant influence on character. These four faculties exist in all of us without exception, but not in perfect balance. So when we say, for instance, that someone is a "thinking type," it means that in any situation he or she tries to be rational. Emotion, which may be the opposite of thinking, will be his or her weakest function. This thinking type can be sensible and reasonable, or calculating and unsympathetic. The emotional type, on the other hand, can often be recognized by exaggerated language—everything is either marvelous or terrible—and in extreme cases they even invent dramas and quarrels out of nothing just to make life more interesting.

The other two faculties are intuition and physical sensation. The sensation type does not only care for food and drink, nice clothes and furniture; he or she is also interested in all forms of physical experience. Many scientists are sensation types as are athletes and nature-lovers. Like sensation, intuition is a form of perception and we all possess it. But it works through that part of the mind which is not under conscious control—consequently it sees meanings and connections which are not obvious to thought or emotion. Inventors and original thinkers are always intuitive, but so, too, are superstitious people who see meanings where none exist.

Thus, sensation tells us what is going on in the world, feeling (that is, emotion) tells us how important it is to ourselves, thinking enables us to interpret it and work out what we should do about it, and intuition tells us what it means to ourselves and others. All four faculties are essential, and all are present in every one of us. But some people are guided chiefly by one, others by another. In addition, Jung also observed a division of the human personality into the extrovert and the introvert, which cuts across these four types.

A disadvantage of all these systems of classification is that one cannot tell very easily where to place oneself. Some people are reluctant to admit that they act to please their emotions. So they deceive themselves for years by trying to belong to whichever type they think is the "best." Of course, there is no best; each has its faults and each has its good points.

The advantage of the signs of the Zodiac is that they simplify classification. Not only that, but your date of birth is personal—it is unarguably yours. What better way to know yourself than by going back as far as possible to the very moment of your birth? And this is precisely what your horoscope is all about, as we shall see in the next section.

WHAT IS A HOROSCOPE?

If you had been able to take a picture of the skies at the moment of your birth, that photograph would be your horoscope. Lacking such a snapshot, it is still possible to recreate the picture—and this is at the basis of the astrologer's art. In other words, your horoscope is a representation of the skies with the planets in the exact positions they occupied at the time you were born.

The year of birth tells an astrologer the positions of the distant, slow-moving planets Jupiter, Saturn, Uranus, Neptune, and Pluto. The month of birth indicates the Sun sign, or birth sign as it is commonly called, as well as indicating the positions of the rapidly moving planets Venus, Mercury, and Mars. The day and time of birth will locate the position of our Moon. And the moment—the exact hour and minute—of birth determines the houses through what is called the Ascendant, or Rising sign.

With this information the astrologer consults various tables to calculate the specific positions of the Sun, Moon, and other planets relative to your birthplace at the moment you were born. Then he or she locates them by means of the Zodiac.

The Zodiac

The Zodiac is a band of stars (constellations) in the skies, centered on the Sun's apparent path around the Earth, and is divided into twelve equal segments, or signs. What we are actually dividing up is the Earth's path around the Sun. But from our point of view here on Earth, it seems as if the Sun is making a great circle around our planet in the sky, so we say it is the Sun's apparent path. This twelvefold division, the Zodiac, is a reference system for the astrologer. At any given moment the planets—and in astrology both the Sun and Moon are considered to be planets—can all be located at a specific point along this path.

Now where in all this are you, the subject of the horoscope? Your character is largely determined by the sign the Sun is in. So that is where the astrologer looks first in your horoscope, at your Sun sign.

The Sun Sign and the Cusp

There are twelve signs in the Zodiac, and the Sun spends approximately one month in each sign. But because of the motion of the Earth around the Sun—the Sun's apparent motion—the dates when the Sun enters and leaves each sign may change from year to year. Some people born near the cusp, or edge, of a sign have difficulty determining which is their Sun sign. But in this book a Table of Cusps is provided for the years 1900 to 2000 (page 5) so you can find out what your true Sun sign is.

Here are the twelve signs of the Zodiac, their ancient zodiacal symbol, and the dates when the Sun enters and leaves each sign for the year 2000. Remember, these dates may change from year to year.

ARIES	Ram	March 20–April 19
TAURUS	Bull	April 19–May 20
GEMINI	Twins	May 20–June 20
CANCER	Crab	June 20–July 22
LEO	Lion	July 22–August 22
VIRGO	Virgin	August 22–September 22
LIBRA	Scales	September 22–October 22
SCORPIO	Scorpion	October 22–November 21
SAGITTARIUS	Archer	November 21–December 21
CAPRICORN	Sea Goat	December 21–January 20
AQUARIUS	Water Bearer	January 20–February 19
PISCES	Fish	February 19–March 20

It is possible to draw significant conclusions and make meaningful predictions based simply on the Sun sign of a person. There are many people who have been amazed at the accuracy of the description of their own character based only on the Sun sign. But an astrologer needs more information than just your Sun sign to interpret the photograph that is your horoscope.

The Rising Sign and the Zodiacal Houses

An astrologer needs the exact time and place of your birth in order to construct and interpret your horoscope. The illustration on the next page shows the flat chart, or natural wheel, an astrologer uses. Note the inner circle of the wheel labeled 1 through 12. These 12 divisions are known as the houses of the Zodiac.

18 / WHAT IS A HOROSCOPE?

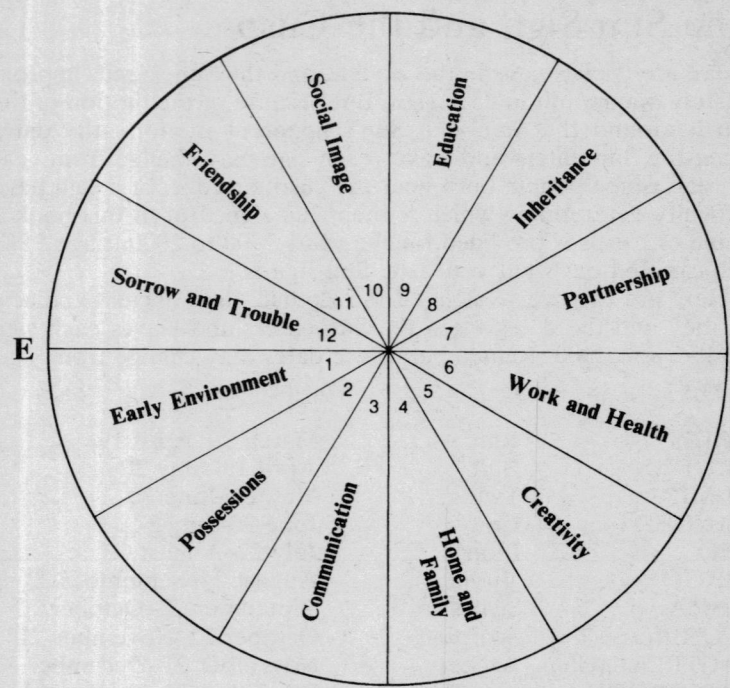

The 1st house always starts from the position marked E, which corresponds to the eastern horizon. The rest of the houses 2 through 12 follow around in a "counterclockwise" direction. The point where each house starts is known as a cusp, or edge.

The cusp, or edge, of the 1st house (point E) is where an astrologer would place your Rising sign, the Ascendant. And, as already noted, the exact time of your birth determines your Rising sign. Let's see how this works.

As the Earth rotates on its axis once every 24 hours, each one of the twelve signs of the Zodiac appears to be "rising" on the horizon, with a new one appearing about every 2 hours. Actually it is the turning of the Earth that exposes each sign to view, but in our astrological work we are discussing apparent motion. This Rising sign marks the Ascendant, and it colors the whole orientation of a horoscope. It indicates the sign governing the 1st house of the chart, and will thus determine which signs will govern all the other houses.

To visualize this idea, imagine two color wheels with twelve divisions superimposed upon each other. For just as the Zodiac is divided into twelve constellations that we identify as the signs, another twelvefold division is used to denote the houses. Now imagine one wheel (the signs) moving slowly while the other wheel (the houses) remains still. This analogy may help you see how the signs keep shifting the "color" of the houses as the Rising sign continues to change every two hours. To simplify things, a Table of Rising Signs has been provided (pages 8–9) for your specific Sun sign.

Once your Rising sign has been placed on the cusp of the 1st house, the signs that govern the rest of the 11 houses can be placed on the chart. In any individual's horoscope the signs do not necessarily correspond with the houses. For example, it could be that a sign covers part of two adjacent houses. It is the interpretation of such variations in an individual's horoscope that marks the professional astrologer.

But to gain a workable understanding of astrology, it is not necessary to go into great detail. In fact, we just need a description of the houses and their meanings, as is shown in the illustration above and in the table below.

THE 12 HOUSES OF THE ZODIAC

1st	Individuality, body appearance, general outlook on life	Personality house
2nd	Finance, possessions, ethical principles, gain or loss	Money house
3rd	Relatives, communication, short journeys, writing, education	Relatives house
4th	Family and home, parental ties, land and property, security	Home house
5th	Pleasure, children, creativity, entertainment, risk	Pleasure house
6th	Health, harvest, hygiene, work and service, employees	Health house
7th	Marriage and divorce, the law, partnerships and alliances	Marriage house
8th	Inheritance, secret deals, sex, death, regeneration	Inheritance house
9th	Travel, sports, study, philosophy and religion	Travel house
10th	Career, social standing, success and honor	Business house
11th	Friendship, social life, hopes and wishes	Friends house
12th	Troubles, illness, secret enemies, hidden agendas	Trouble house

The Planets in the Houses

An astrologer, knowing the exact time and place of your birth, will use tables of planetary motion in order to locate the planets in your horoscope chart. He or she will determine which planet or planets are in which sign and in which house. It is not uncommon, in an individual's horoscope, for there to be two or more planets in the same sign and in the same house.

The characteristics of the planets modify the influence of the Sun according to their natures and strengths.

Sun: Source of life. Basic temperament according to the Sun sign. The conscious will. Human potential.
Moon: Emotions. Moods. Customs. Habits. Changeable. Adaptive. Nurturing.
Mercury: Communication. Intellect. Reasoning power. Curiosity. Short travels.
Venus: Love. Delight. Charm. Harmony. Balance. Art. Beautiful possessions.
Mars: Energy. Initiative. War. Anger. Adventure. Courage. Daring. Impulse.
Jupiter: Luck. Optimism. Generous. Expansive. Opportunities. Protection.
Saturn: Pessimism. Privation. Obstacles. Delay. Hard work. Research. Lasting rewards after long struggle.
Uranus: Fashion. Electricity. Revolution. Independence. Freedom. Sudden changes. Modern science.
Neptune: Sensationalism. Theater. Dreams. Inspiration. Illusion. Deception.
Pluto: Creation and destruction. Total transformation. Lust for power. Strong obsessions.

Superimpose the characteristics of the planets on the functions of the house in which they appear. Express the result through the character of the Sun sign, and you will get the basic idea.

Of course, many other considerations have been taken into account in producing the carefully worked out predictions in this book: the aspects of the planets to each other; their strength according to position and sign; whether they are in a house of exaltation or decline; whether they are natural enemies or not; whether a planet occupies its own sign; the position of a planet in relation to its own house or sign; whether the sign is male or female; whether the sign is a fire, earth, water, or air sign. These are only a few of the colors on the astrologer's pallet which he or she must mix with the inspiration of the artist and the accuracy of the mathematician.

How To Use These Predictions

A person reading the predictions in this book should understand that they are produced from the daily position of the planets for a group of people and are not, of course, individually specialized. To get the full benefit of them our readers should relate the predictions to their own character and circumstances, coordinate them, and draw their own conclusions from them.

If you are a serious observer of your own life, you should find a definite pattern emerging that will be a helpful and reliable guide.

The point is that we always retain our free will. The stars indicate certain directional tendencies but we are not compelled to follow. We can do or not do, and wisdom must make the choice.

We all have our good and bad days. Sometimes they extend into cycles of weeks. It is therefore advisable to study daily predictions in a span ranging from the day before to several days ahead.

Daily predictions should be taken very generally. The word "difficult" does not necessarily indicate a whole day of obstruction or inconvenience. It is a warning to you to be cautious. Your caution will often see you around the difficulty before you are involved. This is the correct use of astrology.

In another section (pages 78–84), detailed information is given about the influence of the Moon as it passes through each of the twelve signs of the Zodiac. There are instructions on how to use the Moon Tables (pages 85–92), which provide Moon Sign Dates throughout the year as well as the Moon's role in health and daily affairs. This information should be used in conjunction with the daily forecasts to give a fuller picture of the astrological trends.

HISTORY OF ASTROLOGY

The origins of astrology have been lost far back in history, but we do know that reference is made to it as far back as the first written records of the human race. It is not hard to see why. Even in primitive times, people must have looked for an explanation for the various happenings in their lives. They must have wanted to know why people were different from one another. And in their search they turned to the regular movements of the Sun, Moon, and stars to see if they could provide an answer.

It is interesting to note that as soon as man learned to use his tools in any type of design, or his mind in any kind of calculation, he turned his attention to the heavens. Ancient cave dwellings reveal dim crescents and circles representative of the Sun and Moon, rulers of day and night. Mesopotamia and the civilization of Chaldea, in itself the foundation of those of Babylonia and Assyria, show a complete picture of astronomical observation and well-developed astrological interpretation.

Humanity has a natural instinct for order. The study of anthropology reveals that primitive people—even as far back as prehistoric times—were striving to achieve a certain order in their lives. They tried to organize the apparent chaos of the universe. They had the desire to attach meaning to things. This demand for order has persisted throughout the history of man. So that observing the regularity of the heavenly bodies made it logical that primitive peoples should turn heavenward in their search for an understanding of the world in which they found themselves so random and alone.

And they did find a significance in the movements of the stars. Shepherds tending their flocks, for instance, observed that when the cluster of stars now known as the constellation Aries was in sight, it was the time of fertility and they associated it with the Ram. And they noticed that the growth of plants and plant life corresponded with different phases of the Moon, so that certain times were favorable for the planting of crops, and other times were not. In this way, there grew up a tradition of seasons and causes connected with the passage of the Sun through the twelve signs of the Zodiac.

Astrology was valued so highly that the king was kept informed of the daily and monthly changes in the heavenly bodies, and the results of astrological studies regarding events of the future. Head astrologers were clearly men of great rank and position, and the office was said to be a hereditary one.

Omens were taken, not only from eclipses and conjunctions of the Moon or Sun with one of the planets, but also from storms and earthquakes. In the eastern civilizations, particularly, the reverence inspired by astrology appears to have remained unbroken since the very earliest days. In ancient China, astrology, astronomy, and religion went hand in hand. The astrologer, who was also an astronomer, was part of the official government service and had his own corner in the Imperial Palace. The duties of the Imperial astrologer, whose office was one of the most important in the land, were clearly defined, as this extract from early records shows:

> This exalted gentleman must concern himself with the stars in the heavens, keeping a record of the changes and movements of the Planets, the Sun and the Moon, in order to examine the movements of the terrestrial world with the object of prognosticating good and bad fortune. He divides the territories of the nine regions of the empire in accordance with their dependence on particular celestial bodies. All the fiefs and principalities are connected with the stars and from this their prosperity or misfortune should be ascertained. He makes prognostications according to the twelve years of the Jupiter cycle of good and evil of the terrestrial world. From the colors of the five kinds of clouds, he determines the coming of floods or droughts, abundance or famine. From the twelve winds, he draws conclusions about the state of harmony of heaven and earth, and takes note of good and bad signs that result from their accord or disaccord. In general, he concerns himself with five kinds of phenomena so as to warn the Emperor to come to the aid of the government and to allow for variations in the ceremonies according to their circumstances.

The Chinese were also keen observers of the fixed stars, giving them such unusual names as Ghost Vehicle, Sun of Imperial Concubine, Imperial Prince, Pivot of Heaven, Twinkling Brilliance, Weaving Girl. But, great astrologers though they may have been, the Chinese lacked one aspect of mathematics that the Greeks applied to astrology—deductive geometry. Deductive geometry was the basis of much classical astrology in and after the time of the Greeks, and this explains the different methods of prognostication used in the East and West.

Down through the ages the astrologer's art has depended, not so much on the uncovering of new facts, though this is important, as on the interpretation of the facts already known. This is the essence of the astrologer's skill.

But why should the signs of the Zodiac have any effect at all on the formation of human character? It is easy to see why people thought they did, and even now we constantly use astrological expressions in our everyday speech. The thoughts of "lucky star," "ill-fated," "star-crossed," "mooning around," are interwoven into the very structure of our language.

Wherever the concept of the Zodiac is understood and used, it could well appear to have an influence on the human character. Does this mean, then, that the human race, in whose civilization the idea of the twelve signs of the Zodiac has long been embedded, is divided into only twelve types? Can we honestly believe that it is really as simple as that? If so, there must be pretty wide ranges of variation within each type. And if, to explain the variation, we call in heredity and environment, experiences in early childhood, the thyroid and other glands, and also the four functions of the mind together with extroversion and introversion, then one begins to wonder if the original classification was worth making at all. No sensible person believes that his favorite system explains everything. But even so, he will not find the system much use at all if it does not even save him the trouble of bothering with the others.

In the same way, if we were to put every person under only one sign of the Zodiac, the system becomes too rigid and unlike life. Besides, it was never intended to be used like that. It may be convenient to have only twelve types, but we know that in practice there is every possible gradation between aggressiveness and timidity, or between conscientiousness and laziness. How, then, do we account for this?

A person born under any given Sun sign can be mainly influenced by one or two of the other signs that appear in their individual horoscope. For instance, famous persons born under the sign of Gemini include Henry VIII, whom nothing and no one could have induced to abdicate, and Edward VIII, who did just that. Obviously, then, the sign Gemini does not fully explain the complete character of either of them.

Again, under the opposite sign, Sagittarius, were both Stalin, who was totally consumed with the notion of power, and Charles V, who freely gave up an empire because he preferred to go into a monastery. And we find under Scorpio many uncompromising characters such as Luther, de Gaulle, Indira Gandhi, and Montgomery, but also Petain, a successful commander whose name later became synonymous with collaboration.

A single sign is therefore obviously inadequate to explain the differences between people; it can only explain resemblances, such as the combativeness of the Scorpio group, or the far-reaching devotion of Charles V and Stalin to their respective ideals—the Christian heaven and the Communist utopia.

But very few people have only one sign in their horoscope chart. In addition to the month of birth, the day and, even more, the hour to the nearest minute if possible, ought to be considered. Without this, it is impossible to have an actual horoscope, for the word horoscope literally means "a consideration of the hour."

The month of birth tells you only which sign of the Zodiac was occupied by the Sun. The day and hour tell you what sign was occupied by the Moon. And the minute tells you which sign was rising on the eastern horizon. This is called the Ascendant, and, as some astrologers believe, it is supposed to be the most important thing in the whole horoscope.

The Sun is said to signify one's heart, that is to say, one's deepest desires and inmost nature. This is quite different from the Moon, which signifies one's superficial way of behaving. When the ancient Romans referred to the Emperor Augustus as a Capricorn, they meant that he had the Moon in Capricorn. Or, to take another example, a modern astrologer would call Disraeli a Scorpion because he had Scorpio Rising, but most people would call him Sagittarius because he had the Sun there. The Romans would have called him Leo because his Moon was in Leo.

So if one does not seem to fit one's birth month, it is always worthwhile reading the other signs, for one may have been born at a time when any of them were rising or occupied by the Moon. It also seems to be the case that the influence of the Sun develops as life goes on, so that the month of birth is easier to guess in people over the age of forty. The young are supposed to be influenced mainly by their Ascendant, the Rising sign, which characterizes the body and physical personality as a whole.

It is nonsense to assume that all people born at a certain time will exhibit the same characteristics, or that they will even behave in the same manner. It is quite obvious that, from the very moment of its birth, a child is subject to the effects of its environment, and that this in turn will influence its character and heritage to a decisive extent. Also to be taken into account are education and economic conditions, which play a very important part in the formation of one's character as well.

People have, in general, certain character traits and qualities which, according to their environment, develop in either a positive or a negative manner. Therefore, selfishness (inherent selfishness, that is) might emerge as unselfishness; kindness and consideration as cruelty and lack of consideration toward others. In the same way, a naturally constructive person may, through frustration, become destructive, and so on. The latent characteristics with which people are born can, therefore, through environment and good or bad training, become something that would appear to be its opposite, and so give the lie to the astrologer's description of their character. But this is not the case. The true character is still there, but it is buried deep beneath these external superficialities.

Careful study of the character traits of various signs of the Zodiac are of immeasurable help, and can render beneficial service to the intelligent person. Undoubtedly, the reader will already have discovered that, while he is able to get on very well with some people, he just "cannot stand" others. The causes sometimes seem inexplicable. At times there is intense dislike, at other times immediate sympathy. And there is, too, the phenomenon of love at first sight, which is also apparently inexplicable. People appear to be either sympathetic or unsympathetic toward each other for no apparent reason.

Now if we look at this in the light of the Zodiac, we find that people born under different signs are either compatible or incompatible with each other. In other words, there are good and bad interrelating factors among the various signs. This does not, of course, mean that humanity can be divided into groups of hostile camps. It would be quite wrong to be hostile or indifferent toward people who happen to be born under an incompatible sign. There is no reason why everybody should not, or cannot, learn to control and adjust their feelings and actions, especially after they are aware of the positive qualities of other people by studying their character analyses, among other things.

Every person born under a certain sign has both positive and negative qualities, which are developed more or less according to our free will. Nobody is entirely good or entirely bad, and it is up to each of us to learn to control ourselves on the one hand and at the same time to endeavor to learn about ourselves and others.

It cannot be emphasized often enough that it is free will that determines whether we will make really good use of our talents and abilities. Using our free will, we can either overcome our failings or allow them to rule us. Our free will enables us to exert sufficient willpower to control our failings so that they do not harm ourselves or others.

Astrology can reveal our inclinations and tendencies. Astrology can tell us about ourselves so that we are able to use our free will to overcome our shortcomings. In this way astrology helps us do our best to become needed and valuable members of society as well as helpmates to our family and our friends. Astrology also can save us a great deal of unhappiness and remorse.

Yet it may seem absurd that an ancient philosophy could be a prop to modern men and women. But below the materialistic surface of modern life, there are hidden streams of feeling and thought. Symbology is reappearing as a study worthy of the scholar; the psychosomatic factor in illness has passed from the writings of the crank to those of the specialist; spiritual healing in all its forms is no longer a pious hope but an accepted phenomenon. And it is into this context that we consider astrology, in the sense that it is an analysis of human types.

Astrology and medicine had a long journey together, and only parted company a couple of centuries ago. There still remain in medical language such astrological terms as "saturnine," "choleric," and "mercurial," used in the diagnosis of physical tendencies. The herbalist, for long the handyman of the medical profession, has been dominated by astrology since the days of the Greeks. Certain herbs traditionally respond to certain planetary influences, and diseases must therefore be treated to ensure harmony between the medicine and the disease.

But the stars are expected to foretell and not only to diagnose.

Astrological forecasting has been remarkably accurate, but often it is wide of the mark. The brave person who cares to predict world events takes dangerous chances. Individual forecasting is less clear cut; it can be a help or a disillusionment. Then we come to the nagging question: if it is possible to foreknow, is it right to foretell? This is a point of ethics on which it is hard to pronounce judgment. The doctor faces the same dilemma if he finds that symptoms of a mortal disease are present in his patient and that he can only prognosticate a steady decline. How much to tell an individual in a crisis is a problem that has perplexed many distinguished scholars. Honest and conscientious astrologers in this modern world, where so many people are seeking guidance, face the same problem.

Five hundred years ago it was customary to call in a learned man who was an astrologer who was probably also a doctor and a philosopher. By his knowledge of astrology, his study of planetary influences, he felt himself qualified to guide those in distress. The world has moved forward at a fantastic rate since then, and yet people are still uncertain of themselves. At first sight it seems fantastic in the light of modern thinking that they turn to the most ancient of all studies, and get someone to calculate a horoscope for them. But is it *really* so fantastic if you take a second look? For astrology is concerned with tomorrow, with survival. And in a world such as ours, tomorrow and survival are the keywords for the twenty-first century.

ASTROLOGICAL BRIDGE TO THE 21st CENTURY

As the last decade of the twentieth century comes to a close, planetary aspects for its final years connect you with the future. Major changes completed in 1995 and 1996 give rise to new planetary cycles that form the bridge to the twenty-first century and new horizons. The years 1996 through 1999 and into the year 2000 reveal hidden paths and personal hints for achieving your potential, for making the most of your message from the planets.

All the major planets begin new cycles in the late 1990s. Jupiter, planet of good fortune, transits four zodiacal signs from 1996 through 1999 and goes through a complete cycle in each of the elements earth, air, fire, and water. Jupiter is in Capricorn, then in Aquarius, next in Pisces, and finally in Aries as the century turns. With the dawning of the twenty-first century, each new yearly Jupiter cycle follows the natural progression of the Zodiac, from Aries in 2000, then Taurus in 2001, next Gemini in 2002, and so on through Pisces in 2011. The beneficent planet Jupiter promotes your professional and educational goals while urging informed choice and deliberation. Jupiter sharpens your focus and hones your skills. And while safeguarding good luck, Jupiter can turn unusual risks into achievable aims.

Saturn, planet of reason and responsibility, has begun a new cycle in the spring of 1996 when it entered fiery Aries. Saturn in Aries through March 1999 heightens a longing for independence. Your movements are freed from everyday restrictions, allowing you to travel, to explore, to act on a variety of choices. With Saturn in Aries you get set to blaze a new trail. Saturn enters earthy Taurus in March 1999 for a three-year stay over the turn of the century into the year 2002. Saturn in Taurus inspires industry and affection. Practicality, perseverance, and planning can reverse setbacks and minimize risk. Saturn in Taurus lends beauty, order, and structure to your life. In order to take advantage of opportunity through responsibility, to persevere against adversity, look to beautiful planet Saturn.

Uranus, planet of innovation and surprise, started an important new cycle in January of 1996. At that time Uranus entered its natural home in airy Aquarius. Uranus in Aquarius into the year 2003 has a profound effect on your personality and the lens through which you see the world. A basic change in the way you project yourself is just one impact of Uranus in Aquarius. More significantly, a whole new consciousness is evolving. Winds of change blowing your way emphasize movement and freedom. Uranus in Aquarius poses involvement in the larger community beyond self, family, friends, lovers, associates. Radical ideas and progressive thought signal a journey of liberation. As the century turns, follow Uranus on the path of humanitarianism. While you carve a prestigious niche in public life, while you preach social reform and justice, you will be striving to make the world a better place for all people.

Neptune, planet of vision and mystery, is in earthy Capricorn until late 1998. Neptune in Capricorn excites creativity while restraining fanciful thinking. Wise use of resources helps you build persona and prestige. Then Neptune enters airy Aquarius during November 1998 and is there into the year 2011. Neptune in Aquarius, the sign of the Water Bearer, represents two sides of the coin of wisdom: inspiration and reason. Here Neptune stirs powerful currents bearing a rich and varied harvest, the fertile breeding ground for idealistic aims and practical considerations. Neptune's fine intuition tunes in to your dreams, your imagination, your spirituality. You can never turn your back on the mysteries of life. Uranus and Neptune, the planets of enlightenment and renewed idealism both in the sign of Aquarius, give you glimpses into the future, letting you peek through secret doorways into the twenty-first century.

Pluto, planet of beginnings and endings, has completed one cycle of growth November 1995 in the sign of Scorpio. Pluto in Scorpio marked a long period of experimentation and rejuvenation. Then Pluto entered the fiery sign of Sagittarius on November 10, 1995 and is there into the year 2007. Pluto in Sagittarius during its long stay of twelve years can create significant change. The great power of Pluto in Sagittarius may already be starting its transformation of your character and lifestyle. Pluto in Sagittarius takes you on a new journey of exploration and learning. The awakening you experience on intellectual and artistic levels heralds a new cycle of growth. Uncompromising Pluto, seeker of truth, challenges your identity, persona, and self-expression. Uncovering the real you, Pluto holds the key to understanding and meaningful communication. Pluto in Sagittarius can be the guiding light illuminating the first decade of the twenty-first century. Good luck is riding on the waves of change.

THE SIGNS OF THE ZODIAC

Dominant Characteristics

Aries: March 21–April 20

The Positive Side of Aries

The Aries has many positive points to his character. People born under this first sign of the Zodiac are often quite strong and enthusiastic. On the whole, they are forward-looking people who are not easily discouraged by temporary setbacks. They know what they want out of life and they go out after it. Their personalities are strong. Others are usually quite impressed by the Ram's way of doing things. Quite often they are sources of inspiration for others traveling the same route. Aries men and women have a special zest for life that can be contagious; for others, they are a fine example of how life should be lived.

The Aries person usually has a quick and active mind. He is imaginative and inventive. He enjoys keeping busy and active. He generally gets along well with all kinds of people. He is interested in mankind, as a whole. He likes to be challenged. Some would say he thrives on opposition, for it is when he is set against that he often does his best. Getting over or around obstacles is a challenge he generally enjoys. All in all, Aries is quite positive and young-thinking. He likes to keep abreast of new things that are happening in the world. Aries are often fond of speed. They like things to be done quickly, and this sometimes aggravates their slower colleagues and associates.

The Aries man or woman always seems to remain young. Their whole approach to life is youthful and optimistic. They never say die, no matter what the odds. They may have an occasional setback, but it is not long before they are back on their feet again.

The Negative Side of Aries

Everybody has his less positive qualities—and Aries is no exception. Sometimes the Aries man or woman is not very tactful in communicating with others; in his hurry to get things done he is apt to be a little callous or inconsiderate. Sensitive people are likely to find him somewhat sharp-tongued in some situations. Often in his eagerness to get the show on the road, he misses the mark altogether and cannot achieve his aims.

At times Aries can be too impulsive. He can occasionally be stubborn and refuse to listen to reason. If things do not move quickly enough to suit the Aries man or woman, he or she is apt to become rather nervous or irritable. The uncultivated Aries is not unfamiliar with moments of doubt and fear. He is capable of being destructive if he does not get his way. He can overcome some of his emotional problems by steadily trying to express himself as he really is, but this requires effort.

Taurus: April 21–May 20

The Positive Side of Taurus

The Taurus person is known for his ability to concentrate and for his tenacity. These are perhaps his strongest qualities. The Taurus man or woman generally has very little trouble in getting along with others; it's his nature to be helpful toward people in need. He can always be depended on by his friends, especially those in trouble.

Taurus generally achieves what he wants through his ability to persevere. He never leaves anything unfinished but works on something until it has been completed. People can usually take him at his word; he is honest and forthright in most of his dealings. The Taurus person has a good chance to make a success of his life because of his many positive qualities. The Taurus who aims high seldom falls short of his mark. He learns well by experience. He is thorough and does not believe in shortcuts of any kind. The Bull's thoroughness pays off in the end, for through his deliberateness he learns how to rely on himself and what he has learned. The Taurus person tries to get along with others, as a rule. He is not overly critical and likes people to be themselves. He is a tolerant person and enjoys peace and harmony—especially in his home life.

Taurus is usually cautious in all that he does. He is not a person who believes in taking unnecessary risks. Before adopting any one line of action, he will weigh all of the pros and cons. The Taurus person is steadfast. Once his mind is made up it seldom changes. The person born under this sign usually is a good family person—reliable and loving.

The Negative Side of Taurus

Sometimes the Taurus man or woman is a bit too stubborn. He won't listen to other points of view if his mind is set on something. To others, this can be quite annoying. Taurus also does not like to be told what to do. He becomes rather angry if others think him not too bright. He does not like to be told he is wrong, even when he is. He dislikes being contradicted.

Some people who are born under this sign are very suspicious of others—even of those persons close to them. They find it difficult to trust people fully. They are often afraid of being deceived or taken advantage of. The Bull often finds it difficult to forget or forgive. His love of material things sometimes makes him rather avaricious and petty.

Gemini: May 21–June 20

The Positive Side of Gemini

The person born under this sign of the Heavenly Twins is usually quite bright and quick-witted. Some of them are capable of doing many different things. The Gemini person very often has many different interests. He keeps an open mind and is always anxious to learn new things.

Gemini is often an analytical person. He is a person who enjoys making use of his intellect. He is governed more by his mind than by his emotions. He is a person who is not confined to one view; he can often understand both sides to a problem or question. He knows how to reason, how to make rapid decisions if need be.

He is an adaptable person and can make himself at home almost anywhere. There are all kinds of situations he can adapt to. He is a person who seldom doubts himself; he is sure of his talents and his ability to think and reason. Gemini is generally most satisfied

when he is in a situation where he can make use of his intellect. Never short of imagination, he often has strong talents for invention. He is rather a modern person when it comes to life; Gemini almost always moves along with the times—perhaps that is why he remains so youthful throughout most of his life.

Literature and art appeal to the person born under this sign. Creativity in almost any form will interest and intrigue the Gemini man or woman.

The Gemini is often quite charming. A good talker, he often is the center of attraction at any gathering. People find it easy to like a person born under this sign because he can appear easy-going and usually has a good sense of humor.

The Negative Side of Gemini

Sometimes the Gemini person tries to do too many things at one time—and as a result, winds up finishing nothing. Some Twins are easily distracted and find it rather difficult to concentrate on one thing for too long a time. Sometimes they give in to trifling fancies and find it rather boring to become too serious about any one thing. Some of them are never dependable, no matter what they promise.

Although the Gemini man or woman often appears to be well-versed on many subjects, this is sometimes just a veneer. His knowledge may be only superficial, but because he speaks so well he gives people the impression of erudition. Some Geminis are sharp-tongued and inconsiderate; they think only of themselves and their own pleasure.

Cancer: June 21–July 20

The Positive Side of Cancer

The Moon Child's most positive point is his understanding nature. On the whole, he is a loving and sympathetic person. He would never go out of his way to hurt anyone. The Cancer man or woman is often very kind and tender; they give what they can to others. They hate to see others suffering and will do what they can to help someone in less fortunate circumstances than themselves. They are often very concerned about the world. Their interest in people generally goes beyond that of just their own families and close friends; they have a deep sense of community and respect humanitarian values. The Moon Child means what he says, as a rule; he is honest about his feelings.

The Cancer man or woman is a person who knows the art of patience. When something seems difficult, he is willing to wait until the situation becomes manageable again. He is a person who knows how to bide his time. Cancer knows how to concentrate on one thing at a time. When he has made his mind up he generally sticks with what he does, seeing it through to the end.

Cancer is a person who loves his home. He enjoys being surrounded by familiar things and the people he loves. Of all the signs, Cancer is the most maternal. Even the men born under this sign often have a motherly or protective quality about them. They like to take care of people in their family—to see that they are well loved and well provided for. They are usually loyal and faithful. Family ties mean a lot to the Cancer man or woman. Parents and in-laws are respected and loved. Young Cancer responds very well to adults who show faith in him. The Moon Child has a strong sense of tradition. He is very sensitive to the moods of others.

The Negative Side of Cancer

Sometimes Cancer finds it rather hard to face life. It becomes too much for him. He can be a little timid and retiring, when things don't go too well. When unfortunate things happen, he is apt to just shrug and say, "Whatever will be will be." He can be fatalistic to a fault. The uncultivated Cancer is a bit lazy. He doesn't have very much ambition. Anything that seems a bit difficult he'll gladly leave to others. He may be lacking in initiative. Too sensitive, when he feels he's been injured, he'll crawl back into his shell and nurse his imaginary wounds. The immature Moon Child often is given to crying when the smallest thing goes wrong.

Some Cancers find it difficult to enjoy themselves in environments outside their homes. They make heavy demands on others, and need to be constantly reassured that they are loved. Lacking such reassurance, they may resort to sulking in silence.

Leo: July 21–August 21

The Positive Side of Leo

Often Leos make good leaders. They seem to be good organizers and administrators. Usually they are quite popular with others. Whatever group it is that they belong to, the Leo man or woman is almost sure to be or become the leader. Loyalty, one of the Lion's noblest traits, enables him or her to maintain this leadership position.

Leo is generous most of the time. It is his best characteristic. He or she likes to give gifts and presents. In making others happy, the Leo person becomes happy himself. He likes to splurge when spending money on others. In some instances it may seem that the Lion's generosity knows no boundaries. A hospitable person, the Leo man or woman is very fond of welcoming people to his house and entertaining them. He is never short of company.

Leo has plenty of energy and drive. He enjoys working toward some specific goal. When he applies himself correctly, he gets what he wants most often. The Leo person is almost never unsure of himself. He has plenty of confidence and aplomb. He is a person who is direct in almost everything he does. He has a quick mind and can make a decision in a very short time.

He usually sets a good example for others because of his ambitious manner and positive ways. He knows how to stick to something once he's started. Although Leo may be good at making a joke, he is not superficial or glib. He is a loving person, kind and thoughtful.

There is generally nothing small or petty about the Leo man or woman. He does what he can for those who are deserving. He is a person others can rely upon at all times. He means what he says. An honest person, generally speaking, he is a friend who is valued and sought out.

The Negative Side of Leo

Leo, however, does have his faults. At times, he can be just a bit too arrogant. He thinks that no one deserves a leadership position except him. Only he is capable of doing things well. His opinion of himself is often much too high. Because of his conceit, he is

sometimes rather unpopular with a good many people. Some Leos are too materialistic; they can only think in terms of money and profit.

Some Leos enjoy lording it over others—at home or at their place of business. What is more, they feel they have the right to. Egocentric to an impossible degree, this sort of Leo cares little about how others think or feel. He can be rude and cutting.

Virgo: August 22–September 22

The Positive Side of Virgo

The person born under the sign of Virgo is generally a busy person. He knows how to arrange and organize things. He is a good planner. Above all, he is practical and is not afraid of hard work.

Often called the sign of the Harvester, Virgo knows how to attain what he desires. He sticks with something until it is finished. He never shirks his duties, and can always be depended upon. The Virgo person can be thoroughly trusted at all times.

The man or woman born under this sign tries to do everything to perfection. He doesn't believe in doing anything halfway. He always aims for the top. He is the sort of a person who is always learning and constantly striving to better himself—not because he wants more money or glory, but because it gives him a feeling of accomplishment.

The Virgo man or woman is a very observant person. He is sensitive to how others feel, and can see things below the surface of a situation. He usually puts this talent to constructive use.

It is not difficult for the Virgo to be open and earnest. He believes in putting his cards on the table. He is never secretive or underhanded. He's as good as his word. The Virgo person is generally plainspoken and down to earth. He has no trouble in expressing himself.

The Virgo person likes to keep up to date on new developments in his particular field. Well-informed, generally, he sometimes has a keen interest in the arts or literature. What he knows, he knows well. His ability to use his critical faculties is well-developed and sometimes startles others because of its accuracy.

Virgos adhere to a moderate way of life; they avoid excesses. Virgo is a responsible person and enjoys being of service.

The Negative Side of Virgo

Sometimes a Virgo person is too critical. He thinks that only he can do something the way it should be done. Whatever anyone else does is inferior. He can be rather annoying in the way he quibbles over insignificant details. In telling others how things should be done, he can be rather tactless and mean.

Some Virgos seem rather emotionless and cool. They feel emotional involvement is beneath them. They are sometimes too tidy, too neat. With money they can be rather miserly. Some Virgos try to force their opinions and ideas on others.

Libra: September 23–October 22

The Positive Side of Libra

Libras love harmony. It is one of their most outstanding character traits. They are interested in achieving balance; they admire beauty and grace in things as well as in people. Generally speaking, they are kind and considerate people. Libras are usually very sympathetic. They go out of their way not to hurt another person's feelings. They are outgoing and do what they can to help those in need.

People born under the sign of Libra almost always make good friends. They are loyal and amiable. They enjoy the company of others. Many of them are rather moderate in their views; they believe in keeping an open mind, however, and weighing both sides of an issue fairly before making a decision.

Alert and intelligent, Libra, often known as the Lawgiver, is always fair-minded and tries to put himself in the position of the other person. They are against injustice; quite often they take up for the underdog. In most of their social dealings, they try to be tactful and kind. They dislike discord and bickering, and most Libras strive for peace and harmony in all their relationships.

The Libra man or woman has a keen sense of beauty. They appreciate handsome furnishings and clothes. Many of them are artistically inclined. Their taste is usually impeccable. They know how to use color. Their homes are almost always attractively arranged and inviting. They enjoy entertaining people and see to it that their guests always feel at home and welcome.

Libra gets along with almost everyone. He is well-liked and socially much in demand.

The Negative Side of Libra

Some people born under this sign tend to be rather insincere. So eager are they to achieve harmony in all relationships that they will even go so far as to lie. Many of them are escapists. They find facing the truth an ordeal and prefer living in a world of make-believe.

In a serious argument, some Libras give in rather easily even when they know they are right. Arguing, even about something they believe in, is too unsettling for some of them.

Libras sometimes care too much for material things. They enjoy possessions and luxuries. Some are vain and tend to be jealous.

Scorpio: October 23–November 22

The Positive Side of Scorpio

The Scorpio man or woman generally knows what he or she wants out of life. He is a determined person. He sees something through to the end. Scorpio is quite sincere, and seldom says anything he doesn't mean. When he sets a goal for himself he tries to go about achieving it in a very direct way.

The Scorpion is brave and courageous. They are not afraid of hard work. Obstacles do not frighten them. They forge ahead until they achieve what they set out for. The Scorpio man or woman has a strong will.

Although Scorpio may seem rather fixed and determined, inside he is often quite tender and loving. He can care very much for others. He believes in sincerity in all relationships. His feelings about someone tend to last; they are profound and not superficial.

The Scorpio person is someone who adheres to his principles no matter what happens. He will not be deterred from a path he believes to be right.

Because of his many positive strengths, the Scorpion can often achieve happiness for himself and for those that he loves.

He is a constructive person by nature. He often has a deep understanding of people and of life, in general. He is perceptive and unafraid. Obstacles often seem to spur him on. He is a positive person who enjoys winning. He has many strengths and resources; challenge of any sort often brings out the best in him.

The Negative Side of Scorpio

The Scorpio person is sometimes hypersensitive. Often he imagines injury when there is none. He feels that others do not bother to recognize him for his true worth. Sometimes he is given to excessive boasting in order to compensate for what he feels is neglect.

Scorpio can be proud, arrogant, and competitive. They can be sly when they put their minds to it and they enjoy outwitting persons or institutions noted for their cleverness.

Their tactics for getting what they want are sometimes devious and ruthless. They don't care too much about what others may think. If they feel others have done them an injustice, they will do their best to seek revenge. The Scorpion often has a sudden, violent temper; and this person's interest in sex is sometimes quite unbalanced or excessive.

Sagittarius: November 23–December 20

The Positive Side of Sagittarius

People born under this sign are honest and forthright. Their approach to life is earnest and open. Sagittarius is often quite adult in his way of seeing things. They are broad-minded and tolerant people. When dealing with others the person born under the sign of the Archer is almost always open and forthright. He doesn't believe in deceit or pretension. His standards are high. People who associate with Sagittarius generally admire and respect his tolerant viewpoint.

The Archer trusts others easily and expects them to trust him. He is never suspicious or envious and almost always thinks well of others. People always enjoy his company because he is so friendly and easygoing. The Sagittarius man or woman is often good-humored. He can always be depended upon by his friends, family, and co-workers.

The person born under this sign of the Zodiac likes a good joke every now and then. Sagittarius is eager for fun and laughs, which makes him very popular with others.

A lively person, he enjoys sports and outdoor life. The Archer is fond of animals. Intelligent and interesting, he can begin an

animated conversation with ease. He likes exchanging ideas and discussing various views.

He is not selfish or proud. If someone proposes an idea or plan that is better than his, he will immediately adopt it. Imaginative yet practical, he knows how to put ideas into practice.

The Archer enjoys sport and games, and it doesn't matter if he wins or loses. He is a forgiving person, and never sulks over something that has not worked out in his favor.

He is seldom critical, and is almost always generous.

The Negative Side of Sagittarius

Some Sagittarius are restless. They take foolish risks and seldom learn from the mistakes they make. They don't have heads for money and are often mismanaging their finances. Some of them devote much of their time to gambling.

Some are too outspoken and tactless, always putting their feet in their mouths. They hurt others carelessly by being honest at the wrong time. Sometimes they make promises which they don't keep. They don't stick close enough to their plans and go from one failure to another. They are undisciplined and waste a lot of energy.

Capricorn: December 21–January 19

The Positive Side of Capricorn

The person born under the sign of Capricorn, known variously as the Mountain Goat or Sea Goat, is usually very stable and patient. He sticks to whatever tasks he has and sees them through. He can always be relied upon and he is not averse to work.

An honest person, Capricorn is generally serious about whatever he does. He does not take his duties lightly. He is a practical person and believes in keeping his feet on the ground.

Quite often the person born under this sign is ambitious and knows how to get what he wants out of life. The Goat forges ahead and never gives up his goal. When he is determined about something, he almost always wins. He is a good worker—a hard worker. Although things may not come easy to him, he will not complain, but continue working until his chores are finished.

He is usually good at business matters and knows the value of money. He is not a spendthrift and knows how to put something away for a rainy day; he dislikes waste and unnecessary loss.

Capricorn knows how to make use of his self-control. He can apply himself to almost anything once he puts his mind to it. His ability to concentrate sometimes astounds others. He is diligent and does well when involved in detail work.

The Capricorn man or woman is charitable, generally speaking, and will do what is possible to help others less fortunate. As a friend, he is loyal and trustworthy. He never shirks his duties or responsibilities. He is self-reliant and never expects too much of the other fellow. He does what he can on his own. If someone does him a good turn, then he will do his best to return the favor.

The Negative Side of Capricorn

Like everyone, Capricorn, too, has faults. At times, the Goat can be overcritical of others. He expects others to live up to his own high standards. He thinks highly of himself and tends to look down on others.

His interest in material things may be exaggerated. The Capricorn man or woman thinks too much about getting on in the world and having something to show for it. He may even be a little greedy.

He sometimes thinks he knows what's best for everyone. He is too bossy. He is always trying to organize and correct others. He may be a little narrow in his thinking.

Aquarius: January 20–February 18

The Positive Side of Aquarius

The Aquarius man or woman is usually very honest and forthright. These are his two greatest qualities. His standards for himself are generally very high. He can always be relied upon by others. His word is his bond.

Aquarius is perhaps the most tolerant of all the Zodiac personalities. He respects other people's beliefs and feels that everyone is entitled to his own approach to life.

He would never do anything to injure another's feelings. He is never unkind or cruel. Always considerate of others, the Water

Bearer is always willing to help a person in need. He feels a very strong tie between himself and all the other members of mankind.

The person born under this sign, called the Water Bearer, is almost always an individualist. He does not believe in teaming up with the masses, but prefers going his own way. His ideas about life and mankind are often quite advanced. There is a saying to the effect that the average Aquarius is fifty years ahead of his time.

Aquarius is community-minded. The problems of the world concern him greatly. He is interested in helping others no matter what part of the globe they live in. He is truly a humanitarian sort. He likes to be of service to others.

Giving, considerate, and without prejudice, Aquarius have no trouble getting along with others.

The Negative Side of Aquarius

Aquarius may be too much of a dreamer. He makes plans but seldom carries them out. He is rather unrealistic. His imagination has a tendency to run away with him. Because many of his plans are impractical, he is always in some sort of a dither.

Others may not approve of him at all times because of his unconventional behavior. He may be a bit eccentric. Sometimes he is so busy with his own thoughts that he loses touch with the realities of existence.

Some Aquarius feel they are more clever and intelligent than others. They seldom admit to their own faults, even when they are quite apparent. Some become rather fanatic in their views. Their criticism of others is sometimes destructive and negative.

Pisces: February 19–March 20

The Positive Side of Pisces

Known as the sign of the Fishes, Pisces has a sympathetic nature. Kindly, he is often dedicated in the way he goes about helping others. The sick and the troubled often turn to him for advice and assistance. Possessing keen intuition, Pisces can easily understand people's deepest problems.

He is very broad-minded and does not criticize others for their faults. He knows how to accept people for what they are. On the whole, he is a trustworthy and earnest person. He is loyal to his friends and will do what he can to help them in time of need. Generous and good-natured, he is a lover of peace; he is often willing to help others solve their differences. People who have taken a wrong turn in life often interest him and he will do what he can to persuade them to rehabilitate themselves.

He has a strong intuitive sense and most of the time he knows how to make it work for him. Pisces is unusually perceptive and often knows what is bothering someone before that person, himself, is aware of it. The Pisces man or woman is an idealistic person, basically, and is interested in making the world a better place in which to live. Pisces believes that everyone should help each other. He is willing to do more than his share in order to achieve cooperation with others.

The person born under this sign often is talented in music or art. He is a receptive person; he is able to take the ups and downs of life with philosophic calm.

The Negative Side of Pisces

Some Pisces are often depressed; their outlook on life is rather glum. They may feel that they have been given a bad deal in life and that others are always taking unfair advantage of them. Pisces sometimes feel that the world is a cold and cruel place. The Fishes can be easily discouraged. The Pisces man or woman may even withdraw from the harshness of reality into a secret shell of his own where he dreams and idles away a good deal of his time.

Pisces can be lazy. He lets things happen without giving the least bit of resistance. He drifts along, whether on the high road or on the low. He can be lacking in willpower.

Some Pisces people seek escape through drugs or alcohol. When temptation comes along they find it hard to resist. In matters of sex, they can be rather permissive.

Sun Sign Personalities

ARIES: Hans Christian Andersen, Pearl Bailey, Marlon Brando, Wernher Von Braun, Charlie Chaplin, Joan Crawford, Da Vinci, Bette Davis, Doris Day, W. C. Fields, Alec Guinness, Adolf Hitler, William Holden, Thomas Jefferson, Nikita Khrushchev, Elton John, Arturo Toscanini, J. P. Morgan, Paul Robeson, Gloria Steinem, Sarah Vaughn, Vincent van Gogh, Tennessee Williams

TAURUS: Fred Astaire, Charlotte Brontë, Carol Burnett, Irving Berlin, Bing Crosby, Salvador Dali, Tchaikovsky, Queen Elizabeth II, Duke Ellington, Ella Fitzgerald, Henry Fonda, Sigmund Freud, Orson Welles, Joe Louis, Lenin, Karl Marx, Golda Meir, Eva Peron, Bertrand Russell, Shakespeare, Kate Smith, Benjamin Spock, Barbra Streisand, Shirley Temple, Harry Truman

GEMINI: Ruth Benedict, Josephine Baker, Rachel Carson, Carlos Chavez, Walt Whitman, Bob Dylan, Ralph Waldo Emerson, Judy Garland, Paul Gauguin, Allen Ginsberg, Benny Goodman, Bob Hope, Burl Ives, John F. Kennedy, Peggy Lee, Marilyn Monroe, Joe Namath, Cole Porter, Laurence Olivier, Harriet Beecher Stowe, Queen Victoria, John Wayne, Frank Lloyd Wright

CANCER: "Dear Abby," Lizzie Borden, David Brinkley, Yul Brynner, Pearl Buck, Marc Chagall, Princess Diana, Babe Didrikson, Mary Baker Eddy, Henry VIII, John Glenn, Ernest Hemingway, Lena Horne, Oscar Hammerstein, Helen Keller, Ann Landers, George Orwell, Nancy Reagan, Rembrandt, Richard Rodgers, Ginger Rogers, Rubens, Jean-Paul Sartre, O. J. Simpson

LEO: Neil Armstrong, James Baldwin, Lucille Ball, Emily Brontë, Wilt Chamberlain, Julia Child, William J. Clinton, Cecil B. De Mille, Ogden Nash, Amelia Earhart, Edna Ferber, Arthur Goldberg, Alfred Hitchcock, Mick Jagger, George Meany, Annie Oakley, George Bernard Shaw, Napoleon, Jacqueline Onassis, Henry Ford, Francis Scott Key, Andy Warhol, Mae West, Orville Wright

VIRGO: Ingrid Bergman, Warren Burger, Maurice Chevalier, Agatha Christie, Sean Connery, Lafayette, Peter Falk, Greta Garbo, Althea Gibson, Arthur Godfrey, Goethe, Buddy Hackett, Michael Jackson, Lyndon Johnson, D. H. Lawrence, Sophia Loren, Grandma Moses, Arnold Palmer, Queen Elizabeth I, Walter Reuther, Peter Sellers, Lily Tomlin, George Wallace

LIBRA: Brigitte Bardot, Art Buchwald, Truman Capote, Dwight D. Eisenhower, William Faulkner, F. Scott Fitzgerald, Gandhi, George Gershwin, Micky Mantle, Helen Hayes, Vladimir Horowitz, Doris Lessing, Martina Navratalova, Eugene O'Neill, Luciano Pavarotti, Emily Post, Eleanor Roosevelt, Bruce Springsteen, Margaret Thatcher, Gore Vidal, Barbara Walters, Oscar Wilde

SCORPIO: Vivien Leigh, Richard Burton, Art Carney, Johnny Carson, Billy Graham, Grace Kelly, Walter Cronkite, Marie Curie, Charles de Gaulle, Linda Evans, Indira Gandhi, Theodore Roosevelt, Rock Hudson, Katherine Hepburn, Robert F. Kennedy, Billie Jean King, Martin Luther, Georgia O'Keeffe, Pablo Picasso, Jonas Salk, Alan Shepard, Robert Louis Stevenson

SAGITTARIUS: Jane Austen, Louisa May Alcott, Woody Allen, Beethoven, Willy Brandt, Mary Martin, William F. Buckley, Maria Callas, Winston Churchill, Noel Coward, Emily Dickinson, Walt Disney, Benjamin Disraeli, James Doolittle, Kirk Douglas, Chet Huntley, Jane Fonda, Chris Evert Lloyd, Margaret Mead, Charles Schulz, John Milton, Frank Sinatra, Steven Spielberg

CAPRICORN: Muhammad Ali, Isaac Asimov, Pablo Casals, Dizzy Dean, Marlene Dietrich, James Farmer, Ava Gardner, Barry Goldwater, Cary Grant, J. Edgar Hoover, Howard Hughes, Joan of Arc, Gypsy Rose Lee, Martin Luther King, Jr., Rudyard Kipling, Mao Tse-tung, Richard Nixon, Gamal Nasser, Louis Pasteur, Albert Schweitzer, Stalin, Benjamin Franklin, Elvis Presley

AQUARIUS: Marian Anderson, Susan B. Anthony, Jack Benny, John Barrymore, Mikhail Baryshnikov, Charles Darwin, Charles Dickens, Thomas Edison, Clark Gable, Jascha Heifetz, Abraham Lincoln, Yehudi Menuhin, Mozart, Jack Nicklaus, Ronald Reagan, Jackie Robinson, Norman Rockwell, Franklin D. Roosevelt, Gertrude Stein, Charles Lindbergh, Margaret Truman

PISCES: Edward Albee, Harry Belafonte, Alexander Graham Bell, Chopin, Adelle Davis, Albert Einstein, Golda Meir, Jackie Gleason, Winslow Homer, Edward M. Kennedy, Victor Hugo, Mike Mansfield, Michelangelo, Edna St. Vincent Millay, Liza Minelli, John Steinbeck, Linus Pauling, Ravel, Renoir, Diana Ross, William Shirer, Elizabeth Taylor, George Washington

The Signs and Their Key Words

		POSITIVE	NEGATIVE
ARIES	self	courage, initiative, pioneer instinct	brash rudeness, selfish impetuosity
TAURUS	money	endurance, loyalty, wealth	obstinacy, gluttony
GEMINI	mind	versatility	capriciousness, unreliability
CANCER	family	sympathy, homing instinct	clannishness, childishness
LEO	children	love, authority, integrity	egotism, force
VIRGO	work	purity, industry, analysis	faultfinding, cynicism
LIBRA	marriage	harmony, justice	vacillation, superficiality
SCORPIO	sex	survival, regeneration	vengeance, discord
SAGITTARIUS	travel	optimism, higher learning	lawlessness
CAPRICORN	career	depth	narrowness, gloom
AQUARIUS	friends	human fellowship, genius	perverse unpredictability
PISCES	confinement	spiritual love, universality	diffusion, escapism

The Elements and Qualities of The Signs

Every sign has both an *element* and a *quality* associated with it. The element indicates the basic makeup of the sign, and the quality describes the kind of activity associated with each.

Element	Sign	Quality	Sign
FIRE	ARIES LEO SAGITTARIUS	CARDINAL	ARIES LIBRA CANCER CAPRICORN
EARTH	TAURUS VIRGO CAPRICORN	FIXED	TAURUS LEO SCORPIO AQUARIUS
AIR	GEMINI LIBRA AQUARIUS		
WATER	CANCER SCORPIO PISCES	MUTABLE	GEMINI VIRGO SAGITTARIUS PISCES

Signs can be grouped together according to their element and quality. Signs of the same element share many basic traits in common. They tend to form stable configurations and ultimately harmonious relationships. Signs of the same quality are often less harmonious, but they share many dynamic potentials for growth as well as profound fulfillment.

Further discussion of each of these sign groupings is provided on the following pages.

The Fire Signs

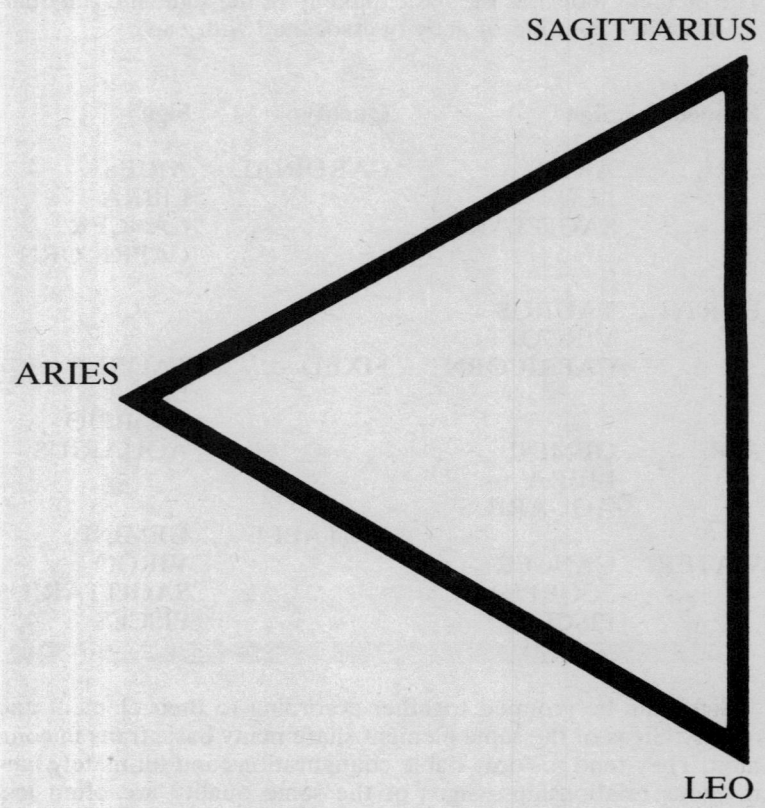

This is the fire group. On the whole these are emotional, volatile types, quick to anger, quick to forgive. They are adventurous, powerful people and act as a source of inspiration for everyone. They spark into action with immediate exuberant impulses. They are intelligent, self-involved, creative, and idealistic. They all share a certain vibrancy and glow that outwardly reflects an inner flame and passion for living.

The Earth Signs

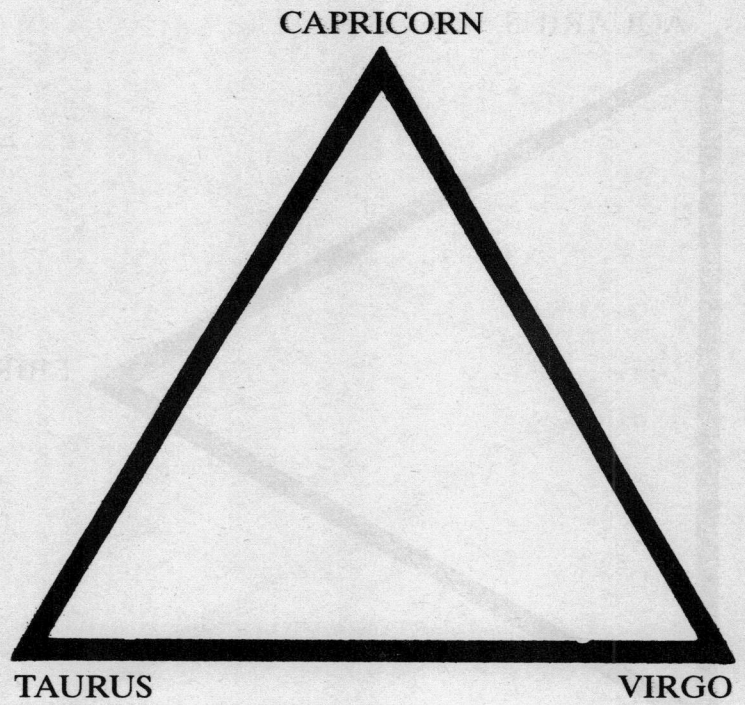

This is the earth group. They are in constant touch with the material world and tend to be conservative. Although they are all capable of spartan self-discipline, they are earthy, sensual people who are stimulated by the tangible, elegant, and luxurious. The thread of their lives is always practical, but they do fantasize and are often attracted to dark, mysterious, emotional people. They are like great cliffs overhanging the sea, forever married to the ocean but always resisting erosion from the dark, emotional forces that thunder at their feet.

The Air Signs

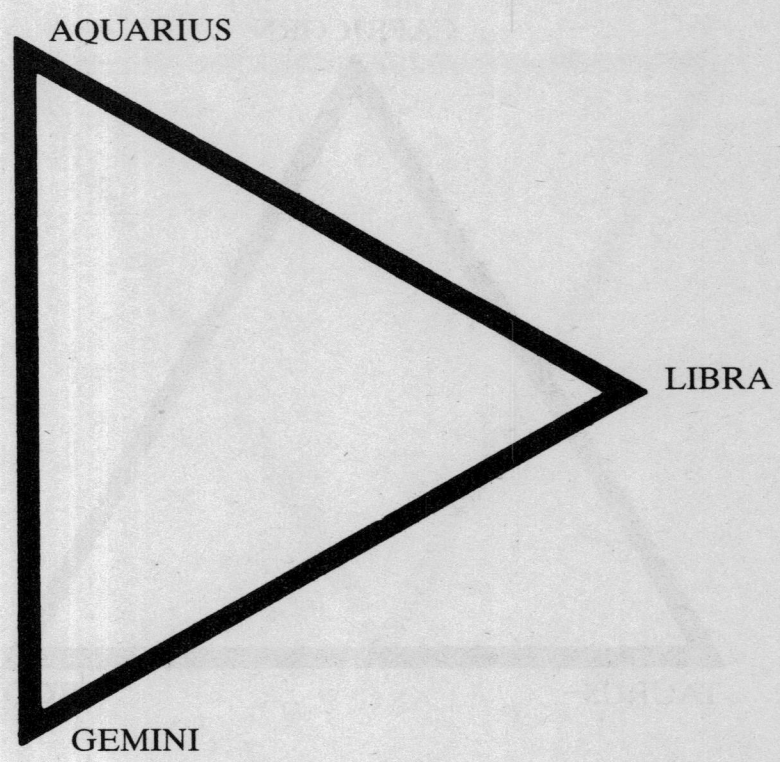

This is the air group. They are light, mental creatures desirous of contact, communication, and relationship. They are involved with people and the forming of ties on many levels. Original thinkers, they are the bearers of human news. Their language is their sense of word, color, style, and beauty. They provide an atmosphere suitable and pleasant for living. They add change and versatility to the scene, and it is through them that we can explore new territory of human intelligence and experience.

The Water Signs

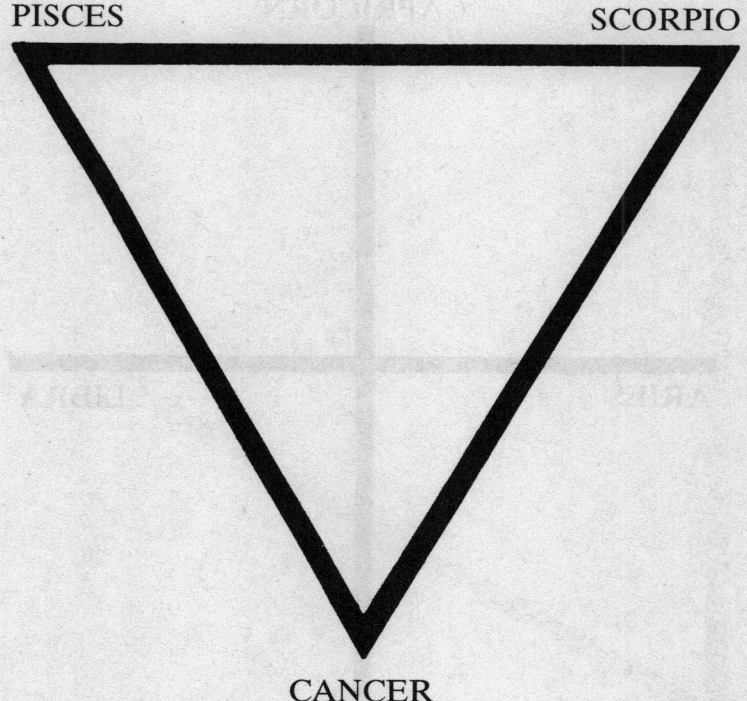

This is the water group. Through the water people, we are all joined together on emotional, nonverbal levels. They are silent, mysterious types whose magic hypnotizes even the most determined realist. They have uncanny perceptions about people and are as rich as the oceans when it comes to feeling, emotion, or imagination. They are sensitive, mystical creatures with memories that go back beyond time. Through water, life is sustained. These people have the potential for the depths of darkness or the heights of mysticism and art.

The Cardinal Signs

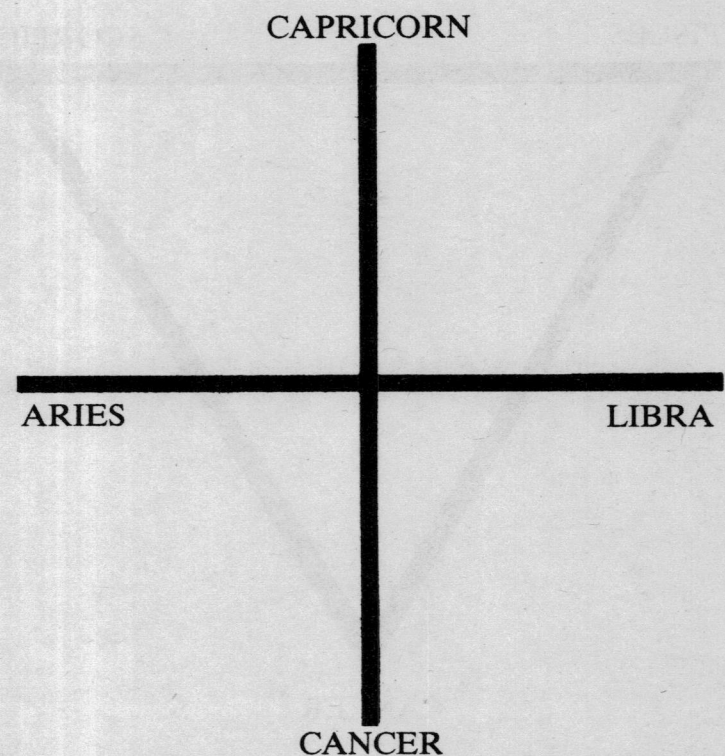

Put together, this is a clear-cut picture of dynamism, activity, tremendous stress, and remarkable achievement. These people know the meaning of great change since their lives are often characterized by significant crises and major successes. This combination is like a simultaneous storm of summer, fall, winter, and spring. The danger is chaotic diffusion of energy; the potential is irrepressible growth and victory.

The Fixed Signs

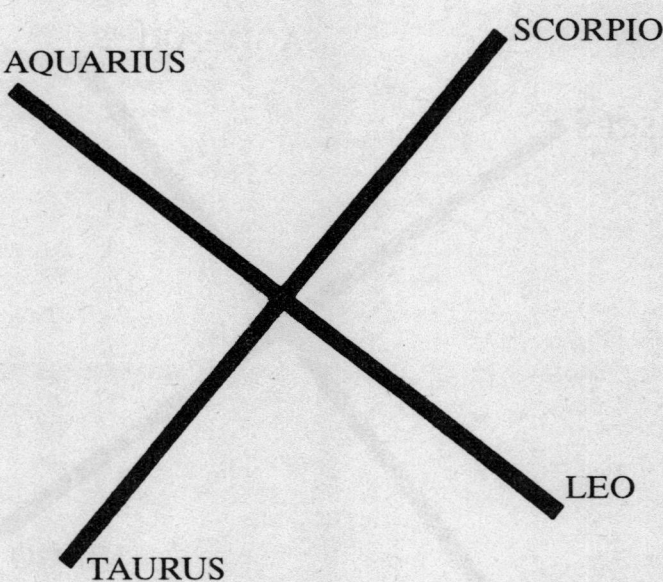

Fixed signs are always establishing themselves in a given place or area of experience. Like explorers who arrive and plant a flag, these people claim a position from which they do not enjoy being deposed. They are staunch, stalwart, upright, trusty, honorable people, although their obstinacy is well-known. Their contribution is fixity, and they are the angels who support our visible world.

The Mutable Signs

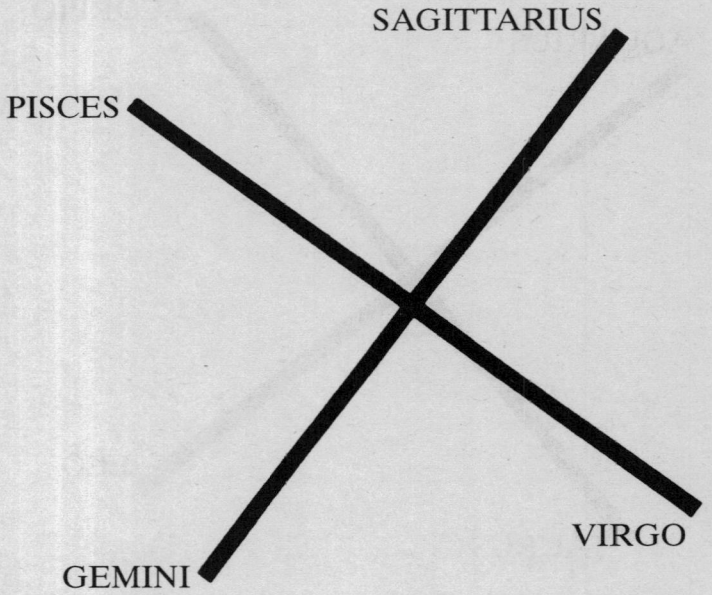

Mutable people are versatile, sensitive, intelligent, nervous, and deeply curious about life. They are the translators of all energy. They often carry out or complete tasks initiated by others. Combinations of these signs have highly developed minds; they are imaginative and jumpy and think and talk a lot. At worst their lives are a Tower of Babel. At best they are adaptable and ready creatures who can assimilate one kind of experience and enjoy it while anticipating coming changes.

THE PLANETS OF THE SOLAR SYSTEM

This section describes the planets of the solar system. In astrology, both the Sun and the Moon are considered to be planets. Because of the Moon's influence in our day-to-day lives, the Moon is described in a separate section following this one.

The Planets and the Signs They Rule

The signs of the Zodiac are linked to the planets in the following way. Each sign is governed or ruled by one or more planets. No matter where the planets are located in the sky at any given moment, they still rule their respective signs, and when they travel through the signs they rule, they have special dignity and their effects are stronger.

Following is a list of the planets and the signs they rule. After looking at the list, read the definitions of the planets and see if you can determine how the planet ruling *your* Sun sign has affected your life.

SIGNS	RULING PLANETS
Aries	Mars, Pluto
Taurus	Venus
Gemini	Mercury
Cancer	Moon
Leo	Sun
Virgo	Mercury
Libra	Venus
Scorpio	Mars, Pluto
Sagittarius	Jupiter
Capricorn	Saturn
Aquarius	Saturn, Uranus
Pisces	Jupiter, Neptune

Characteristics of the Planets

The following pages give the meaning and characteristics of the planets of the solar system. They all travel around the Sun at different speeds and different distances. Taken with the Sun, they all distribute individual intelligence and ability throughout the entire chart.

The planets modify the influence of the Sun in a chart according to their own particular natures, strengths, and positions. Their positions must be calculated for each year and day, and their function and expression in a horoscope will change as they move from one area of the Zodiac to another.

We start with a description of the sun.

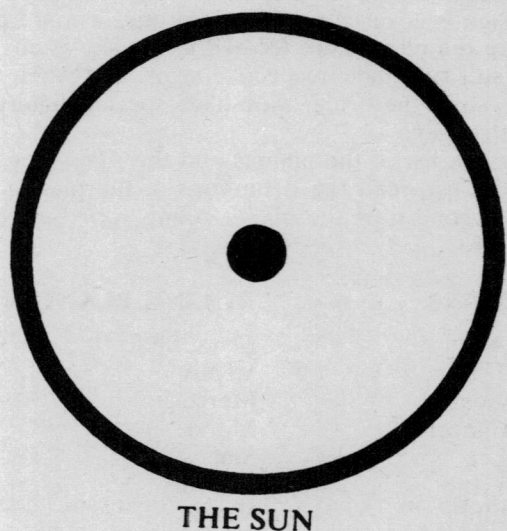

THE SUN

SUN

This is the center of existence. Around this flaming sphere all the planets revolve in endless orbits. Our star is constantly sending out its beams of light and energy without which no life on Earth would be possible. In astrology it symbolizes everything we are trying to become, the center around which all of our activity in life will always revolve. It is the symbol of our basic nature and describes the natural and constant thread that runs through everything that we do from birth to death on this planet.

To early astrologers, the Sun seemed to be another planet because it crossed the heavens every day, just like the rest of the bodies in the sky.

It is the only star near enough to be seen well—it is, in fact, a dwarf star. Approximately 860,000 miles in diameter, it is about ten times as wide as the giant planet Jupiter. The next nearest star is nearly 300,000 times as far away, and if the Sun were located as far away as most of the bright stars, it would be too faint to be seen without a telescope.

Everything in the horoscope ultimately revolves around this singular body. Although other forces may be prominent in the charts of some individuals, still the Sun is the total nucleus of being and symbolizes the complete potential of every human being alive. It is vitality and the life force. Your whole essence comes from the position of the Sun.

You are always trying to express the Sun according to its position by house and sign. Possibility for all development is found in the Sun, and it marks the fundamental character of your personal radiations all around you.

It is the symbol of strength, vigor, wisdom, dignity, ardor, and generosity, and the ability for a person to function as a mature individual. It is also a creative force in society. It is consciousness of the gift of life.

The underdeveloped solar nature is arrogant, pushy, undependable, and proud, and is constantly using force.

MERCURY

Mercury is the planet closest to the Sun. It races around our star, gathering information and translating it to the rest of the system. Mercury represents your capacity to understand the desires of your own will and to translate those desires into action.

In other words it is the planet of mind and the power of communication. Through Mercury we develop an ability to think, write, speak, and observe—to become aware of the world around us. It colors our attitudes and vision of the world, as well as our capacity to communicate our inner responses to the outside world. Some people who have serious disabilities in their power of verbal communication have often wrongly been described as people lacking intelligence.

Although this planet (and its position in the horoscope) indicates your power to communicate your thoughts and perceptions to the world, intelligence is something deeper. Intelligence is distributed throughout all the planets. It is the relationship of the planets to each other that truly describes what we call intelligence. Mercury rules speaking, language, mathematics, draft and design, students, messengers, young people, offices, teachers, and any pursuits where the mind of man has wings.

VENUS

Venus is beauty. It symbolizes the harmony and radiance of a rare and elusive quality: beauty itself. It is refinement and delicacy, softness and charm. In astrology it indicates grace, balance, and the aesthetic sense. Where Venus is we see beauty, a gentle drawing in of energy and the need for satisfaction and completion. It is a special touch that finishes off rough edges. It is sensitivity, and affection, and it is always the place for that other elusive phenomenon: love. Venus describes our sense of what is beautiful and loving. Poorly developed, it is vulgar, tasteless, and self-indulgent. But its ideal is the flame of spiritual love—Aphrodite, goddess of love, and the sweetness and power of personal beauty.

MARS

Mars is raw, crude energy. The planet next to Earth but outward from the Sun is a fiery red sphere that charges through the horoscope with force and fury. It represents the way you reach out for new adventure and new experience. It is energy and drive, initiative, courage, and daring. It is the power to start something and see it through. It can be thoughtless, cruel and wild, angry and hostile, causing cuts, burns, scalds, and wounds. It can stab its way through a chart, or it can be the symbol of healthy spirited adventure, well-channeled constructive power to begin and keep up the drive. If you have trouble starting things, if you lack the get-up-and-go to start the ball rolling, if you lack aggressiveness and self-confidence, chances are there's another planet influencing your Mars. Mars rules soldiers, butchers, surgeons, salesmen—any field that requires daring, bold skill, operational technique, or self-promotion.

JUPITER

This is the largest planet of the solar system. Scientists have recently learned that Jupiter reflects more light than it receives from the Sun. In a sense it is like a star itself. In astrology it rules good luck and good cheer, health, wealth, optimism, happiness, success, and joy. It is the symbol of opportunity and always opens the way for new possibilities in your life. It rules exuberance, enthusiasm, wisdom, knowledge, generosity, and all forms of expansion in general. It rules actors, statesmen, clerics, professional people, religion, publishing, and the distribution of many people over large areas.

Sometimes Jupiter makes you think you deserve everything, and you become sloppy, wasteful, careless and rude, prodigal and lawless, in the illusion that nothing can ever go wrong. Then there is the danger of overconfidence, exaggeration, undependability, and overindulgence.

Jupiter is the minimization of limitation and the emphasis on spirituality and potential. It is the thirst for knowledge and higher learning.

SATURN

Saturn circles our system in dark splendor with its mysterious rings, forcing us to be awakened to whatever we have neglected in the past. It will present real puzzles and problems to be solved, causing delays, obstacles, and hindrances. By doing so, Saturn stirs our own sensitivity to those areas where we are laziest.

Here we must patiently develop *method*, and only through painstaking effort can our ends be achieved. It brings order to a horoscope and imposes reason just where we are feeling least reasonable. By creating limitations and boundary, Saturn shows the consequences of being human and demands that we accept the changing cycles inevitable in human life. Saturn rules time, old age, and sobriety. It can bring depression, gloom, jealousy, and greed, or serious acceptance of responsibilities out of which success will develop. With Saturn there is nothing to do but face facts. It rules laborers, stones, granite, rocks, and crystals of all kinds.

THE OUTER PLANETS: URANUS, NEPTUNE, PLUTO

Uranus, Neptune, Pluto are the outer planets. They liberate human beings from cultural conditioning, and in that sense are the lawbreakers. In early times it was thought that Saturn was the last planet of the system—the outer limit beyond which we could never go. The discovery of the next three planets ushered in new phases of human history, revolution, and technology.

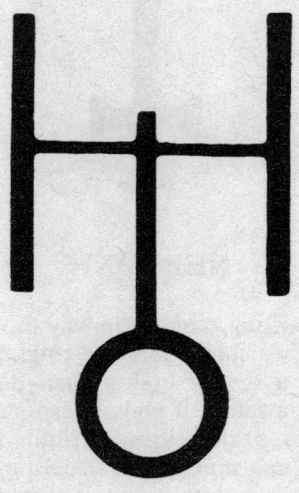

URANUS

Uranus rules unexpected change, upheaval, revolution. It is the symbol of total independence and asserts the freedom of an individual from all restriction and restraint. It is a breakthrough planet and indicates talent, originality, and genius in a horoscope. It usually causes last-minute reversals and changes of plan, unwanted separations, accidents, catastrophes, and eccentric behavior. It can add irrational rebelliousness and perverse bohemianism to a personality or a streak of unaffected brilliance in science and art. It rules technology, aviation, and all forms of electrical and electronic advancement. It governs great leaps forward and topsy-turvy situations, and *always* turns things around at the last minute. Its effects are difficult to predict, since it rules sudden last-minute decisions and events that come like lightning out of the blue.

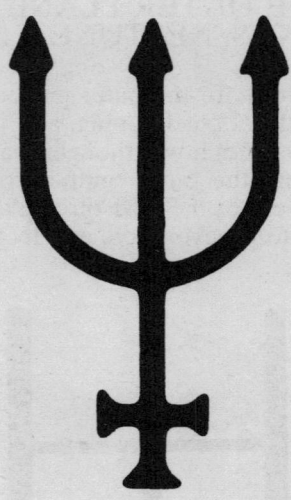

NEPTUNE

Neptune dissolves existing reality the way the sea erodes the cliffs beside it. Its effects are subtle like the ringing of a buoy's bell in the fog. It suggests a reality higher than definition can usually describe. It awakens a sense of higher responsibility often causing guilt, worry, anxieties, or delusions. Neptune is associated with all forms of escape and can make things seem a certain way so convincingly that you are absolutely sure of something that eventually turns out to be quite different.

It is the planet of illusion and therefore governs the invisible realms that lie beyond our ordinary minds, beyond our simple factual ability to prove what is "real." Treachery, deceit, disillusionment, and disappointment are linked to Neptune. It describes a vague reality that promises eternity and the divine, yet in a manner so complex that we cannot really fathom it at all. At its worst Neptune is a cheap intoxicant; at its best it is the poetry, music, and inspiration of the higher planes of spiritual love. It has dominion over movies, photographs, and much of the arts.

PLUTO

Pluto lies at the outpost of our system and therefore rules finality in a horoscope—the final closing of chapters in your life, the passing of major milestones and points of development from which there is no return. It is a final wipeout, a closeout, an evacuation. It is a distant, subtle but powerful catalyst in all transformations that occur. It creates, destroys, then recreates. Sometimes Pluto starts its influence with a minor event or insignificant incident that might even go unnoticed. Slowly but surely, little by little, everything changes, until at last there has been a total transformation in the area of your life where Pluto has been operating. It rules mass thinking and the trends that society first rejects, then adopts, and finally outgrows.

Pluto rules the dead and the underworld—all the powerful forces of creation and destruction that go on all the time beneath, around, and above us. It can bring a lust for power with strong obsessions.

It is the planet that rules the metamorphosis of the caterpillar into a butterfly, for it symbolizes the capacity to change totally and forever a person's lifestyle, way of thought, and behavior.

THE MOON IN EACH SIGN

The Moon is the nearest planet to the Earth. It exerts more observable influence on us from day to day than any other planet. The effect is very personal, very intimate, and if we are not aware of how it works it can make us quite unstable in our ideas. And the annoying thing is that at these times we often see our own instability but can do nothing about it. A knowledge of what can be expected may help considerably. We can then be prepared to stand strong against the Moon's negative influences and use its positive ones to help us to get ahead. Who has not heard of going with the tide?

The Moon reflects, has no light of its own. It reflects the Sun—the life giver—in the form of vital movement. The Moon controls the tides, the blood rhythm, the movement of sap in trees and plants. Its nature is inconstancy and change so it signifies our moods, our superficial behavior—walking, talking, and especially thinking. Being a true reflector of other forces, the Moon is cold, watery like the surface of a still lake, brilliant and scintillating at times, but easily ruffled and disturbed by the winds of change.

The Moon takes about 27⅓ days to make a complete transit of the Zodiac. It spends just over 2¼ days in each sign. During that time it reflects the qualities, energies, and characteristics of the sign and, to a degree, the planet which rules the sign. When the Moon in its transit occupies a sign incompatible with our own birth sign, we can expect to feel a vague uneasiness, perhaps a touch of irritableness. We should not be discouraged nor let the feeling get us down, or, worse still, allow ourselves to take the discomfort out on others. Try to remember that the Moon has to change signs within 55 hours and, provided you are not physically ill, your mood will probably change with it. It is amazing how frequently depression lifts with the shift in the Moon's position. And, of course, when the Moon is transiting a sign compatible or sympathetic to yours, you will probably feel some sort of stimulation or just be plain happy to be alive.

In the horoscope, the Moon is such a powerful indicator that competent astrologers often use the sign it occupied at birth as the birth sign of the person. This is done particularly when the Sun is on the cusp, or edge, of two signs. Most experienced astrologers, however, coordinate both Sun and Moon signs by reading and confirming from one to the other and secure a far more accurate and personalized analysis.

For these reasons, the Moon tables which follow this section (see pages 86–92) are of great importance to the individual. They show the days and the exact times the Moon will enter each sign of the Zodiac for the year. Remember, you have to adjust the indicated times to local time. The corrections, already calculated for most of the main cities, are at the beginning of the tables. What follows now is a guide to the influences that will be reflected to the Earth by the Moon while it transits each of the twelve signs. The influence is at its peak about 26 hours after the Moon enters a sign. As you read the daily forecast, check the Moon sign for any given day and glance back at this guide.

MOON IN ARIES

This is a time for action, for reaching out beyond the usual self-imposed limitations and faint-hearted cautions. If you have plans in your head or on your desk, put them into practice. New ventures, applications, new jobs, new starts of any kind—all have a good chance of success. This is the period when original and dynamic impulses are being reflected onto Earth. Such energies are extremely vital and favor the pursuit of pleasure and adventure in practically every form. Sick people should feel an improvement. Those who are well will probably find themselves exuding confidence and optimism. People fond of physical exercise should find their bodies growing with tone and well-being. Boldness, strength, determination should characterize most of your activities with a readiness to face up to old challenges. Yesterday's problems may seem petty and exaggerated—so deal with them. Strike out alone. Self-reliance will attract others to you. This is a good time for making friends. Business and marriage partners are more likely to be impressed with the man and woman of action. Opposition will be overcome or thrown aside with much less effort than usual. CAUTION: Be dominant but not domineering.

MOON IN TAURUS

The spontaneous, action-packed person of yesterday gives way to the cautious, diligent, hardworking "thinker." In this period ideas will probably be concentrated on ways of improving finances. A great deal of time may be spent figuring out and going over schemes and plans. It is the right time to be careful with detail.

People will find themselves working longer than usual at their desks. Or devoting more time to serious thought about the future. A strong desire to put order into business and financial arrangements may cause extra work. Loved ones may complain of being neglected and may fail to appreciate that your efforts are for their ultimate benefit. Your desire for system may extend to criticism of arrangements in the home and lead to minor upsets. Health may be affected through overwork. Try to secure a reasonable amount of rest and relaxation, although the tendency will be to "keep going" despite good advice. Work done conscientiously in this period should result in a solid contribution to your future security. CAUTION: Try not to be as serious with people as the work you are engaged in.

MOON IN GEMINI
The humdrum of routine and too much work should suddenly end. You are likely to find yourself in an expansive, quicksilver world of change and self-expression. Urges to write, to paint, to experience the freedom of some sort of artistic outpouring, may be very strong. Take full advantage of them. You may find yourself finishing something you began and put aside long ago. Or embarking on something new which could easily be prompted by a chance meeting, a new acquaintance, or even an advertisement. There may be a yearning for a change of scenery, the feeling to visit another country (not too far away), or at least to get away for a few days. This may result in short, quick journeys. Or, if you are planning a single visit, there may be some unexpected changes or detours on the way. Familiar activities will seem to give little satisfaction unless they contain a fresh element of excitement or expectation. The inclination will be toward untried pursuits, particularly those that allow you to express your inner nature. The accent is on new faces, new places. CAUTION: Do not be too quick to commit yourself emotionally.

MOON IN CANCER
Feelings of uncertainty and vague insecurity are likely to cause problems while the Moon is in Cancer. Thoughts may turn frequently to the warmth of the home and the comfort of loved ones. Nostalgic impulses could cause you to bring out old photographs and letters and reflect on the days when your life seemed to be much more rewarding and less demanding. The love and understanding of parents and family may be important, and, if it is not forthcoming, you may have to fight against bouts of self-pity. The cordiality of friends and the thought of good times with them that are sure to be repeated will help to restore you to a happier frame

of mind. The desire to be alone may follow minor setbacks or rebuffs at this time, but solitude is unlikely to help. Better to get on the telephone or visit someone. This period often causes peculiar dreams and upsurges of imaginative thinking which can be helpful to authors of occult and mystical works. Preoccupation with the personal world of simple human needs can overshadow any material strivings. CAUTION: Do not spend too much time thinking—seek the company of loved ones or close friends.

MOON IN LEO
New horizons of exciting and rather extravagant activity open up. This is the time for exhilarating entertainment, glamorous and lavish parties, and expensive shopping sprees. Any merrymaking that relies upon your generosity as a host has every chance of being a spectacular success. You should find yourself right in the center of the fun, either as the life of the party or simply as a person whom happy people like to be with. Romance thrives in this heady atmosphere and friendships are likely to explode unexpectedly into serious attachments. Children and younger people should be attracted to you and you may find yourself organizing a picnic or a visit to a fun-fair, the movies, or the beach. The sunny company and vitality of youthful companions should help you to find some unsuspected energy. In career, you could find an opening for promotion or advancement. This should be the time to make a direct approach. The period favors those engaged in original research. CAUTION: Bask in popularity, not in flattery.

MOON IN VIRGO
Off comes the party cap and out steps the busy, practical worker. He wants to get his personal affairs straight, to rearrange them, if necessary, for more efficiency, so he will have more time for more work. He clears up his correspondence, pays outstanding bills, makes numerous phone calls. He is likely to make inquiries, or sign up for some new insurance and put money into gilt-edged investment. Thoughts probably revolve around the need for future security—to tie up loose ends and clear the decks. There may be a tendency to be "finicky," to interfere in the routine of others, particularly friends and family members. The motive may be a genuine desire to help with suggestions for updating or streamlining their affairs, but these will probably not be welcomed. Sympathy may be felt for less fortunate sections of the community and a flurry of some sort of voluntary service is likely. This may be accompanied by strong feelings of responsibility on several fronts and health may suffer from extra efforts made. CAUTION: Everyone may not want your help or advice.

MOON IN LIBRA
These are days of harmony and agreement and you should find yourself at peace with most others. Relationships tend to be smooth and sweet-flowing. Friends may become closer and bonds deepen in mutual understanding. Hopes will be shared. Progress by cooperation could be the secret of success in every sphere. In business, established partnerships may flourish and new ones get off to a good start. Acquaintances could discover similar interests that lead to congenial discussions and rewarding exchanges of some sort. Love, as a unifying force, reaches its optimum. Marriage partners should find accord. Those who wed at this time face the prospect of a happy union. Cooperation and tolerance are felt to be stronger than dissension and impatience. The argumentative are not quite so loud in their bellowings, nor as inflexible in their attitudes. In the home, there should be a greater recognition of the other point of view and a readiness to put the wishes of the group before selfish insistence. This is a favorable time to join an art group. CAUTION: Do not be too independent—let others help you if they want to.

MOON IN SCORPIO
Driving impulses to make money and to economize are likely to cause upsets all around. No area of expenditure is likely to be spared the ax, including the household budget. This is a time when the desire to cut down on extravagance can become near fanatical. Care must be exercised to try to keep the aim in reasonable perspective. Others may not feel the same urgent need to save and may retaliate. There is a danger that possessions of sentimental value will be sold to realize cash for investment. Buying and selling of stock for quick profit is also likely. The attention turns to organizing, reorganizing, tidying up at home and at work. Neglected jobs could suddenly be done with great bursts of energy. The desire for solitude may intervene. Self-searching thoughts could disturb. The sense of invisible and mysterious energies in play could cause some excitability. The reassurance of loves ones may help. CAUTION: Be kind to the people you love.

MOON IN SAGITTARIUS
These are days when you are likely to be stirred and elevated by discussions and reflections of a religious and philosophical nature. Ideas of faraway places may cause unusual response and excitement. A decision may be made to visit someone overseas, perhaps a person whose influence was important to your earlier character development. There could be a strong resolution to get away from present intellectual patterns, to learn new subjects, and to meet

more interesting people. The superficial may be rejected in all its forms. An impatience with old ideas and unimaginative contacts could lead to a change of companions and interests. There may be an upsurge of religious feeling and metaphysical inquiry. Even a new insight into the significance of astrology and other occult studies is likely under the curious stimulus of the Moon in Sagittarius. Physically, you may express this need for fundamental change by spending more time outdoors: sports, gardening, long walks appeal. CAUTION: Try to channel any restlessness into worthwhile study.

MOON IN CAPRICORN
Life in these hours may seem to pivot around the importance of gaining prestige and honor in the career, as well as maintaining a spotless reputation. Ambitious urges may be excessive and could be accompanied by quite acquisitive drives for money. Effort should be directed along strictly ethical lines where there is no possibility of reproach or scandal. All endeavors are likely to be characterized by great earnestness, and an air of authority and purpose which should impress those who are looking for leadership or reliability. The desire to conform to accepted standards may extend to sharp criticism of family members. Frivolity and unconventional actions are unlikely to amuse while the Moon is in Capricorn. Moderation and seriousness are the orders of the day. Achievement and recognition in this period could come through community work or organizing for the benefit of some amateur group. CAUTION: Dignity and esteem are not always self-awarded.

MOON IN AQUARIUS
Moon in Aquarius is in the second last sign of the Zodiac where ideas can become disturbingly fine and subtle. The result is often a mental "no-man's land" where imagination cannot be trusted with the same certitude as other times. The dangers for the individual are the extremes of optimism and pessimism. Unless the imagination is held in check, situations are likely to be misread, and rosy conclusions drawn where they do not exist. Consequences for the unwary can be costly in career and business. Best to think twice and not speak or act until you think again. Pessimism can be a cruel self-inflicted penalty for delusion at this time. Between the two extremes are strange areas of self-deception which, for example, can make the selfish person think he is actually being generous. Eerie dreams which resemble the reality and even seem to continue into the waking state are also possible. CAUTION: Look for the fact and not just for the image in your mind.

MOON IN PISCES
Everything seems to come to the surface now. Memory may be crystal clear, throwing up long-forgotten information which could be valuable in the career or business. Flashes of clairvoyance and intuition are possible along with sudden realizations of one's own nature, which may be used for self-improvement. A talent, never before suspected, may be discovered. Qualities not evident before in friends and marriage partners are likely to be noticed. As this is a period in which the truth seems to emerge, the discovery of false characteristics is likely to lead to disenchantment or a shift in attachments. However, when qualities are accepted, it should lead to happiness and deeper feeling. Surprise solutions could bob up for old problems. There may be a public announcement of the solving of a crime or mystery. People with secrets may find someone has "guessed" correctly. The secrets of the soul or the inner self also tend to reveal themselves. Religious and philosophical groups may make some interesting discoveries. CAUTION: Not a time for activities that depend on secrecy.

NOTE: When you read your daily forecasts, use the Moon Sign Dates that are provided in the following section of Moon Tables. Then you may want to glance back here for the Moon's influence in a given sign.

MOON TABLES

CORRECTION FOR NEW YORK TIME, FIVE HOURS WEST OF GREENWICH

Atlanta, Boston, Detroit, Miami, Washington, Montreal, Ottawa, Quebec, Bogota, Havana, Lima, Santiago .. Same time

Chicago, New Orleans, Houston, Winnipeg, Churchill, Mexico City .... Deduct 1 hour

Albuquerque, Denver, Phoenix, El Paso, Edmonton, Helena .... Deduct 2 hours

Los Angeles, San Francisco, Reno, Portland, Seattle, Vancouver .... Deduct 3 hours

Honolulu, Anchorage, Fairbanks, Kodiak .... Deduct 5 hours

Nome, Samoa, Tonga, Midway .... Deduct 6 hours

Halifax, Bermuda, San Juan, Caracas, La Paz, Barbados .... Add 1 hour

St. John's, Brasilia, Rio de Janeiro, Sao Paulo, Buenos Aires, Montevideo .... Add 2 hours

Azores, Cape Verde Islands .... Add 3 hours

Canary Islands, Madeira, Reykjavik .... Add 4 hours

London, Paris, Amsterdam, Madrid, Lisbon, Gibraltar, Belfast, Rabat .... Add 5 hours

Frankfurt, Rome, Oslo, Stockholm, Prague, Belgrade .... Add 6 hours

Bucharest, Beirut, Tel Aviv, Athens, Istanbul, Cairo, Alexandria, Cape Town, Johannesburg .... Add 7 hours

Moscow, Leningrad, Baghdad, Dhahran, Addis Ababa, Nairobi, Teheran, Zanzibar .... Add 8 hours

Bombay, Calcutta, Sri Lanka .... Add 10 ½ hours

Hong Kong, Shanghai, Manila, Peking, Perth ...... Add 13 hours

Tokyo, Okinawa, Darwin, Pusan .... Add 14 hours

Sydney, Melbourne, Port Moresby, Guam .... Add 15 hours

Auckland, Wellington, Suva, Wake .... Add 17 hours

2000 MOON SIGN DATES—
NEW YORK TIME

JANUARY
Day Moon Enters
1. Scorp.
2. Sagitt. 4:33 pm
3. Sagitt.
4. Sagitt.
5. Capric. 5:25 am
6. Capric.
7. Aquar. 5:54 pm
8. Aquar.
9. Aquar.
10. Pisces 5:00 am
11. Pisces
12. Aries 1:49 pm
13. Aries
14. Taurus 7:39 pm
15. Taurus
16. Gemini 10:26 pm
17. Gemini
18. Cancer 11:02 pm
19. Cancer
20. Leo 10:59 pm
21. Leo
22. Leo
23. Virgo 0:08 am
24. Virgo
25. Libra 4:10 am
26. Libra
27. Scorp. 0:02 pm
28. Scorp.
29. Sagitt. 11:19 pm
30. Sagitt.
31. Sagitt.

FEBRUARY
Day Moon Enters
1. Capric. 0:11 pm
2. Capric.
3. Capric.
4. Aquar. 0:32 am
5. Aquar.
6. Pisces 11:03 am
7. Pisces
8. Aries 7:18 pm
9. Aries
10. Aries
11. Taurus 1:22 am
12. Taurus
13. Gemini 5:24 am
14. Gemini
15. Cancer 7:46 am
16. Cancer
17. Leo 9:12 am
18. Leo
19. Virgo 10:54 am
20. Virgo
21. Libra 2:22 pm
22. Libra
23. Scorp. 8:59 pm
24. Scorp.
25. Scorp.
26. Sagitt. 7:11 am
27. Sagitt.
28. Capric. 7:46 pm
29. Capric.

MARCH
Day Moon Enters
1. Capric.
2. Aquar. 8:15 am
3. Aquar.
4. Pisces 6:31 pm
5. Pisces
6. Pisces
7. Aries 1:55 am
8. Aries
9. Taurus 7:02 am
10. Taurus
11. Gemini 10:47 am
12. Gemini
13. Cancer 1:52 pm
14. Cancer
15. Leo 4:44 pm
16. Leo
17. Virgo 7:49 pm
18. Virgo
19. Libra 11:58 pm
20. Libra
21. Libra
22. Scorp. 6:19 am
23. Scorp.
24. Sagitt. 3:44 pm
25. Sagitt.
26. Sagitt.
27. Capric. 3:52 am
28. Capric.
29. Aquar. 4:35 pm
30. Aquar.
31. Aquar.

Summer time to be considered where applicable.

2000 MOON SIGN DATES— NEW YORK TIME

APRIL
Day Moon Enters
1. Pisces 3:13 am
2. Pisces
3. Aries 10:23 am
4. Aries
5. Taurus 2:30 pm
6. Taurus
7. Gemini 4:59 pm
8. Gemini
9. Cancer 7:17 pm
10. Cancer
11. Leo 10:17 pm
12. Leo
13. Leo
14. Virgo 2:20 am
15. Virgo
16. Libra 7:37 am
17. Libra
18. Scorp. 2:36 pm
19. Scorp.
20. Sagitt. 11:59 pm
21. Sagitt.
22. Sagitt.
23. Capric. 11:48 am
24. Capric.
25. Capric.
26. Aquar. 0:43 am
27. Aquar.
28. Pisces 0:07 pm
29. Pisces
30. Aries 7:56 pm

MAY
Day Moon Enters
1. Aries
2. Taurus 11:55 pm
3. Taurus
4. Taurus
5. Gemini 1:24 am
6. Gemini
7. Cancer 2:15 am
8. Cancer
9. Leo 4:02 am
10. Leo
11. Virgo 7:42 am
12. Virgo
13. Libra 1:28 pm
14. Libra
15. Scorp. 9:17 pm
16. Scorp.
17. Scorp.
18. Sagitt. 7:10 am
19. Sagitt.
20. Capric. 7:02 pm
21. Capric.
22. Capric.
23. Aquar. 8:01 am
24. Aquar.
25. Pisces 8:08 pm
26. Pisces
27. Pisces
28. Aries 5:09 am
29. Aries
30. Taurus 10:03 am
31. Taurus

JUNE
Day Moon Enters
1. Gemini 11:35 am
2. Gemini
3. Cancer 11:31 am
4. Cancer
5. Leo 11:47 am
6. Leo
7. Virgo 1:58 pm
8. Virgo
9. Libra 7:00 pm
10. Libra
11. Libra
12. Scorp. 0:56 am
13. Scorp.
14. Sagitt. 1:19 pm
15. Sagitt.
16. Sagitt.
17. Capric. 1:28 am
18. Capric.
19. Aquar. 2:27 pm
20. Aquar.
21. Aquar.
22. Pisces 2:53 am
23. Pisces
24. Aries 0:56 pm
25. Aries
26. Taurus 7:20 pm
27. Taurus
28. Gemini 10:00 pm
29. Gemini
30. Cancer 10:10 pm

Summer time to be considered where applicable.

2000 MOON SIGN DATES—
NEW YORK TIME

JULY
Day Moon Enters
1. Cancer
2. Leo   9:39 pm
3. Leo
4. Virgo   10:20 pm
5. Virgo
6. Virgo
7. Libra   1:48 am
8. Libra
9. Scorp.   8:49 am
10. Scorp.
11. Sagitt. 7:07 pm
12. Sagitt.
13. Sagitt.
14. Capric. 7:29 am
15. Capric.
16. Aquar.   8:28 pm
17. Aquar.
18. Aquar.
19. Pisces   8:45 am
20. Pisces
21. Aries   7:10 pm
22. Aries
23. Aries
24. Taurus   2:45 am
25. Taurus
26. Gemini   7:02 am
27. Gemini
28. Cancer   8:31 am
29. Cancer
30. Leo   8:25 am
31. Leo

AUGUST
Day Moon Enters
1. Virgo   8:28 am
2. Virgo
3. Libra   10:32 am
4. Libra
5. Scorp.   4:05 pm
6. Scorp.
7. Scorp.
8. Sagitt.   1:31 am
9. Sagitt.
10. Capric. 1:45 pm
11. Capric.
12. Capric.
13. Aquar.   2:44 am
14. Aquar.
15. Pisces   2:42 pm
16. Pisces
17. Pisces
18. Aries   0:45 am
19. Aries
20. Taurus   8:32 am
21. Taurus
22. Gemini   1:56 pm
23. Gemini
24. Cancer   5:01 pm
25. Cancer
26. Leo   6:18 pm
27. Leo
28. Virgo   6:56 pm
29. Virgo
30. Libra   8:34 pm
31. Libra

SEPTEMBER
Day Moon Enters
1. Libra
2. Scorp.   0:56 am
3. Scorp.
4. Sagitt.   9:09 am
5. Sagitt.
6. Capric.   8:48 pm
7. Capric.
8. Capric.
9. Aquar.   9:45 am
10. Aquar.
11. Pisces   9:35 pm
12. Pisces
13. Pisces
14. Aries   7:01 am
15. Aries
16. Taurus   2:06 pm
17. Taurus
18. Gemini   7:23 pm
19. Gemini
20. Cancer   11:17 pm
21. Cancer
22. Cancer
23. Leo   2:01 am
24. Leo
25. Virgo   4:03 am
26. Virgo
27. Libra   6:23 am
28. Libra
29. Scorp.   10:31 am
30. Scorp.

Summer time to be considered where applicable.

2000 MOON SIGN DATES—
NEW YORK TIME

OCTOBER
Day Moon Enters
1. Sagitt. 5:51 pm
2. Sagitt.
3. Sagitt.
4. Capric. 4:43 am
5. Capric.
6. Aquar. 5:34 pm
7. Aquar.
8. Aquar.
9. Pisces 5:37 am
10. Pisces
11. Aries 2:52 pm
12. Aries
13. Taurus 9:07 pm
14. Taurus
15. Taurus
16. Gemini 1:20 am
17. Gemini
18. Cancer 4:38 am
19. Cancer
20. Leo 7:43 am
21. Leo
22. Virgo 10:53 am
23. Virgo
24. Libra 2:31 pm
25. Libra
26. Scorp. 7:24 pm
27. Scorp.
28. Scorp.
29. Sagitt. 2:41 am
30. Sagitt.
31. Capric. 1:03 pm

NOVEMBER
Day Moon Enters
1. Capric.
2. Capric.
3. Aquar. 1:42 am
4. Aquar.
5. Pisces 2:14 pm
6. Pisces
7. Pisces
8. Aries 0:03 am
9. Aries
10. Taurus 6:13 am
11. Taurus
12. Gemini 9:28 am
13. Gemini
14. Cancer 11:22 am
15. Cancer
16. Leo 1:20 pm
17. Leo
18. Virgo 4:16 pm
19. Virgo
20. Libra 8:36 pm
21. Libra
22. Libra
23. Scorp. 2:34 am
24. Scorp.
25. Sagitt. 10:34 am
26. Sagitt.
27. Capric. 8:58 pm
28. Capric.
29. Capric.
30. Aquar. 9:28 am

DECEMBER
Day Moon Enters
1. Aquar.
2. Pisces 10:24 pm
3. Pisces
4. Pisces
5. Aries 9:18 am
6. Aries
7. Taurus 4:28 pm
8. Taurus
9. Gemini 7:51 pm
10. Gemini
11. Cancer 8:50 pm
12. Cancer
13. Leo 9:10 pm
14. Leo
15. Virgo 10:31 pm
16. Virgo
17. Virgo
18. Libra 2:02 am
19. Libra
20. Scorp. 8:13 am
21. Scorp.
22. Sagitt. 4:58 pm
23. Sagitt.
24. Sagitt.
25. Capric. 3:55 am
26. Capric.
27. Aquar. 4:26 pm
28. Aquar.
29. Aquar.
30. Pisces 5:28 am
31. Pisces

Summer time to be considered where applicable.

2000 PHASES OF THE MOON—
NEW YORK TIME

New Moon	First Quarter	Full Moon	Last Quarter
Jan. 6	Jan. 14	Jan. 20	Jan. 28
Feb. 5	Feb. 12	Feb. 19	Feb. 26
March 5	March 13	March 19	March 27
April 4	April 11	April 18	April 26
May 3	May 10	May 18	May 26
June 2	June 8	June 16	June 24
July 1	July 8	July 16	July 24
July 30	Aug. 6	Aug. 15	Aug. 22
Aug. 29	Sept. 5	Sept. 13	Sept. 20
Sept. 27	Oct. 5	Oct. 13	Oct. 20
Oct. 27	Nov. 4	Nov. 11	Nov. 18
Nov. 25	Dec. 3	Dec. 11	Dec. 17
Dec. 25	Jan. 2 ('01)	Jan. 9 ('01)	Jan. 17 ('01)

Each phase of the Moon lasts approximately seven to eight days, during which the Moon's shape gradually changes as it comes out of one phase and goes into the next.

There will be a partial solar eclipse during the New Moon phase on February 5, July 1, July 30, and December 25.

There will be a lunar eclipse during the Full Moon phase on January 20 and July 16.

2000 FISHING GUIDE

	Good	Best
January	14-18-21-22-23-24	6-19-20-28
February	5-17-18-19-20-21-27	12-16-22
March	13-17-18-19	6-20-21-22-23-28
April	4-15-16-21-26	11-17-18-19-20
May	10-18-19-20	4-15-16-17-21-26
June	2-9-14-15-16-19-25	13-17-18
July	13-14-17-18-19-31	1-8-15-16-24
August	13-14-15-18-22-29	7-12-16-17
September	5-10-11-14-15-16-27	12-13-21
October	11-12-13-16-20	5-10-14-15-27
November	4-8-9-10-12-13-14	11-18-25
December	10-11-14	4-8-9-12-13-18-25

2000 PLANTING GUIDE

	Aboveground Crops	Root Crops
January	7-10-11-15-16-19-20	1-25-26-27-28-29
February	7-8-11-12-16	2-3-22-23-24-25-29
March	6-10-14	1-5-20-21-22-23-27-28
April	6-10-11-17	1-2-19-20-24-25-29-30
May	4-7-8-14-15-16-17	3-21-22-26-27-31
June	4-10-11-12-13	17-18-22-23-27-28
July	2-7-8-9-10-11-15	20-21-24-25-29
August	4-5-6-7-11-12-31	16-17-21-25-26
September	1-2-3-7-8-12-28-29-30	17-18-21-22
October	1-4-5-6-10-27-28	14-15-18-19-25-26
November	1-2-6-7-28-29	11-15-21-22-23-24
December	3-4-8-9-26-31	12-13-18-19-20-21

	Pruning	Weeds and Pests
January	1-28-29	3-4-21-22-23-24-30-31
February	24-25	4-20-27-28
March	5-23	3-4-25-26-30-31
April	1-2-19-20-29-30	21-22-26-27
May	26-27	1-2-19-20-24-25-29
June	22-23	20-21-25-26-29-30
July	20-21-29	17-18-22-23-27
August	16-17-25-26	18-19-23-24-27-28
September	21-22	15-19-20-23-24-25-26
October	18-19	13-16-17-21-22-23
November	15-23-24	13-17-18-19-20
December	12-13-21	11-14-15-16-17-23-24

MOON'S INFLUENCE OVER PLANTS

Centuries ago it was established that seeds planted when the Moon is in signs and phases called Fruitful will produce more growth than seeds planted when the Moon is in a Barren sign.

Fruitful Signs: Taurus, Cancer, Libra, Scorpio, Capricorn, Pisces
Barren Signs: Aries, Gemini, Leo, Virgo, Sagittarius, Aquarius
Dry Signs: Aries, Gemini, Sagittarius, Aquarius

Activity	Moon In
Mow lawn, trim plants	**Fruitful sign:** 1st & 2nd quarter
Plant flowers	**Fruitful sign:** 2nd quarter; best in Cancer and Libra
Prune	**Fruitful sign:** 3rd & 4th quarter
Destroy pests; spray	**Barren sign:** 4th quarter
Harvest potatoes, root crops	**Dry sign:** 3rd & 4th quarter; Taurus, Leo, and Aquarius

MOON'S INFLUENCE OVER YOUR HEALTH

ARIES	Head, brain, face, upper jaw
TAURUS	Throat, neck, lower jaw
GEMINI	Hands, arms, lungs, shoulders, nervous system
CANCER	Esophagus, stomach, breasts, womb, liver
LEO	Heart, spine
VIRGO	Intestines, liver
LIBRA	Kidneys, lower back
SCORPIO	Sex and eliminative organs
SAGITTARIUS	Hips, thighs, liver
CAPRICORN	Skin, bones, teeth, knees
AQUARIUS	Circulatory system, lower legs
PISCES	Feet, tone of being

Try to avoid work being done on that part of the body when the Moon is in the sign governing that part.

MOON'S INFLUENCE OVER DAILY AFFAIRS

The Moon makes a complete transit of the Zodiac every 27 days 7 hours and 43 minutes. In making this transit the Moon forms different aspects with the planets and consequently has favorable or unfavorable bearings on affairs and events for persons according to the sign of the Zodiac under which they were born.

When the Moon is in conjunction with the Sun it is called a New Moon; when the Moon and Sun are in opposition it is called a Full Moon. From New Moon to Full Moon, first and second quarter—which takes about two weeks—the Moon is increasing or waxing. From Full Moon to New Moon, third and fourth quarter, the Moon is decreasing or waning.

Activity	Moon In
Business: buying and selling new, requiring public support	Sagittarius, Aries, Gemini, Virgo 1st and 2nd quarter
meant to be kept quiet	3rd and 4th quarter
Investigation	3rd and 4th quarter
Signing documents	1st & 2nd quarter, Cancer, Scorpio, Pisces
Advertising	2nd quarter, Sagittarius
Journeys and trips	1st & 2nd quarter, Gemini, Virgo
Renting offices, etc.	Taurus, Leo, Scorpio, Aquarius
Painting of house/apartment	3rd & 4th quarter, Taurus, Scorpio, Aquarius
Decorating	Gemini, Libra, Aquarius
Buying clothes and accessories	Taurus, Virgo
Beauty salon or barber shop visit	1st & 2nd quarter, Taurus, Leo, Libra, Scorpio, Aquarius
Weddings	1st & 2nd quarter

LIBRA

LIBRA

Character Analysis

People born under the sign of Libra are generally quite kind and sympathetic. They dislike seeing others suffer and do what they can to help those in dire straits. Another outstanding characteristic of a Libra is love of harmony and beauty. They generally have a deep appreciation for all forms of art. Libra only feels comfortable in places that radiate harmony and beauty. They are often willing to sacrifice to make their environment suit their tastes.

Libras like people. They are often afraid of being alone. They love company. Others like them for their charm and gentle ways. They are happiest when with others. A Libra alone is likely to fall into a depressed state easily. Being with others helps them to keep their spirits up even during difficult moments. A Libra rarely goes through life alone. They need permanent and reliable relationships. Often they marry early in life.

Libra has a kind and gentle nature. They would never go out of their way to hurt someone. Libra is considerate of others feelings. They will always keep up their end of a bargain. He or she is cooperative and courteous—sometimes to a fault.

The Libra man or woman is someone who is constantly weighing both sides of a problem. This characteristic is represented by the Scales, which is the zodiacal symbol for Libra. Libras are difficult people to satisfy. They want to make sure they are right in all the decisions they make. They may take a long time before coming to a decision. They may even change their minds several times in the process of weighing the pros and cons.

Balance is central to the Libra man or woman, just as balance typifies the function of the Scales. Outwardly Libra remains calm and intelligent in order to present the face of harmony, while inwardly he or she is mulling over the consequences of a proposed action. Libra's interest in harmony extends to social and business relationships. These individuals seldom hold a grudge. They put unpleasant things out of mind. Libra easily forgives and forgets.

Both men and women born under this sign are a bit soft in their dispositions. Sometimes others take advantage of this. The Libra person searches for a world where all things are beautiful and well-balanced—a place where harmony reigns. Because such a search would be useless in the real world, Libra takes refuge in daydreaming and flights of fancy. The harshness they might meet in life makes them unhappy. They may have an intricate fantasy world where they retreat when the going gets too rough.

Libra is gentle and easygoing. They seldom go where they know they are not wanted. Their interest in beauty and art leads them along the less troublesome and conflicting roads of life.

Libra can often achieve what he wants through friendly persuasion. Because of his calm, others often find him a port in a storm. He will tell people what he knows they want to hear in order to bolster their confidence and to avoid unpleasantness. He is tactful and knows how to use his gentleness to his own advantage. People may try to take advantage of him, but when he has his wits about him, this is rather difficult. Even when others think they see through him, they find him a difficult nut to crack. He is so strong in his ways of persuasion that he is almost never undermined.

The Libra man or woman is even-tempered generally, but can flare up when cornered. Still and all, they cool off quite rapidly and are willing to let bygones be bygones. Libra understands others quite deeply because of his sympathetic nature; it is quite easy for him to put himself in another's place. He is considerate of other people's opinions no matter how wrong they may seem.

Libra is fair-minded. He dislikes it when someone is mistreated or cheated out of a chance that is rightfully his. Injustice infuriates him. In all matters, he tries to make the right decision. He may take his time about coming to a conclusion.

In most social affairs, Libra is quite popular and charming. People like Libras because of their pleasant, easygoing ways. Most Libras have a lot of friends. All kinds of people attract Libra. They seldom make preferences on a superficial basis.

Harmony plays an important part in the life of every Libra. He or she will try to preserve it at all costs. Harsh realities disturb the Libra man or woman so at times they are given to lying in order to preserve peace and harmony.

Health

Libras are generally well-groomed and graceful. Their features, for the most part, are small. They are interested in maintaining good health and would never do anything that might encourage illness—even in a slight way. Quite often the man or woman born under this sign is not terribly vigorous and may require lots of rest in order to feel fit. Although they may never say no to a social obligation, Libra often tires quickly as a result of socializing. If they do not have proper rest, they are easily irritated.

Still, Libra is built well and strongly. In spite of this, they are not what you could really call strong. Their resistance is not always what it should be; they can catch colds easily. Still, they have remarkable powers of recovery and do not stay out of commission for very long. In spite of the fact that Libra is delicate, they are surprisingly resilient.

The weakest points of a Libra's body are the kidneys, spine, and loins. When they do fall ill, one of these three points is often affected.

Libra women are often remarkably beautiful. They seldom have problems attracting the opposite sex. Their voices are generally soft and their eyes lively.

Even though the Libra man may not look terribly strong, he is often capable of handling work that would exhaust someone who is bigger or seemingly more vigorous.

Libras become somewhat out of sorts when ill. Being sick tends to make them finicky and ill-humored. They like sympathy when in this condition. When their whims are not satisfied, they may complain about being neglected or unloved.

Occupation

The Libra man or woman is usually pleasant to work with. They like to cooperate with others. They will not oppose authority unless they feel it is unjust. Libra is flexible. It is not difficult for them to shift from one phase of an operation to another.

Environment may have an uncommonly strong influence on Libra. It may spur him or her on to greater heights or slow them down. Sometimes Libra needs to be inspired by the activities of those working in the immediate vicinity. They will sometimes look at the other fellow to see how he is working before they begin on their own.

Libra likes to work in pleasant surroundings. They abhor filth and disorder. They do what they can to bring about the working conditions best suited to their nature. Libra people are not attracted to work that is likely to be strenuous or untidy.

Libra people make good business partners. They are quite good at making the proper decisions at the right time. The person born under this sign knows how to weigh the pros and cons of an argument or problem. People often turn to Libra to make the right decision. Others find it easy to believe in Libra's powers of reasoning. They seldom make a wrong move. Libra can always be relied upon to do what is proper.

On the whole Libra is rather moderate or conservative in most things. This stems from their desire to avoid extremes—especially if they are apt to bring about controversy. Secrets are safe with Libra, especially if they might do someone some harm.

The person born under this sign is often quite intelligent. They have the ability to reason well and to analyze. Philosophical argument does not frighten them, and they can hold their own in almost any intellectual debate. They have a talent for objectivity, putting themselves in another's shoes quite easily. As a mediator Libra is excellent. People born under the sign of the Scales also make good diplomats.

Often called the Lawgiver, the Libra man or woman plays a powerful role as a mediator. In law, Libra can be of service to many, maintaining the peacekeeping and arbitration functions of society. These men and woman make competent judges and lawyers.

Libra can view things calmly and rationally. He or she is not easily swayed by emotions if truth or justice is at stake. Libra wants what is good for everybody concerned. They tend to look at things the way they are. They are not prone to make a mountain out of a molehill. In moments of confusion, Libra's mind is as clear as a bell.

Because of their natural objectivity, many Libras turn out to be admirable scientists and mathematicians. Also, Libra knows how to criticize without hurting. So these men and women could do well as reviewers of books, plays, films, and art in general.

Most Libras are good in creative matters. Anything to do with art or aesthetics appeals to them most of the time. Some of them make good painters, writers, or musicians. The person under this sign sometimes ignores surges of inspiration when they overcome him for fear of being too self-indulgent. The strong Libra knows how to seize these moments to further creative aims and interests. Some of the greatest painters in the world were born under the sign of Libra.

Because Libra is so good at persuasion, they make invaluable salespeople. They possess so much charm that their customers often buy more than they originally intended. Because of their rare beauty, Libra men and women often do well in the field of modeling or acting.

Libra is capable of spending more money than they actually have. During their lifetime, great sums are apt to come into their hands. They do not care too much about money, though. They are generous to a fault, and find it hard to refuse people who claim they are in need.

Libra usually has expensive tastes. They find it hard to save money. Because they like people and a busy social life, the person born under this sign often spends considerable sums in entertainment. Luxuries are as important to Libra at times as necessities are to someone else.

In spite of their light ways with money, Libra is no fool. They know well how to discourage someone who is only interested in them for their finances.

Home and Family

Home is important to the average Libra. It must be a place where they can relax and feel comfortable. It must radiate charm, beauty, and harmony. A popular person, the Libra man or woman loves to entertain. Nothing excites them more than company of good friends and acquaintances. Libra usually makes a good host. They know how to put guests at ease. People like to visit Libra because of their charming and easygoing ways.

The furnishings in a Libra's home are usually of excellent taste. They like ornamental furnishings, things that are often a bit ostentatious. No Libra home is without its paintings or pieces of sculpture. The Libra woman or man is often excellent at interior decorating. They may have a habit of changing the interior of their house quite often.

The Libra person is refined in nature and is not fond of getting their hands soiled. They would rather leave the rough tasks for others to do. If they have enough money, they'll see to it that someone comes to the house several times a week to clean up. There are always flowers and plants in the Libra home. In general, they are fond of light gardening.

There is usually a definite relationship between the Libra woman and her home. It usually complements or supplements her charm and personality.

The person born under Libra is generally a good parent. He or she does what they can to bring up youngsters properly. Libra never tries to influence the children unnecessarily. Libra lets them develop along natural lines, never forcing them into a mold he or she has designed. One thing a Libra respects in a child is originality and individuality.

The Libra parent is far from strict, yet the children seldom turn out spoiled. The Libra mother or father will correct or punish whenever it is absolutely necessary. Most of the time, the children listen to them because of their calm sure way. Kids have faith in their Libra parent and usually respect their judgment. Children like being with Libra adults because in them they have a sympathetic friend—someone who can understand their point of view.

Libras as children are often happy and friendly. Parents find them ideal because they are so agreeable and cooperative. They never challenge their parents' authority and do what is expected of them most of the time. Libra children are often creative. Whenever they show signs of artistic ability, they should be encouraged. Some of them are great daydreamers at school and have to be encouraged and inspired in order to do their best.

Social Relationships

The Libra man or woman usually makes a good friend because of their even disposition and easygoing ways. Others turn to Libra in time of need. He or she always is able to advise someone in a helpful manner. Generally, Libra is honest and sincere in their dealings with associates and friends. However, he or she may feel a bit envious if friends have nicer things.

Libras do not enjoy being alone and perhaps this is the reason they are so friendly. They enjoy being popular and well-liked. They seldom disappoint people who believe in them. All in all, they are quite cooperative and easy to get along with. They can be counted on to do the right thing at all times.

The person born under this sign usually becomes angry rather quickly. However, he quickly gets over it and is willing to kiss and make up within a short time after his explosion. Whatever he does he will try to avoid hurting someone else's feelings. He is not cruel or petty. That is not his nature.

The Libra person is a good conversationalist. Often at parties they are the center of attention. People generally have the impression that Libra is well-informed and rather aristocratic. Whenever Libra is upset or disturbed—off balance, so to speak—they try not to let it show.

Love and Marriage

In matters of love and romance, Libra is without equal. They are well-informed on everything that has to do with romance. Love is essential to Libras because they are born under the love planet Venus. As sons and daughters of Venus, Libras are affectionate and gentle, truly considerate of their mate or lover.

At times, the Libra man or woman may be uncertain of their feelings. They may go through a series of love affairs before they really know what they are looking for in a mate. Libra is fickle. He or she can be quite passionate in a love affair, then some days later break it off or lose interest for no apparent reason. It is just one of Libra's ways—difficult as it may be to understand.

Libra is easily attracted to members of the opposite sex and enjoys their company immensely. People find the Libra charm difficult to resist. Some people born under this seventh sign of the Zodiac are somewhat sentimental and are easily moved. This quality often appeals to their lovers or admirers. When Libras desire to transfer their affection, they usually do so with much tact and consideration.

Libras are often passionate lovers in spite of their calm and gentle ways. Their calm fronts often hide a hot temperament. When in love, they'll forsake their usual lamb-like ways for those of a ram.

The Libra woman expects to be handled with kid gloves by the man who professes to love her. She enjoys small courtesies and enjoys having things done for her.

Libra people are generally quite well suited for marriage or permanent love relationships. Although they may go from one romance to the other quite easily, what they are always in search of is permanent union. They are quite domestic by nature and enjoy setting up house and attending to family affairs. Some of them marry quite young. Although they may not be faithful at all times, they are honest in their intention of being steadfast.

The Libra person enjoys home life. A place for entertaining and sharing the company of loved ones, the home is something special. Libra is usually a very considerate partner. A mate may find it a difficult task keeping up. Libra's ease in social relationships is a quality that is rare to come by.

In spite of an occasional post-marital fling that they may find difficult to pass up from time to time, Libras shun all thoughts of divorce or separation. They do what they can to keep the marriage together and will try to keep serious faults under wraps. Libra is not likely to be open about indiscretions for fear of upsetting a mate and the relationship.

Romance and the Libra Woman

Libra women are quite passionate and affectionate. Most of them possess a mysterious charm which makes them much in demand with the opposite sex. The Libra woman is never short of admirers. She may have a difficult time trying to make up her mind about which one to settle down with, but she does what she can to enjoy herself during her state of indecision. She may go from one affair to the other without any regrets or misgivings. Others may accuse her of being a great flirt, but in all love relationships she is quite sincere. She is changeable and impulsive, though, which makes it hard for her to be consistent in her affections at times.

The Libra woman adjusts to married life very well. When she has found the right man, she is willing to do all she can to keep their life a peaceful and harmonious one. In spite of her inclination to flirt, the Libra woman usually remains faithful after she has married. At times, she may find herself strongly attracted to another man. But she knows how to control herself and would do nothing that might jeopardize her marriage.

The Libra woman is usually poised and charming in a stand-offish way. Underneath, however, she may be very passionate and loving. Her husband may find her more romantic than he expected. She is the kind of woman most men adore. There is something helpless yet seductive about her. She is not the sort of woman who would like to wear the pants in the family. She is only too glad to let someone else manage everything. She likes being taken care of.

Although she may seem terribly dependent and clinging, when the situation calls for her to take things over, she can do this quite ably. She's the kind of a woman who generally gets things her own way. Her charm and beauty are indeed irresistible.

The Libra woman makes an ideal wife. She knows how to arrange things in a home so that they radiate peace, harmony, and beauty. When guests arrive, she knows how to make them feel comfortable immediately. She makes an excellent hostess. Her husband is apt to find her an invaluable companion. He can discuss things with her at his ease. The Libra woman is quite intelligent and has no difficulty in discussing matters that many women fail to understand or master.

She is a lover of a busy social life. However, she would be willing to give up all the glitter and laughter of party going if it interfered with her duties as a wife or mother.

Her tastes are rather expensive. She may run up bills without giving it much thought. If her husband can afford her extravagance, chances are he won't complain. He is apt to feel that his charming wife is worth the extra expense.

The Libra woman makes an understanding mother. It is important to her that her children get a chance to develop their real personalities. She is quite persuasive in a gentle way.

Romance and the Libra Man

Libra men have no trouble at all in attracting members of the opposite sex. Women find them charming and handsome. They are usually quite considerate of their women friends and know how to make them feel important and loved. The Libra man is quite a lover. He is not at a loss when it comes to romancing, for he finds love one of the most important things there is about life.

One fault, however, is the Libra man's ability to change from one love to another with appalling ease. He is always sincere in his love interests, but sometimes he finds it difficult to remain in love with the same person for a long period of time.

Women like him because he seems to know what is right; he never does the wrong thing, no matter what the occasion. His interest in the arts and such matters impress women. His sensitivity is another quality they often admire. The Libra man does not stint when it comes to demonstrating his affection for the woman he believes he loves. However, he is quite crestfallen if the woman should indicate that she is not ready to reciprocate.

Once he settles down, the Libra man makes a good husband and father. He is well suited to family life. Home is important to him. He likes to entertain close friends and relatives frequently. He is generally a very considerate and lively host. It is important that the Libra man find the right woman for his married life. If he has selected someone who finds it difficult to show the same interest in him that he shows in her, he will begin to look elsewhere for companionship. However, he is interested in having stability in his home and will do what he can to keep things in order.

He may be difficult to please at times, particularly if his wife does not share his refined tastes. If his wife has a practical mind, so much the better. Generally, Libra has a poor head for financial matters and is apt to let money slip through his fingers like water.

As a father he is quite considerate and encouraging. He is anxious to see his children express themselves as they desire. Yet he will not tolerate spoiled behavior. Children respect his gentle ways, and they do what they can to please him.

Woman—Man

LIBRA WOMAN
ARIES MAN

In some ways, the Aries man resembles his zodiacal symbol the Ram, roaming the meadow in search of good grazing land. He has an insatiable thirst for knowledge. He's ambitious and is apt to have his finger in many pies. He can do with a woman like you—someone attractive, quick-witted, and smart.

He is not interested in a clinging vine for a mate. He wants someone who is there when he needs her, someone who listens and understands what he says, someone who can give advice if he should ever need it—which is not likely to be often. The Aries man wants a woman who will look good on his arm without hanging on it too heavily.

He is looking for a woman who has both feet on the ground and yet is mysterious and enticing—a kind of domestic Helen of Troy whose face or fine dinner can launch a thousand business deals if need be. That woman he's in search of sounds a little like you, doesn't she? If the shoe fits, put it on. You won't regret it.

The Aries man makes a good husband. He is faithful and attentive. He is an affectionate kind of man. He'll make you feel needed and loved. Love is a serious matter for the Aries man. He does not believe in flirting or playing the field—especially after he's found the woman of his dreams. He'll expect you to be as constant in your affection as he is in his. He'll expect you to be one hundred percent his; he won't put up with any nonsense while romancing you.

The Aries man may be fairly progressive and modern about many things. However, when it comes to pants wearing, he's downright conventional: it's strictly male attire. The best role you can take in the relationship is a supporting one. He's the boss and that's that. Once you have learned to accept the role playing, you'll find the going easy.

The Aries man, with his endless energy and drive, likes to relax in the comfort of his home at the end of the day. The good homemaker can be sure of holding his love. He's keen on watching the news from a comfortable armchair. If you see to it that everything in the house is where he expects to find it, you'll have no difficulty keeping the relationship on an even keel.

Life and love with an Aries man may be just the medicine you need. He'll be a good provider. He'll spoil you if he's financially able to do so.

Aries is your zodiacal mate, as well as your zodiacal opposite, so the Aries-Libra couple will make wonderful parents together. Kids take to Aries like ducks to water. His quick mind and energetic behavior appeal to the young. His ability to jump from one thing to another will delight the kids and keep them active. The Aries father is young at heart and will spoil children every chance he gets. You will set standards for their growing up and see to it that they observe social etiquette and good manners.

LIBRA WOMAN
TAURUS MAN

If you've got your heart set on a man born under the sign of Taurus, you'll have to learn the art of being patient. Taurus take their time about everything—even love.

The steady and deliberate Taurus man is a little slow on the draw. It may take him quite a while before he gets around to popping that question. For the woman who doesn't mind twiddling her thumbs, the waiting and anticipating will almost always pay off in the end. Taurus men want to make sure that every step they take is a good one—particularly if they feel that the path they're on is one that leads to the altar.

If you are in the mood for a whirlwind romance, you had better cast your net in shallower waters. Moreover, most Taurus prefer to do the angling themselves. They are not keen on women taking the lead. If she does, he might drop her like a dead fish. If you let yourself get caught on his terms, you'll find that he's fallen for you—hook, line, and sinker.

The Taurus man is fond of a comfortable home life. It is very important to him. If you keep those home fires burning you will have no trouble keeping that flame in your Bull's heart aglow. You have a talent for homemaking; use it. Your taste in furnishings is excellent. You know how to make a house come to life with colors and decorations.

Taurus, the strong, steady, and protective Bull, may not be your idea of a man on the move. Still, he's reliable. Perhaps he could be the anchor for your dreams and plans. He could help you to acquire a more balanced outlook and approach to your life. If you're given to impulsiveness, he could help you to curb it. He's the man who is always there when you need him.

When you tie the knot with a man born under Taurus, you can put away fears about creditors pounding on the front door. Taurus are practical about everything including bill paying. When he carries you over that threshold, you can be certain that the entire house is paid for, not only the doorsill.

As a wife, you won't have to worry about putting aside your many interests for the sake of back-breaking house chores. Your Taurus hubby will see to it that you have all the latest time-saving appliances and comforts.

Taurus, born under the planet Venus just as you are, has much affection for the children, and he has no trouble demonstrating his love and warmth. Yet the Taurus father does not believe in spoiling the kids. He believes that children have a place, and that place is mainly to be seen but not heard. He is an excellent disciplinarian. With your cooperation, he will see to it that the youngsters grow up to be polite, obedient, and respectful.

LIBRA WOMAN
GEMINI MAN

The Gemini man is quite a catch. Many a woman has set her cap for him and failed to bag him. Generally, Gemini men are intelligent, witty, and outgoing. Many of them tend to be versatile and multitalented. The Gemini man could easily wind up being your better half.

One thing that causes a Twin's mind and affection to wander is a bore. But it is unlikely that a socially chic woman like Libra would ever allow herself to be accused of being that. The Gemini man who has caught your heart will admire you for your ideas and intellect—perhaps even more than for your homemaking talents and good looks.

The woman who hitches up with a Twin needn't feel that once she's made her marriage vows she'll have to store her interests and ambition in the attic somewhere. The Gemini man will admire you for your zeal and liveliness. He's the kind of guy who won't scowl if you let him shift for himself in the kitchen once in a while. In fact, he'll enjoy the challenge of wrestling with pots and pans himself for a change. Chances are, too, that he might turn out to be a better cook than you—that is, if he isn't already.

The man born under the sign of the Twins is a very active person. There aren't many women who have enough pep to keep up with him, but this should be no problem for the airy Libra female.

The Gemini man is a dreamer, planner, and idealist. A woman with a strong personality could easily fill the role of rudder for her Gemini's ship-without-a-sail. If you are a cultivated, purposeful woman, he won't mind it too much. The intelligent Twin is often aware of his shortcomings and doesn't resent it if someone with better bearings than himself gives him a shove in the right direction—when it's needed. The average Gemini does not have serious ego hang-ups and will even accept a well-deserved chewing out from his mate quite good-naturedly.

When you team up with a Gemini man, you'll probably always have a houseful of people to entertain—interesting people, too, which suits your Libra sociability. Geminis find it hard to tolerate antisocial characters who have little to say.

People born under Gemini generally have two sides to their natures, as different as night and day. It's very easy for them to be happy-go-lucky one minute, then down in the dumps the next. They hate to be bored and will generally do anything to make their lives interesting, vivid, and action-packed.

Gemini men are always attractive to the opposite sex. He'll flirt occasionally, but it will never amount to anything serious.

The Gemini father and the Libra mother combine the airy qualities basic to both your zodiacal signs, and as a result the children will grow up in a very open, tolerant environment. The Gemini father is a pushover for the kids. He loves them so much, he generally lets them do what they want. His sense of humor is infectious, so the youngsters will naturally come to see the fun and funny sides of life. You will have to introduce a few rules and regulations.

LIBRA WOMAN
CANCER MAN

Chances are you won't hit it off too well with the man born under Cancer if your plans are love. But then, Cupid has been known to do some pretty unlikely things. The Cancer man is very sensitive—thin-skinned and occasionally moody. You've got to keep on your toes—and not step on his—if you're determined to make a go of the relationship.

The Cancer man may be lacking in some of the qualities you seek in a man. But when it comes to being faithful and being a good provider, he's hard to beat.

The perceptive woman will not mistake the Crab's quietness for sullenness or his thriftiness for penny-pinching. In some respects, he is like that wise old owl out on a limb; he may look like he's dozing but actually he hasn't missed a thing.

Cancer people often possess a well of knowledge about human behavior. They can come across with some pretty helpful advice to those in trouble or in need. He can certainly guide you in making investments both in time and money. He may not say much, but he's always got his wits about him.

The Crab may not be the match or catch for the sociable Libra woman. At times, you are likely to find him downright dull. True to his sign, he can be fairly cranky and crabby when handled the wrong way. He is perhaps more sensitive than he should be.

If you're smarter than your Cancer friend, be smart enough not to let him know. Never give him the idea that you think he's a little short on brainpower. It would send him scurrying back into his shell—and all that ground lost in the relationship will perhaps never be recovered.

The Crab is most himself at home. Once settled down for the night or the weekend, wild horses couldn't drag him farther than the gatepost—that is, unless those wild horses were dispatched by his mother. The Crab is sometimes a Momma's boy. If his mate does not put her foot down, he will see to it that his mother always comes first. No self-respecting wife would ever allow herself to play second fiddle to her mother-in-law. With a little bit of tact, however, she'll find that slipping into that number-one position is as easy as pie (that legendary one his mother used to bake).

If you pamper your Cancer man, you'll find that Mother turns up less and less, at the front door as well as in conversations.

Cancers make proud, patient, and protective fathers. But they can be a little too protective. Their sheltering instincts can interfere with a youngster's natural inclination to test the waters outside the home. Still, the Cancer father doesn't want to see his kids learning about life the hard way from the streets. Your qualities of grace and refinement, fairness and tolerance will help the youngsters cope with a variety of life situations.

LIBRA WOMAN
LEO MAN

For the woman who enjoys being swept off her feet in a romantic whirlwind fashion, Leo is the sign of love. When the Lion puts his mind to romancing, he doesn't stint. It's all wining and dining and dancing till the wee hours of the morning.

Leo is all heart and knows how to make his woman feel like a woman. The girl in constant search of a man she can look up to need go no farther: Leo is ten-feet tall—in spirit if not in stature. He's a man not only in full control of his faculties but in full control of just about any situation he finds himself in. He's a winner.

The Leo man may not look like Tarzan, but he knows how to roar and beat his chest if he has to. The woman who has had her fill of weak-kneed men finds in a Leo someone she can at last lean upon. He can support you not only physically but spiritually as well. He's good at giving advice that pays off.

Leos are direct people. They don't believe in wasting time or effort. They almost never make unwise investments.

Many Leos rise to the top of their profession. Through example, they often prove to be a source of great inspiration to others.

Although he's a ladies' man, the Leo man is very particular about his ladies. His standards are high when it comes to love interests. The idealistic and cultivated Libra should have no trouble keeping her balance on the pedestal the Lion sets her on. Leo believes that romance should be played on a fair give-and-take basis. He won't stand for any monkey business in a love relationship. It's all or nothing.

You'll find him a frank, off-the-shoulder person. He generally says what is on his mind.

If you decide upon a Leo man for a mate, you must be prepared to stand behind him full force. He expects it—and usually deserves it. He's the head of the house and can handle that position without a hitch. He knows how to go about breadwinning. If he has his way, and most Leos do have their own way, he'll see to it that you'll have all the luxuries you crave and the comforts you need.

It's unlikely that the romance in your marriage will ever die out. Lions need love like flowers need sunshine. They're everamorous and generally expect full attention and affection from their mates. Leos are fond of going out on the town. They love to give parties, as well as go to them.

Leo fathers have a tendency to spoil the children—up to a point. That point is reached when the children become the center of attention, and Leo feels neglected. Then the Leo father becomes strict and insists that his rules be followed. You will have your hands full pampering both your Leo mate and the children. As long as he comes first in your affections, the family will be happy and loving.

LIBRA WOMAN
VIRGO MAN

The Virgo man is all business—at least he may seem so to you. He is usually very cool, calm, and collected. He's perhaps too much of a fussbudget to wake up deep romantic interests in the Venus-born Libra woman.

Torrid romancing to Virgo is just so much sentimental mush. He can do without it and can make that quite evident in short order. He's keen on chastity and, if necessary, he can lead a sedentary, sexless life without caring too much about the fun others think he's missing.

In short, you might find the Virgo man a first-class dud. He doesn't have much of an imagination; flights of fancy don't interest him. He is always correct and likes to be handled correctly. Almost everything about him is orderly, with a place for everything and everything in its place.

He does have an honest-to-goodness heart, believe it or not. The woman who finds herself strangely attracted to his cool, feet-flat-on-the-ground ways will discover that his is a constant heart, not one that goes in for flings or sordid affairs. Virgos take an awfully long time to warm up to someone. A practical man, even in matters of the heart, he wants to know just what kind of person you are before he takes a chance on you.

The impulsive date had better not make the mistake of kissing her Virgo friend on the street—even if it's only a peck on the cheek. He's not at all demonstrative and hates public displays of affection. Love, according to him, should be kept within the confines of one's home—with the curtains drawn.

Once he believes that you are on the level with him as far as your love is concerned, you'll see how fast he can lose his cool. Virgos are considerate, gentle lovers. He'll spend a long time, though, getting to know you. He'll like you before he loves you.

A romance with a Virgo man can be a sometime—or, rather, a one-time—thing. If the bottom ever falls out, don't bother reaching for the adhesive tape. Nine times out of ten he won't care about patching up. He's a once-burnt-twice-shy guy. When he crosses your telephone number out of his address book, he's crossing you out of his life—for good.

Neat as a pin, he's thumbs-down on what he considers sloppy housekeeping. An ashtray with just one stubbed out cigarette in it can annoy him even if it's only two seconds old. Glassware should always sparkle and shine if you want to keep him happy.

If you marry him, keep your sunny-side up.

The Virgo father appreciates courtesy, good manners, and proper etiquette as much, if not more, than you do. He will instill a sense of order in the household, and he expects the children to respect his wishes. He is very concerned about the kids' health and hygiene, so he may try to restrict their freedom. You'll have to step in and let the youngsters break a few rules now and then.

LIBRA WOMAN
LIBRA MAN

If there's a Libra man in your life, you may have found the male complement to your side of the Libra equation for balance and harmony. Men born under this sign have a way with women. You'll always feel at ease in a Libra's company. You can be yourself when you're with him.

The Libra man can be moody at times. His moodiness is often puzzling. One moment he comes on hard and strong with declarations of his love, the next moment you find that he's left you like yesterday's mashed potatoes. He'll come back, though; don't worry. Libras are like that. Deep down inside he really knows what he wants even though he may not appear to.

You'll appreciate his admiration of beauty and harmony. If you're dressed to the teeth and never looked lovelier, you'll get a ready compliment—and one that's really deserved. Libras don't indulge in idle flattery. If they don't like something, they are tactful enough to remain silent.

Libras will go to great lengths to preserve peace and harmony—even tell a fat lie if necessary. They don't like showdowns or disagreeable confrontations. The frank woman is all for getting whatever is bothering her off her chest and out into the open, even if it comes out all wrong. To the Libra man, making a clean breast of everything seems like sheer folly sometimes.

One of you Libras may lose your patience while waiting for the other to make up your mind. It takes ages sometimes for Libra to make a decision. You both weigh all sides carefully before committing to anything. You both dillydally—at least about small things—and often find it difficult to come to a decision.

All in all, the Libra man is kind, considerate, and fair. He is interested in the real truth. He'll try to balance everything out until he has all the correct answers. It's not difficult for him to see both sides of a story.

Libras are not show-offs. Generally, they are well-balanced, modest people. Honest, wholesome, and affectionate, they are serious about every love encounter they have. If he should find that the woman he's dating is not really suited to him, he will end the relationship in such a tactful manner that no hard feelings will come about.

The Libra father is patient and fair. He can be firm without exercising undue strictness or discipline. Although he can be a harsh judge at times, with the kids he will radiate sweetness and light in the hope that they will grow up imitating his gentle manner. Together, the Libra couple will set a sterling example of graciousness and charm for the youngsters to follow.

LIBRA WOMAN
SCORPIO MAN

Many find the Scorpio's sting a fate worse than death. When his anger breaks loose, you had better clear out of the vicinity.

The average Scorpio may strike you as a brute. He'll stick pins into the balloons of your plans and dreams if they don't line up with what he thinks is right. If you do anything to irritate him—just anything—you'll wish you hadn't. He'll give you a sounding out that would make you pack your bags and go back to mother—if you were that kind of woman.

The Scorpio man hates being tied down to home life. He would rather be out on the battlefield of life, belting away at whatever he feels is a just and worthy cause, instead of staying home nestled in a comfortable armchair with the evening paper. If you are a woman who has a homemaking streak, don't keep those home fires burning too brightly, too long; you may run out of firewood.

As passionate as he is in business affairs and politics, the Scorpio man still has plenty of pepper and ginger stored away for lovemaking.

Most women are easily attracted to him—perhaps you are no exception. Those who allow a man born under this sign to sweep them off their feet soon find that they are dealing with a cauldron of seething excitement. The Scorpio is passionate with a capital P, you can be sure of that. But he's capable of dishing out as much pain as pleasure.

Scorpios are blunt. An insult is likely to whiz out of his mouth quicker than a compliment.

If you're the kind of woman who can keep a stiff upper lip, take it on the chin, turn a deaf ear, and all that, because you feel you are still under his love spell in spite of everything—lots of luck.

If you have decided to take the bitter with the sweet, prepare yourself for a lot of ups and downs. Chances are you won't have as much time for your own affairs and interests as you'd like. The Scorpio's love of power may cause you to be at his constant beck and call.

Scorpios like fathering large families. He is proud of his children, but often he fails to live up to his responsibilities as a parent. In spite of the extremes in his personality, the Scorpio man is able to transform the conflicting characteristics within himself when he becomes a father. When he takes his fatherly duties seriously, he is a powerful teacher. He believes in preparing his children for the hard knocks life sometimes delivers. He is adept with difficult youngsters because he knows how to tap the best in each child.

LIBRA WOMAN
SAGITTARIUS MAN

If you've set your cap for a man born under the sign of Sagittarius, you may have to apply an awful lot of strategy before you can persuade him to get down on bended knee. Although some Sagittarius may be marriage-shy, they're not ones to skitter away from romance. You'll find a love relationship with an Archer—whether a fling or the real thing—a very enjoyable experience.

As a rule, Sagittarius are bright, happy, healthy people. They have a strong sense of fair play. Often they are a source of inspiration to others. They are full of drive and ideas.

You'll be taken by the Archer's infectious grin and his lighthearted friendly nature. If you do wind up being the woman in his life, you'll find that he's apt to treat you more like a buddy than the love of his life. It's just his way. Sagittarius is often more chummy than romantic.

You'll admire his broad-mindedness in most matters—including those of the heart. If, while dating you, he claims that he still wants to play the field, he'll expect you to enjoy the same liberty. Once he's promised to love, honor, and obey, however, he does just that. Marriage for him, once he's taken that big step, is very serious business.

The Sagittarius man is quick-witted. He has a genuine interest in equality. He hates prejudice and injustice. Generally, Archers are good at sports. They love the great outdoors and respect wildlife and wilderness in all its forms.

He's not much of a homebody. Quite often he's occupied with faraway places either in his daydreams or in reality. He enjoys being on the move. He's got ants in his pants and refuses to sit still for long stretches at a time. Humdrum routine—especially at home—bores him.

He likes to surprise people. At the drop of a hat, he may ask you to hop on a plane and dine in some foreign port—most likely down the road and not too far from home by car. He also likes to tease.

He'll take great pride in showing you off to his friends. He'll always be considerate of your feelings. He will never embarrass or disappoint you intentionally.

His friendly, sunshiny nature is capable of attracting many people. Like you, he's very tolerant when it comes to friends. You will most likely spend a great deal of time helping him entertain people and being the gracious Libra hostess for his big parties.

The Sagittarius father can be all thumbs when it comes to tiny tots. He will dote on any son or daughter dutifully, but he may be bewildered by the newborn. The Archer usually becomes comfortable with youngsters once they have passed through the baby stage. As soon as the children are old enough to walk and talk, the Sagittarius dad encourages each and every visible sign of talent and skill in his kids.

LIBRA WOMAN
CAPRICORN MAN

A with-it Libra woman like you is likely to find the average Capricorn man a bit of a drag. The man born under the sign of the Goat is often a closed person and difficult to get to know. Even if you do get to know him, you may not find him very interesting.

In romance, Capricorn men are a little on the rusty side. You'll probably have to make all the passes.

You may find his plodding manner irritating and his conservative, traditional ways downright maddening. He's not one to take chances on anything. If it was good enough for his father, it's good enough for him. He follows a way that is tried and true.

The Capricorn man is habit-bound. Whenever adventure rears its tantalizing head, the Goat will turn the other way.

He may be just as ambitious as you are—perhaps even more so—but his ways of accomplishing his aims are more subterranean or, at least, seem so. He operates from the background a good deal of the time. At a gathering you may never even notice him, but he's there, taking in everything, sizing everyone up—planning his next careful move.

Although Capricorns may be intellectual to a degree, it is not generally the kind of intelligence you appreciate. He may not be as quick or as bright as you; it may take him ages to understand a simple joke.

If you do decide to take up with a man born under this sign, you ought to be pretty good in the cheering up department. The Capricorn man often acts as though he's constantly being followed by a cloud of gloom.

The Capricorn man is most himself when in the comfort and privacy of his own home. The security possible within four walls can make him a happy man. He'll spend as much time as he can at home. If he is loaded down with extra work, he'll bring it home instead of working overtime at the office.

You'll most likely find yourself frequently confronted by his relatives. Family is very important to the Capricorn—his family, that is. They had better take a pretty important place in your life, too, if you want to keep your home a happy one.

Although his caution in most matters may all but drive the luxury-loving Libra woman up the wall, you'll find that his concerned way with money is justified most of the time. He'll plan everything right down to the last penny.

The Capricorn father is a dutiful parent and takes a lifelong interest in seeing that his children make something of themselves. He may not understand their hopes and dreams because he often tries to put his head on their shoulders. The Capricorn father believes that there are certain goals to be achieved, and there is a traditional path to achieving them. He can be quite a scold if the youngsters break the rules. You will have to balance his sometimes rigid approach and smooth things over for the kids.

LIBRA WOMAN
AQUARIUS MAN

Aquarius individuals love everybody—even their worst enemies sometimes. Through your love relationship with an Aquarius you'll find yourself running into all sorts of people, ranging from near-genius to downright insane—and they're all friends of his.

As a rule, Aquarius are extremely friendly and open. Of all the signs, they are perhaps the most tolerant. In the thinking department, they are often miles ahead of others.

You'll most likely find your relationship with this man a challenging one. Your high respect for intelligence and imagination may be reason enough for you to set your heart on a Water Bearer. You'll find that you can learn a lot from him.

In the holding-hands phase of your romance, you may find that your Water Bearer friend has cold feet. Aquarius take quite a bit of warming up before they are ready to come across with that first goodnight kiss. More than likely, he'll just want to be your pal in the beginning. For him, that's an important first step in any relationship—love included.

The poetry and flowers stage—if it ever comes—will come later. Aquarius is all heart. Still, when it comes to tying himself down to one person and for keeps, he is almost always sure to hesitate. He may even try to get out of it if you breathe down his neck too heavily.

The Aquarius man is no Valentino and wouldn't want to be. The kind of love life he's looking for is one that's made up mainly of companionship. Although he may not be very romantic, the memory of his first romance will always hold an important position in his heart. Some Aquarius wind up marrying their childhood sweethearts.

You won't find it difficult to look up to a man born under the sign of the Water Bearer, but you may find the challenge of trying to keep up with him dizzying. He can pierce through the most complicated problem as if it were simple math. You may find him a little too lofty and high-minded, but don't judge him too harshly if that's the case. He's way ahead of his time—your time, too, most likely.

If you marry this man, he'll stay true to you. Don't think that once the honeymoon is over, you'll be chained to the kitchen sink forever. Your Aquarius husband will encourage you to keep active in your own interests and affairs. You'll most likely have a minor tiff now and again but never anything serious.

The Aquarius father has an almost intuitive understanding of children. He sees them as individuals in their own right, not as extensions of himself or as beings who are supposed to take a certain place in the world. He can talk to the kids on a variety of subjects, and his knowledge can be awe-inspiring. You will sometimes have to bring the youngsters back down to earth, but you will appreciate the lessons of tolerance and fairness your Aquarius mate has transmitted to the children.

LIBRA WOMAN
PISCES MAN

The man born under Pisces is quite a dreamer. Sometimes he's so wrapped up in his dreams that he's difficult to reach. To the average, ambitious woman, he may seem a little passive.

He's easygoing most of the time. He seems to take things in his stride. He'll entertain all kinds of views and opinions from just about anyone, nodding or smiling vaguely, giving the impression that he's with them 100 percent while that may not be the case at all. His attitude may be why bother when he is confronted with someone wrong who thinks he's right. The Pisces man will seldom speak his mind if he thinks he'll be rigidly opposed.

The Pisces man is oversensitive at times—he's afraid of getting his feelings hurt. He'll sometimes imagine a personal affront when none's been made. Chances are you'll find this complex of his maddening. At times, you may feel like giving him a swift kick where it hurts the most. It won't do any good, though. It would just add fuel to the fire of his complex.

One thing you will admire about this man is his concern for people who are sickly or troubled. He'll make his shoulder available to anyone in the mood for a good cry. He can listen to one hard-luck story after another without seeming to tire. When his advice is asked, he is capable of coming across with some pretty important words of wisdom. He often knows what's bothering someone before that person is aware of it. It's almost intuitive with Pisces, it seems.

Still, at the end of the day, your Pisces lover looks forward to some peace and quiet. If you've got a problem on your mind, don't dump it into his lap. If you do, you're apt to find him short-tempered. He's a good listener, but he can only take so much.

Pisces men are not aimless although they may seem so at times. The positive sort of Pisces man is quite often successful in his profession and is likely to wind up rich and influential. Material gain, however, is not a direct goal for a man born under the sign of the Fishes.

The weaker Pisces is usually content to stay put on the level where he happens to find himself. He won't complain too much if the roof leaks or the fence is in need of repair. He'll just shrug it off as a minor inconvenience. He's got more important things to think about, he'll say.

Because of their seemingly laissez-faire manner, Pisces fathers and Pisces men in general are immensely popular with children. For tots, Pisces plays the double role of confidant and playmate. It will never enter his mind to discipline a child, no matter how spoiled or incorrigible that child becomes.

Man—Woman

LIBRA MAN
ARIES WOMAN

Aries and Libra are zodiacal mates or zodiacal opposites, depending how individuals of these signs link up in love. For many a mild Libra man, the Aries woman may be a little too bossy and busy. Aries women are ambitious creatures. They tend to lose their patience with thorough and deliberate people, like Libra, who take a lot of time to complete something.

The Aries woman is a fast worker. Sometimes she's so fast she forgets to look where she's going. When she stumbles or falls, it would be nice if you were there to grab her. But Aries women are very proud. They don't like to be criticized when they err. Tongue-wagging can turn them into blocks of ice.

However, don't think that the Aries woman frequently gets tripped up in her plans. Quite often they are capable of taking aim and hitting the bull's-eye. You'll be flabbergasted at times by their accuracy as well as by their ambition.

You are perhaps somewhat slower than the Aries woman in attaining your goals. Still, you are not apt to make mistakes along the way. Libra is seldom ill-prepared.

The Aries woman is sensitive at times. She likes to be handled with gentleness and respect. Let her know that you love her for her brains as well as for her good looks. Never give her cause to become jealous. When your Aries woman sees green, you'd better forget about sharing a rosy future together. Handle her with tender love and care and she's yours.

The Aries woman can be giving if she feels her partner is deserving. She is no iceberg; she responds to the proper masculine flame. She needs a man she can look up to and feel proud of. If the shoe fits, put it on. If not, better put your sneakers back on and quietly tiptoe out of her sight.

She can cause you plenty of heartache if you've made up your mind about her and she hasn't made up hers about you. Aries women are very demanding at times. Some of them tend to be high-strung. They can be difficult if they feel their independence is being hampered.

The cultivated Aries woman makes a wonderful homemaker and hostess. You'll find that she's very clever in decorating; she knows how to use colors. Your house will be tastefully furnished. Both of you see to it that it radiates harmony. Friends and acquaintances will love your Aries wife. She knows how to make everyone feel at home and welcome.

Although the Aries woman may not be keen on burdensome responsibilities, she is fond of children and the joy they bring. She is skilled at juggling both career and motherhood, so her kids will never feel that she is an absentee parent. In fact, as the youngsters grow older, they might want a little more of the liberation that is so important to her.

LIBRA MAN
TAURUS WOMAN

The woman born under the sign of Taurus may lack a little of the sparkle and bubble you often like to find in a woman. The Taurus woman is generally down to earth and never flighty. It's important to her that she keep both feet flat on the ground. She is not fond of bounding all over the place, especially if she's under the impression that there's no profit in it.

On the other hand, if you hit it off with a Taurus woman, you won't be disappointed in the romance area. The Taurus woman is all woman and proud of it, too. She can be very devoted and loving once she decides that her relationship with you is no fly-by-night romance. Basically, she's a passionate person. In sex, she's direct and to the point. If she really loves you, she'll let you know she's yours—and without reservations.

Better not flirt with other women once you've committed yourself to her. She's capable of being very jealous and possessive.

She'll stick by you through thick and thin. It's almost certain that if the going ever gets rough, she won't go running home to her mother. She can adjust to the hard times just as graciously as she can to the good times.

Taurus are, on the whole, even-tempered. They like to be treated with kindness. Luxurious things and artistic objects win their hearts.

You may find her a little cautious and deliberate. She likes to be safe and sure about everything. Let her plod along if she likes. Don't coax her, but just let her take her own sweet time. Everything she does is done thoroughly and, generally, without mistakes.

Don't deride her caution or shyness. It could lead to an explosive scene. The Taurus woman doesn't anger readily but when prodded often enough, she's capable of letting loose with a cyclone of ill will. If you treat her with kindness and consideration, you'll have no cause for complaint.

The Taurus woman loves doing things for her man. She's a whiz in the kitchen and can whip up feasts fit for a king if she thinks they'll be royally appreciated. She may not fully understand you, but she'll adore you and be faithful to you if she feels you're worthy of it.

The Taurus woman, ruled by lovely planet Venus as you are, will share with you the joys and burdens of parenthood. But the Taurus mother seldom puts up with any nonsense from the youngsters. It is not that she is strict, she is just concerned. She likes the children to be well behaved. She can wield an iron fist in a velvet glove.

Nothing pleases a Taurus mother more than a compliment from a neighbor or teacher about her child's behavior. She may have some difficult times with them when they reach adolescence. And some teenagers may inwardly resent their Taurus mother's tutelage. But in later life they are often thankful they were brought up in such a conscientious fashion.

LIBRA MAN
GEMINI WOMAN
You may find a romance with a woman born under the sign of the Twins a many-splendored thing. In her you can find the intellectual companionship you often look for in a friend or mate. A Gemini partner can appreciate your aims and desires because she travels pretty much the same road as you do intellectually—that is, at least part of the way. She may share your interest, but she will lack your tenacity.

She suffers from itchy feet. She can be here, there, all over the place and at the same time, or so it would seem. Her eagerness to move about may make you dizzy, still you'll enjoy and appreciate her liveliness and mental agility.

Geminis often have sparkling personalities. You'll be attracted by her warmth and grace. While she's on your arm you'll probably notice that many male eyes are drawn to her. She may even return a gaze or two, but don't let that worry you. All women born under this sign have nothing against a harmless flirt once in a while. They enjoy this sort of attention. If she feels she is already spoken for, however, she will never let it get out of hand.

Although she may not be as handy as you'd like in the kitchen, you'll never go hungry for a filling and tasty meal. She's as much in a hurry as you are, and won't feel like she's cheating by breaking out the instant mashed potatoes or the frozen peas. She may not be much of a good cook but she is clever. With a dash of this and a suggestion of that, she can make an uninteresting TV dinner taste like a gourmet meal. Then, again, maybe you've struck it rich and have a Gemini who finds complicated recipes a challenge to her intellect. If so, you'll find every meal a tantalizing and mouth-watering surprise.

When you're beating your brains out over the Sunday crossword puzzle and find yourself stuck, just ask your Gemini mate. She'll give you all the right answers without batting an eyelash.

Like you, she loves all kinds of people. You may even find that you're a bit more particular than she. Often all that a Gemini requires is that her friends be interesting—and stay interesting. One thing she's not able to abide is a dullard.

Leave the party organizing to your Gemini sweetheart or mate, and you'll never have a chance to know what a dull moment is. She'll bring the swinger out in you if you give her half a chance.

A Gemini mother enjoys her children, which can be the truest form of love. Like them, she's often restless, adventurous, and easily bored. She will never complain about their fleeting interests because she understands the changes they will go through as they mature.

**LIBRA MAN
CANCER WOMAN**
If you fall in love with a Cancer woman, be prepared for anything. They are sometimes difficult to understand when it comes to love. In one hour, she can unravel a whole gamut of emotions. Her moods will leave you in a tizzy. She'll always keep you guessing, that's for sure.

You may find her a little too uncertain and sensitive for your liking. You'll most likely spend a good deal of time encouraging her, helping her to erase her foolish fears. Tell her she's a living doll a dozen times a day, and you'll be well loved in return.

Be careful of the jokes you make when in her company. Don't let any of them revolve around her, her personal interests, or her family. If you do, you'll most likely reduce her to tears. She can't stand being made fun of. It will take bushels of roses and tons of chocolates—not to mention the apologies—to get her to come back out of her shell.

In matters of money managing, she may not easily come around to your way of thinking. Money will never burn a hole in her pocket. You may get the notion that your Cancer sweetheart or mate is a direct descendant of Scrooge. If she has her way, she'll hang onto the first dollar you earned. She's not only that way with money, but with everything right on up from bakery string to jelly jars. She's a saver. She never throws anything away, no matter how trivial.

Once she returns your love, you'll have an affectionate, self-sacrificing, and devoted woman for keeps. Her love for you will never alter unless you want it to. She'll put you up on a high pedestal and will do everything—even if it's against your will—to keep you there.

Cancer women love home life. For them, marriage is an easy step to make. They're domestic with a capital D. She'll do her best to make your home comfortable and cozy. The Cancer woman is more herself at home than in strange surroundings. She makes an excellent hostess. The best in her comes out when she's in her own environment.

Cancer women are reputed to be the best mothers of all the signs of the Zodiac. She'll make every complaint of her child a major catastrophe. With her, children come first. If you're lucky, you'll run a close second. You'll perhaps see her as too devoted to the children. You may have a hard time convincing her that her apron strings are too long.

LIBRA MAN
LEO WOMAN

If you can manage a partner who likes to kick up her heels every now and again, then the Leo woman was made for you. You'll have to learn to put away jealous fears when you take up with a woman born under this sign, as she's often the kind that makes heads turn and tongues wag. You don't necessarily have to believe any of what you hear. It's most likely just jealous gossip or wishful thinking.

The Leo woman has more than a fair share of grace and glamour. She knows it, generally, and knows how to put it to good use. Needless to say, other women in her vicinity turn green with envy and will try anything to put her out of the running.

If she's captured your heart and fancy, woo her full force if your intention is to eventually win her. Shower her with expensive gifts and promise her the moon if you're in a position to go that far. Then you'll find her resistance beginning to weaken.

It's not that she's such a difficult cookie—she'll probably boast about you once she's decided you're the man for her—but she does enjoy a lot of attention. What's more, she feels she's entitled to it. Her mild arrogance, though, is becoming. The Leo woman knows how to transform the crime of excessive pride into a very charming misdemeanor. It sweeps most men right off their feet. Those who do not succumb to her leonine charm are few and far between.

If you've got an important business deal to clinch and you have doubts as to whether you can bring it off as you should, take your Leo wife along to the business luncheon. It will be a cinch that you'll have that contract—lock, stock, and barrel—in your pocket before the meeting is over. She won't have to say or do anything, just be there at your side. The grouchiest oil magnate can be transformed into a gushing, obedient schoolboy if there's a Leo woman in the room.

If you're rich and want to see to it that you stay that way, don't give your Leo spouse a free hand with the charge accounts and credit cards. When it comes to spending, Leos tend to overdo. If you're poor, you have no worries because the luxury-loving Leo will most likely never recognize your existence let alone consent to marry you.

A Leo mother can be so proud of her children that she is sometimes blind to their faults. Yet when she wants them to learn and take their rightful place in the social scheme of things, the Leo mother can be strict. She is a patient teacher, lovingly explaining the rules the youngsters are expected to follow. Easygoing and friendly, she loves to pal around with the kids and show them off on every occasion.

LIBRA MAN
VIRGO WOMAN

The Virgo woman may be too difficult for you to understand at first. Her waters run deep. Even when you think you know her, don't take any bets on it. She's capable of keeping things hidden in the deep recesses of her womanly soul—things she'll only release when she's sure you're the man she's been looking for.

It may take her some time to come around to this decision. Virgos are finicky about almost everything. Everything has to be letter-perfect before they're satisfied. Many of them have the idea that the only people who can do things correctly are Virgos.

Nothing offends a Virgo woman more than slovenly dress, sloppy character, or a careless display of affection. Make sure your tie is not crooked and your shoes sport a bright shine before you go calling on this lady. Keep your off-color jokes for the locker room; she'll have none of that. Take her arm when crossing the street.

Don't rush the romance. Trying to corner a Virgo woman in the back of a cab may be one way of striking out. Never criticize the way she looks. In fact, the best policy would be to agree with her as much as possible. Still, there's just so much a man can take. All those dos and don'ts you'll have to observe if you want to get to first base with a Virgo may be just a little too much to ask of you.

After a few dates, you may come to the conclusion that she just isn't worth all that trouble. However, the Virgo woman is mysterious enough to keep her men running back for more. Chances are you'll be intrigued by her airs and graces.

If lovemaking means a lot to you, you'll be disappointed at first in the cool ways of your Virgo partner. However, under her glacial facade there lies a hot cauldron of seething excitement. If you're patient and artful in your romantic approach, you'll find that all that caution was well worth the trouble. When Virgos love, they don't stint. It's all or nothing as far as they're concerned. Once they're convinced that they love you, they go all the way, tossing all cares to the wind.

One thing a Virgo woman can't stand in love is hypocrisy. They don't give a hoot about what the neighbors say when their hearts tell them to go ahead. They're very concerned with human truths. So if their hearts stumble upon another fancy, they will be true to that new heartthrob and leave you standing in the rain.

Virgo is honest to her heart and will be as true to you as you are with her. Do her wrong once, though, and it's curtains.

The Virgo mother has high expectations for her children, and she will strive to bring out the very best in them. She is more tender than strict, though, and will nag rather than discipline. But youngsters sense her unconditional love for them, and usually turn out just as she hoped they would.

LIBRA MAN
LIBRA WOMAN
You'll probably find that the woman born under the sign of Libra is worth more than her weight in gold. She's a woman after your own heart, your other half in the astrological scheme of things.

With her, you'll always come first—make no mistake about that. She'll always be behind you 100 percent, no matter what you do. When you ask her advice about almost anything, you'll most likely get a very balanced and realistic opinion. She is good at thinking things out and never lets her emotions run away with her when clear logic is called for.

As a homemaker she is hard to beat. She is very concerned with harmony and balance. You can be sure she'll make your house a joy to live in. She'll see to it that the house is tastefully furnished and decorated. A Libra cannot stand filth or disarray. Anything that does not radiate harmony runs against her orderly grain.

She is chock-full of charm and womanly ways. She can sweep

just about any man off his feet with one winning smile. When it comes to using her brains, she can outthink almost anyone and, sometimes, with half the effort. She is diplomatic enough, though, never to let this become glaringly apparent. She may even turn the conversation around so that you think you were the one who did all the brainwork. She couldn't care less, really, just as long as you wind up doing what is right.

The Libra woman will put you on a high pedestal. You are her man and her idol. She will share the decision making—large or small—with you, although you both have trouble in this area. She's not interested in running things, but she will offer her assistance if she feels you need it.

Some find her approach to reason masculine. However, in the areas of love and affection the Libra woman is all woman. She'll literally shower you with love and kisses during your romance with her. She doesn't believe in holding out. You shouldn't either, if you want to hang on to her.

She is the kind of lover who likes to snuggle up to you in front of the fire on chilly autumn nights. She will bring you breakfast in bed Sunday. She'll be very thoughtful about anything that concerns you. If anyone dares suggest you're not the grandest guy in the world, she'll give that person what-for. She'll defend you till her dying breath. The Libra woman will be everything you want her to be.

The Libra mother is well-balanced and moderate, like you, so together you will create a harmonious household in which young family members can grow up in an environment sensitive to their needs. The Libra mother understands that children need both guidance and encouragement. Her youngsters will never lack for anything that could make their lives easier and richer.

LIBRA MAN
SCORPIO WOMAN

The Scorpio woman can be a whirlwind of passion—perhaps too much passion to suit the moderate Libra man. When her temper flies, you'd better lock up the family heirlooms and take cover. When she chooses to be sweet, then she is on your wavelength. But then her mood mysteriously changes, and you don't have a clue.

The Scorpio woman can be as hot as a tamale or as cool as a cucumber, but whatever mood she's in, she's in it for real. She does not believe in posing or putting on airs.

The Scorpio woman is often sultry and seductive. Her femme fatale charm can pierce through the hardest of hearts like a laser ray. She may not look like Mata Hari (quite often Scorpios resemble the tomboy next door), but once she's fixed you with her tantalizing eyes, you're a goner.

Life with the Scorpio woman will not be all smiles and smooth sailing. When prompted, she can unleash a gale of venom. Generally, she'll have the good grace to keep family battles within the walls of your home. When company visits, she's apt to give the impression that married life with you is one great big joyride. It's just one of her ways of expressing her loyalty to you, at least in front of others. She may fight you tooth and nail in the confines of your living room. But during an evening out, she'll hang onto your arm and have stars in her eyes.

Scorpio women are good at keeping secrets. She may even keep a few buried from you if she feels like it.

Never cross her up on on even the smallest thing. When it comes to revenge, she's an eye-for-an-eye woman. She's not too keen on forgiveness, especially if she feels she's been wronged unfairly. You'd be well-advised not to give her any cause to be jealous, either. When the Scorpio woman sees green, your life will be made far from rosy. Once she's put you in the doghouse, you can be sure that you're going to stay there awhile.

You may find life with a Scorpio woman too draining. Although she may be full of the old paprika, it's quite likely that she's not the partner you'd like to spend the rest of your natural life with. You'd prefer someone gentler and not so hot-tempered, someone who can take the highs with the lows and not bellyache, someone who is flexible and understanding. A woman born under Scorpio can be heavenly, but she can also be the very devil when she chooses.

The Scorpio mother is protective yet encouraging. The opposites within her nature mirror the very contradictions of life itself. Under her skillful guidance, the children learn how to cope with extremes and grow up to become many-faceted individuals.

LIBRA MAN
SAGITTARIUS WOMAN

You'll most likely never come across a more good-natured woman than the one born under the sign of Sagittarius. Generally, they're full of bounce and good cheer. Their sunny disposition seems almost permanent and can be relied upon even on the rainiest of days.

Women born under the sign of the Archer are almost never malicious. If ever they seem to be it is only a regrettable mistake. Archers are often a little short on tact and say literally anything that comes into their heads—no matter what the occasion is. Sometimes the words that tumble out of their mouths seem downright cutting and cruel. Still, no matter what she says, she means well. The Sagittarius woman is quite capable of losing some of her friends, and perhaps even some of yours, through a careless slip of the lip.

On the other hand, you will appreciate her honesty and good intentions. To you, qualities of this sort play an important part in life. With a little patience and practice, you can probably help cure your Sagittarius of her loose tongue. In most cases, she'll give in to your better judgment and try to follow your advice to the letter.

Chances are she'll be the outdoors type of date and partner. Long hikes, fishing trips, and white-water canoeing will most likely appeal to her. She's a busy person. No one could ever call her a slouch. She sets great store in mobility. Her feet are itchy, and she won't sit still for a minute if she doesn't have to.

She is great company most of the time and, generally, lots of fun. Even if your buddies drop by for poker and beer, she won't have any trouble fitting in.

The Sagittarius woman is very kind and sympathetic. If she feels she's made a mistake, she'll be the first to call your attention to it. She's not afraid to own up to her faults and shortcomings.

You might lose your patience with her once or twice. After she's seen how upset her shortsightedness or tendency to blab has made you, she'll do her best to straighten up.

The Sagittarius woman is not the kind who will pry into your business affairs. But she'll always be there, ready to offer advice if you need it. If you come home with red stains on your collar and you say it's paint and not lipstick, she'll believe you.

She'll seldom be suspicious. Your word will almost always be good enough for her.

The Sagittarius mother is a wonderful and loving friend to her children. She is not afraid if a youngster learns some street smarts along the way. She will broaden her children's knowledge and see that they get a well-rounded education.

LIBRA MAN
CAPRICORN WOMAN

If you are not a successful businessman or at least on your way to success, it's quite possible that a Capricorn woman will have no interest in entering your life. Generally, the Goat is a very security-minded female. She'll see to it that she invests her time only in sure things.

Men who whittle away their time with one unsuccessful scheme or another seldom attract a Capricorn. But men who are interested in getting somewhere in life and keep their noses close to the grindstone quite often have a Capricorn woman behind them, helping them to get ahead.

Although she can be a social climber, she is not what you could call cruel or hardhearted. Beneath that cool, seemingly calculating exterior there's a warm and desirable woman. She happens to think that it is just as easy to fall in love with a rich or ambitious man as it is with a poor or lazy one. She's practical.

The Capricorn woman may be keenly interested in rising to the top, but she'll never be aggressive about it. She'll seldom step on someone's feet or nudge competitors away with her elbows. She's quiet about her desires. She sits, waits, and watches. When an opening or opportunity does appear, she'll latch onto it. For an on-the-move man, an ambitious Capricorn wife or lover can be quite an asset. She can probably give you some very good advice about business matters. When you invite the boss and his wife for dinner, she'll charm them both.

The Capricorn woman is thorough in whatever she does: cooking, cleaning, making a success out of life. Capricorns are excellent hostesses as well as guests. Generally, they are beautifully mannered and gracious, no matter what their backgrounds are. They seem to have a built-in sense of what is proper. Crude behavior or a careless faux pas can offend them no end.

If you should marry a woman born under Capricorn you need never worry about her going on a wild shopping spree. Capricorns are careful with every cent that comes into their hands. They understand the value of money better than most women and have no room in their lives for careless spending.

Capricorn women are usually very devoted to family—their own, that is. With them, family ties run very deep. Don't make jokes about her relatives; she won't stand for it. You'd better check her family out before you get down on bended knee. After your marriage you'll undoubtedly be seeing lots of her relatives.

The Capricorn mother is very ambitious for her children. She wants them to have every advantage and to benefit from things she perhaps lacked as a child. She will train her youngsters to be polite and kind and to honor traditional codes of conduct.

LIBRA MAN
AQUARIUS WOMAN
If you find that you've fallen head over heels for a woman born under the sign of the Water Bearer, you'd better fasten your safety belt. It may take you quite a while to actually discover what this woman is like. Even then, you may have nothing to go on but a string of vague hunches.

Aquarius is like a rainbow, full of bright and shining hues. She is like no other woman you've ever known. There is something elusive about her, something delightfully mysterious. You'll most likely never be able to put your finger on it. It's nothing calculated, either. Aquarius women don't believe in phony charm.

There will never be a dull moment in your life with this Water Bearer woman. She seems to radiate adventure and magic. She'll most likely be the most open-minded and tolerant woman you've ever met. She has a strong dislike for injustice and prejudice. Narrow-mindedness runs against her grain.

She is very independent by nature and quite capable of shifting for herself if necessary. She may receive many proposals for marriage from all sorts of people without ever really taking them seriously. Marriage is a very big step for her. She wants to be sure she knows what she's getting into. If she thinks that it will seriously curb her independence and love of freedom, she'll turn you down and return your engagement ring—if indeed she's let the romance get that far.

The line between friendship and romance is a pretty fuzzy one for an Aquarius. It's not difficult for her to remain buddy-buddy with an ex-lover. She's tolerant, remember? So, if you should see her on the arm of an old love, don't jump to any hasty conclusions.

She's not a jealous person herself and doesn't expect you to be, either. You'll find her pretty much of a free spirit most of the time. Just when you think you know her inside out, you'll discover that you don't really know her at all.

She's a very sympathetic and warm person. She can be helpful to people in need of assistance and advice.

She'll seldom be suspicious even if she has every right to be. If she loves a man, she'll forgive him just about anything. If he allows himself a little fling, chances are she'll just turn her head the other way. Her tolerance does have its limits, however, and her man should never press his luck at hanky-panky.

The Aquarius mother is bighearted and seldom refuses her children anything. Her open-minded attitude is easily transmitted to her youngsters. They have every chance of growing up as respectful and tolerant individuals who feel at ease anywhere.

LIBRA MAN
PISCES WOMAN

Many a man dreams of an alluring Pisces woman. You're perhaps no exception. She's soft and cuddly and very domestic. She'll let you be the brains of the family; she's contented to play a behind-the-scenes role in order to help you achieve your goals. The illusion that you are the master of the household is the kind of magic that the Pisces woman is adept at creating.

She can be very ladylike and proper. Your business associates and friends will be dazzled by her warmth and femininity. Although she's a charmer, there is a lot more to her than just a pretty exterior. There is a brain ticking away behind that soft, womanly facade. You may never become aware of it—that is, until you're married to her. It's no cause for alarm, however; she'll most likely never use it against you, only to help you and possibly set you on a more successful path.

If she feels you're botching up your married life through careless behavior or if she feels you could be earning more money than you do, she'll tell you about it. But any wife would, really. She will never try to usurp your position as head and breadwinner of the family.

No one had better dare say one uncomplimentary word about you in her presence. It's likely to cause her to break into tears. Pisces women are usually very sensitive beings. Their reaction to adversity, frustration, or anger is just a plain, good, old-fashioned cry. They can weep buckets when inclined.

She can do wonders with a house. She is very fond of dramatic and beautiful things. There will always be plenty of fresh-cut flowers around the house. She will choose charming artwork and antiques, if they are affordable. She'll see to it that the house is decorated in a dazzling yet welcoming style.

She'll have an extra special dinner prepared for you when you come home from an important business meeting. Don't dwell on the boring details of the meeting, though. But if you need that grand vision, the big idea, to seal a contract or make a conquest, your Pisces woman is sure to confide a secret that will guarantee your success. She is canny and shrewd with money, and once you are on her wavelength you can manage the intricacies on your own.

Treat her with tenderness and generosity, and your relationship will be an enjoyable one. She's most likely fond of chocolates. A bunch of beautiful flowers will never fail to make her eyes light up. See to it that you never forget her birthday or your anniversary. These things are very important to her. If you let them slip your mind, you'll send her into a crying fit that could last a considerable length of time.

If you are patient and kind, you can keep a Pisces woman happy for a lifetime. She, however, is not without her faults. Her sensitivity may get on your nerves after a while. You may find her lacking in practicality and good old-fashioned stoicism. You may even feel that she uses her tears as a method of getting her own way.

The Pisces mother has great faith in her children. She makes a strong, self-sacrificing mother. She will teach her children the value of service to the community while not letting them lose their individuality.

LIBRA
LUCKY NUMBERS 2000

Lucky numbers and astrology can be linked through the movements of the Moon. Each phase of the thirteen Moon cycles vibrates with a sequence of numbers for your Sign of the Zodiac over the course of the year. Using your lucky numbers is a fun system that connects you with tradition.

New Moon	First Quarter	Full Moon	Last Quarter
Jan. 6 8 0 8 6	Jan. 14 4 2 4 9	Jan. 20 3 8 9 5	Jan. 28 6 3 4 7
Feb. 5 3 9 4 6	Feb. 12 6 2 9 8	Feb. 19 5 8 4 9	Feb. 26 6 7 1 3
March 5 5 7 9 5	March 13 5 3 2 8	March 19 4 6 2 8	March 27 9 3 5 9
April 4 9 1 2 7	April 11 5 4 1 6	April 18 2 8 5 6	April 26 9 2 6 8
May 3 2 4 2 0	May 10 1 7 3 8	May 18 5 6 5 8	May 26 1 5 7 3
June 2 7 1 9 6	June 8 6 2 7 4	June 16 5 8 5 1	June 24 0 2 4 9
July 1 5 6 3 8	July 8 8 4 1 2	July 16 2 5 7 2	July 24 1 3 8 6
July 30 4 2 7 3	August 6 3 9 1 4	August 15 6 0 1 3	August 22 8 3 1 9
August 29 1 2 7 4	Sept. 5 4 5 8 0	Sept. 13 1 5 7 3	Sept. 20 1 9 1 7
Sept. 27 6 8 5 6	Oct. 5 6 9 2 0	Oct. 13 4 8 4 2	Oct. 20 1 7 1 6
Oct. 27 2 8 9 3	Nov. 4 3 5 9 2	Nov. 11 2 7 5 4	Nov. 18 1 6 9 5
Nov. 25 8 3 6 8	Dec. 3 8 3 5 0	Dec. 11 1 8 7 4	Dec. 17 9 5 1 7
Dec. 25 2 4 0 8	Jan. 2 ('01) 8 1 6 4	Jan. 9 ('01) 4 3 9 5	Jan. 17 ('01) 2 4 9 7

LIBRA
YEARLY FORECAST 2000

*Forecast for 2000 Concerning Business
and Financial Affairs, Job Prospects,
Travel, Health, Romance and Marriage
for Those Born with the Sun
in the Zodiacal Sign of Libra.
September 23–October 22*

For those born under the influence of the Sun in the zodiacal sign of Libra, ruled by Venus, planet of beauty and refinement, 2000 promises to be a year of sharing and adventure. Your ability to cooperate in close relationships should allow you to create a more stable emotional and financial base for the future. Opportunities to expand your horizons abound as certain restrictions associated with the past begin to fall away. Your view of a partnership situation is likely to be optimistic right from the start of the year, when more mutually favorable terms become possible. Where business matters are concerned, you may need to backtrack and cover old ground at the start of the year. You stand to benefit through reestablishing links with people from your past with whom you previously enjoyed happy relations and shared some marked success. There is room to expand your scope in trade and commerce this year and move closer to realizing some of your long-held dreams. Your money matters are likely to be influenced by your mate or partner's actions. Good fortune relating to other people's finances could have positive repercussions for you. It is likely to be worthwhile to focus on saving, even if you do not have much cash to spare. What begins as an almost insignificant amount could soon build up. With regard to routine occupational affairs, there should be chances to bring more variety into your life if you do not mind frequent changes. Putting in extra hours on the job could also help boost your finances. Travel opportunities this year should be plentiful. An increase in overseas travel is likely during the second half of the year. While job responsibilities could be your main reason for travel in the late summer, you may be able to combine a business trip with time out for pleasure. To protect your overall health and well-being, investigate new avenues for dealing with any ongoing physical problems. Read the available literature on a health matter affecting you. New discoveries could prove to be helpful. Romantically you may be restless in a current relationship, or reluctant to tie yourself down if you are single. An emotional partnership may offer more opportunity to expand your personal horizons than you think, however, so try to keep an open mind.

For professional Libra men and women, successful planning is a major key to business growth. Do not be afraid to devote quite some time to looking over the past, especially if your business is still young. Pinpointing patterns that are developing should help you plan more effectively for the future. Much of your time this year may be usefully employed in making a transition from one business field or interest to another. Be sure to tie up all the loose ends relating to one business before launching another; you should be able to take a far more wholehearted approach once you wipe the slate clean. Building up a network of contacts can be important when it comes to trying to expand into new areas or markets. Your strength of vision is also important this year. If you have the ability to lead with clarity and enthusiasm, those whose support you require are likely to be eager to follow. As a Libra you have plenty of initiative but do not always feel sufficiently motivated or fulfilled when the pressure is singularly on you to produce results. Try to adopt a collective ethic this year. The support of a group, whether colleagues or employees, is vital to both mental inspiration and practical success. Working to raise your business profile and reputation during the first six weeks of this year should help to establish a stronger presence. This, in turn, should subsequently improve profits much faster than you initially anticipate. If you are considering making substantial capital investments, wait until after midsummer to seriously commit yourself. The period between August 2 and September 17 could turn out to be quite an expensive time, with unexpected bills having to be balanced against diminished income.

Where finances are concerned, you have to take it easy this year in order to keep yourself on an even keel after previously sustaining some significant losses. Fortunately, you are unlikely to miss what you do not have. In the year ahead you may well adopt a different attitude toward practical wealth. For example, the quality of relationships is likely to seem more important than the scope of material assets. In any case, you are likely to benefit from your mate or partner's good fortune with finances this year.

There is also a possibility that you will be able to worry less about what you earn after finally clearing certain debts out of the way. You may even be able to save some money as you spend less and thus have a reasonable amount of disposable income to play with. Libra people with capital to invest may find it worth considering joining forces with others who are eager to create greater long-term wealth. Your sense of security this year could relate more to what you have invested than to what you are in a position to earn. You can expect to reap the rewards of previous long-term investments over the months ahead. It could be wise to reinvest some of your bounty so that your prosperity has a chance of continuing. The most expensive areas of life this year could be your social arena and much cherished hobbies. Try to allocate a regular amount for these in your budget, then keep to it. This approach should help to keep your finances on an even keel. The one time in the year when you will tend to be more reckless with your finances than is wise will probably be between December 24 and 31. At that time the atmosphere of Christmas festivities followed by irresistible sales may encourage you to be even more generous than usual. Keep in mind that the most welcome gifts are not necessarily the most impressive or the most expensive.

Routine occupational affairs are going to be significant this year. The first month could bring a rapid increase in your workload. If you can organize a structured routine to accommodate your new duties, you should be able to keep pace with developments with relative ease. You may even be able to get ahead because knowing you have more to handle could have the effect of positively increasing your adrenalin. Extra effort at the start of the year is likely to improve your cash-flow situation as well. If you are willing to take on new responsibilities throughout the year, your daily occupational affairs should be more varied and interesting. A flexible schedule beginning in the middle of February can enable you to fit in more socializing. Business and pleasure may combine more easily than you think; expanding your network of contacts could ease your stress level. Libras with young children may, for example, be able to find a reliable baby-sitter or nanny through new local connections made this year. Finding the time to enjoy lunches and casual conversations with friends can also help break up the monotony of the working day.

Travel opportunities are abundant this year. Long-distance and overseas options could be particularly plentiful over the summer and fall periods. Vacations spent with young people could turn out to be far more varied and enjoyable than you anticipate. It could also be worthwhile trying to find time for a spring break alone with your mate or partner so that you have some quality time as a couple. In the course of day-to-day life it is not always easy to stand back and view problems objectively. Time spent away together affords you the opportunity both to properly relax and to put any ongoing difficulties in perspective. The desire to revisit places which were important to you many years ago could become more pressing in the months ahead. In following these impulses, it is possible that you will get back in touch with important dreams which somehow got lost along the way. The period between February 13 and March 23 is ideal for going away with that special person in your life.

For health reasons, it may be necessary at the start of the year to make more of an effort to protect your well-being, especially if you are generally working harder. A balanced diet and plenty of physical exercise should help keep you in tip-top form. Be careful, though, not to miss out on sleep, particularly if you are constantly feeling low in energy. It may not be until spring that you can take liberties with your sleep pattern, simply because you feel more naturally energized then. If you find it difficult to make time for set meals, or you do not always feel hungry during the day, at least consider increasing your intake of fluids. Warm soups and vitamin-loaded drinks could be the answer if your appetite is regularly low.

Where love is concerned, despite the reputation of Libra people for becoming all-consumed by relationships, your own personal freedom may be the most important item on your agenda this year. Due to past experiences where you have either felt too restricted or became accustomed to a high level of independence, you may be unwilling to commit yourself to anyone else in the months ahead. Nevertheless, partnerships are likely to hold far more scope for personal freedom and discovery than you assume. Try to be open-minded. Someone who understands your needs may be able to give you precisely what you want. Nevertheless, single Libras may feel happier seeing a lover simply when it is convenient rather than making an effort to be there for them.

LIBRA DAILY FORECAST

January–December 2000

JANUARY

1. SATURDAY. Satisfactory. Make the most of this quiet day to get your personal finances in better order. You can make life easier for yourself by beginning a more efficient filing system; as long as you know where to quickly find all bills and receipts, nothing much should go wrong. This is a good time to spend an hour or so with your mate or partner, discussing matters that affect you both. It is all too easy to get so caught up in daily living that you shelve plans and questions that do not need instant attention. Take time now to catch up with these matters. A greater sense of security comes from learning to value yourself more; loved ones can help by offering you their total and unwavering support.

2. SUNDAY. Happy. As a Libra you have a real flair for romance, and today offers the chance to pull out all the stops. Your powers of persuasion should be ample to charm your way into the heart of someone you like a lot, especially if you back up your words with an intimate dinner for two. If you are in charge of youngsters, you can have considerable fun joining in with their creative pursuits such as painting or drawing. Children are sure to respond to having their imagination stimulated, and you are also bound to learn something new. Some friction may erupt if loved ones are too demanding on your time; in the interest of peace, let them have their way.

3. MONDAY. Sensitive. For many Libras this is the beginning of the new working year. Resuming contact with your colleagues is a chance to catch up on the latest news and gossip, but do not get so carried away that you forget to settle down to work. As far as romance is concerned, your relationship may not be going quite according to plan. If friends are giving you less sympathy than you expect, this could be a sign that they see problems in the relationship to which you are turning a blind eye. Although the mail is likely to be heavier than usual, resist the temptation to throw away what appears to be junk mail; otherwise an important piece of information could be overlooked.

4. TUESDAY. Stimulating. Today's extra burst of energy enables you to get routine tasks cleared up in record time, freeing you to pursue more challenging jobs. Procrastination is the thief of time; you will only regret putting off dull or boring chores. Your health should benefit from more exercise. Try to schedule a regular jog or workout, especially if the winter months have tempted you into a more idle lifestyle than usual. A new neighbor or work colleague can bring a fresh focus of interest to your life. At first you might not be interested in their unconventional ways, but they have valuable lessons to share if you are able to keep an open mind.

5. WEDNESDAY. Manageable. Discussions with a partner should prove fruitful providing you both put your cards on the table and do not hold anything back. Be prepared to spend extra time mulling over a new project; the results are likely to be well worth the effort. The wedding of a friend or close relative gives you a good excuse to buy a flattering new outfit. This occasion may bring you into contact with someone who could become a friend or even a lover. Although it is not usually a good idea to bring work home, on some occasions it is necessary. Do so with goodwill this evening, and you'll tackle it more effectively. Do not neglect to take your mate or partner's feelings into account.

6. THURSDAY. Helpful. Sometimes it does not pay to tell everyone all of your business, especially where finances are concerned. Someone in the family could give you a useful investment tip, which at this point need only be revealed to your nearest and dearest. Older relatives may be willing to babysit if an opportunity for you to go out tonight comes up on short notice. It is surprising how much different generations can offer each other, and it will not hurt youngsters to be spoiled just a little from time to time. If you are struggling alone to solve a vexing problem, confide in someone whose judgment you trust absolutely. Guard against any action that might weigh on your conscience.

7. FRIDAY. Tricky. Borrowing money from relatives is not always straightforward. If the feeling of obligation makes the atmosphere a little strained, it might be best to make arrangements to pay back small sums regularly so that they are assured of your good intentions. Although you may have been taking for granted that all is fine with a close relationship, there could be a lot bubbling away under the surface. It is not possible to avoid facing the differences between you and a loved one forever; it might be best to get concerns out in the open without further delay. A family gathering can cause tension, so be especially tactful with your parents or in-laws.

8. SATURDAY. Slow. It is likely to be more difficult than usual to get youngsters organized for practical tasks such as a shopping trip. They probably just do not have the same sense of urgency that you have, and for once you may simply have to proceed at their more relaxed pace. A new romance may have you walking on air, although there might be strings attached. Try to keep a level head no matter how ideal the other person appears to be; the reality is almost bound to be disappointing. Even if you set aside time for a leisure pursuit, the business of the day is apt to encroach on your schedule. The best way to cope is to lower your sights and not expect to achieve too much.

9. SUNDAY. Unsettling. Words said in anger may be regretted but can never be recalled. A lovers' tiff could develop into a full-scale disagreement that puts your relationship at risk if you make comments deliberately aimed to hurt. Your financial situation may have suffered as the result of a bout of recent spending on luxury items. Now is the time to make a firm resolution to get back on the straight and narrow; otherwise things could really get out of control. Friends may try to tempt you to take up a sport that has a high element of risk. Unless you are perfectly comfortable with this, it would be wisest to say a firm and definite no without making any excuses.

10. MONDAY. Variable. There are times when you have to trust your Libra instincts, and this is one of them. A well-calculated business gamble should pay off, but do not take a chance without consulting a partner or someone else who can share responsibility. There may be an opportunity for more creative input into a joint venture. Think big and have confidence in your abilities. As the day goes on, the strain of the busy weekend may begin to catch up with you. You need quiet periods in which to recharge your batteries; it is just not possible to continually live on your nerves. Loved ones may get angry if chores at home are not done exactly as they wish.

11. TUESDAY. Mixed. Handling finances belonging to other people may not be your favorite occupation, but as long as you keep meticulous records of your dealings there is no reason for anything to go wrong. In fact, you could be doing someone a real service. Single Libras are apt to be rather tongue-tied when face-to-face with a possible romantic prospect. The problem arises most often when you put someone on a pedestal without even knowing what they are really like. If you can think of them as an ordinary human being, it should be easier to shake off your shyness. Today's more forgetful mood can snarl up simple tasks unless you keep your mind on what you are doing; concentrate on the moment.

12. WEDNESDAY. Fortunate. After a long period of setbacks, money due you should finally be coming your way. It is important to have a clear idea of what you want to do with it so that it does not just get frittered away with no real benefit to you. A long-standing personal fear can be cleared up with professional help. Everyone has weak spots and phobias; with the variety of specialist counseling services available, there is no need to try to cope alone with serious problem areas. Romance is likely to go your way as long as you are prepared to take quick action. There is no point waiting for the other person to make a move; pluck up your courage and show them you are interested in establishing a relationship.

13. THURSDAY. Good. While it can be all too easy to let romance evaporate from a long-term relationship, this is less likely to happen to Libras than to some other signs. Whenever the flame shows signs of burning low, it should be second nature for you to find ways of rekindling the spark that first brought you together with your mate or partner. Youngsters' schooling may be on your mind right now, although there should not be any particular problems to deal with. However, this might be a good time to discuss with teachers whether extracurricular tutoring or outside activities such as music would be beneficial. Surprise yourself and your loved ones by taking up a new hobby.

14. FRIDAY. Uncertain. The best way to approach the day is in a spirit of reconciliation. Other people seem all too eager to set themselves at cross-purposes with you, and this is not the best time to fight back. If you are planning a wedding or anniversary celebration, you may be wondering whether you have bitten off more than you can chew. Do not take on more than you can cope with; this is an ideal occasion to enlist the help of relatives and friends.

On the home front, you may have a feeling that you are being blamed for something, although it is not clear what. This may be a case where one person is being singled out to shoulder a responsibility that all should be sharing equally.

15. SATURDAY. Cautious. Libras who have been hoping for a romantic weekend would be wise not to get too excited. That special person in your life may have something in mind, but it is probably more along the lines of presuming on your kindness to do them a favor. Financially, it may be necessary to tighten your belt for a while. Do not count your chickens before they hatch; even if you are due to receive money soon, it is not smart to spend it in advance. An elderly relative may cause a few headaches, especially if you are required to take on more responsibility for their welfare than seems fair. Other family members should be asked to get involved along with you.

16. SUNDAY. Disconcerting. Do not let youngsters or pets rule the roost or you will soon be at their mercy. They must learn that the world does not revolve around them, and that you need space for yourself once in a while. Sometimes it is a case of least said, soonest mended where love is concerned. If you have put your foot in it, you will probably only make matters worse by trying to extricate yourself from trouble. Be careful if playing sports; a prior injury could flare up again if you overextend yourself. As time passes, possessions tend to mount up. You may have reached the stage where you need either a larger home or a thorough weeding out of your closets.

17. MONDAY. Demanding. Prepare for some concentrated work and there is little that you cannot achieve. Willpower and a sense of purpose enable you to move mountains; just be sure you do not steamroller over colleagues in the process. Some canny financial planning could go a long way toward providing for a more secure future for yourself and your family. However, this is likely to require quite a considerable investment, which could mean adopting a more modest lifestyle for a while. Demands on your creativity may have been somewhat heavy recently, with the result that you are beginning to suffer from burnout. There is no point pushing yourself on; delegate to others if at all possible.

18. TUESDAY. Changeable. Whatever your mood, you should not be short on bright ideas. The question now is whether you have the patience to work them out fully and put them into action. Romantic affairs are apt to take a turn for the better as interests in common provide a stronger bond between you. Mental rapport is important if you want a relationship that is based on more than sheer physical attraction. Travel may present some difficulties. It is not a good idea to rely on friends to give you rides; they could forget their promise, leaving you high and dry. Start thinking about your summer vacation, but do not plan anything that would strain your budget.

19. WEDNESDAY. Difficult. You may have been antagonizing a colleague without even realizing you were doing so. Their irritation is now apt to be out in the open, and it is up to you both to together sort matters out so that you can continue working on a joint project. Routine paperwork may be causing more headaches than usual because you do not have the patience to settle down to such a dull task. It is vital, however, that you make yourself do so; otherwise you could overlook an important piece of information with unfortunate results. Finally it is possible to make a financial decision that will improve the long-term prospects for you and your mate or partner. Better budgeting is the only way out of a financial hole.

20. THURSDAY. Disquieting. If you let other people ride roughshod over you, such actions could become a habit. This is one time when you must stand up for yourself and make it plain that you are a responsible adult. The impending result of a legal case may have you on tenterhooks. Try to turn your mind to other matters; after all, there is nothing you can do now to affect the outcome. Parents or in-laws may be unusually eager to comment on the way in which you manage your personal relationships. Naturally this is irritating, but remember that things were done differently in their days, so older people may have difficulty understanding your generation's needs and expectations.

21. FRIDAY. Deceptive. Although loved ones may not actually set out to deceive you, they could be withholding important information for their own reasons. There may well be something going on that they are not revealing. Now you have to decide whether or not to challenge them. Youngsters are apt to run you ragged during the course of the day; it will take a lot of energy just to keep an eye on them. Romance needs very careful handling. There is a possibility that you are being led down the garden path by a new romantic partner. You could find yourself left high and dry when a newcomer comes between you. Flirting may seem harmless to you now but could be misinterpreted.

22. SATURDAY. Good. You should be feeling full of goodwill and kindness. Loved ones are sure to appreciate a little extra tender loving care. Even a thoughtful word can do wonders for a person's sense of security, so do not hold back expressing your affection. Shopping can be enjoyable as long as you relax in the process and do not get too anxious. There should be great pleasure in buying gifts for other people. You can rely on your innate good Libra taste to come up with something really special. Social events may ruffle a few feathers, although it is unlikely you will be more than a spectator to any upsets. You may, in fact, be able to act as mediator to make the peace.

23. SUNDAY. Favorable. This is the kind of day when you will be happiest in mixed company. Even if you have not made any definite arrangements, it might be pleasant to invite some friends over for an informal get-together and a light meal. Spend some time reviewing your hopes and wishes for the future. Consider how they have changed over the years, and what you can do to realize them more swiftly. Memories of a past relationship can sometimes be comforting as you screen out the bad times and focus on what was good. All the experience you have had should enrich your present partnership. A friend or relative who is confined to their home would appreciate a visit even if you cannot stay long.

24. MONDAY. Unsettling. The high hopes you had to get a new romance off the ground may be dashed. However, you can shrug this off easier than if you had spent considerable time getting more involved. Libras who rely on creative powers to earn a living should be able to tap into depths of subconscious intuition. Let yourself go; do not try to control the process too much or the inspiration is likely to evaporate. Finances may be a bit strained at the moment. This is not the time to take any risks. Do not be tempted by people who seem to know what they are talking about; it is all too likely that they are merely bluffing. Relax this evening watching a good movie.

25. TUESDAY. Changeable. It may seem as if you have been waiting forever for a payment due you, but there is still some way to go. There is little point tormenting yourself with dreams of how you are going to use the money, especially if there is a special purchase that is just out of reach. Although talking over relationship problems with a close friend can sometimes be beneficial, there are times when it is better to sit down alone and work out just what is going on. No one else can really understand how you and your mate or partner relate, and in the end it is up to you to keep your relationship on the right track. You can boost your confidence by indulging in a new outfit or hairstyle.

26. WEDNESDAY. Reassuring. Youngsters' questions should keep you on your toes. Their comments are often highly perceptive and should not be laughed off; they can come uncomfortably close to the truth. A phone call from a relative with whom you have lost touch gives you a chance to renew the bonds between you. It is important to keep up family ties; you can both offer and receive much mutual support. Libras who write for a living may be able to utilize more self-expression. Because your understanding of the world is unique, you have a lot to offer other people. Even routine tasks can be pleasurable if you go out of your way to adopt a positive attitude.

27. THURSDAY. Stressful. As a Libra it is difficult for you to endure upsets within a relationship because you are very likely to suffer if the atmosphere is unsettled. For this reason you should not be rocking the boat right now, almost goading your mate or partner into disagreeing with you. If the results of being overly optimistic about your financial resources have caught up with you, it may be necessary to rethink routine spending and cut back on luxury items. Where business is concerned, it is important not to overstretch current resources. Be realistic about what you can commit to, and do not mislead others into thinking the company is more powerful than it really is.

28. FRIDAY. Difficult. A shock announcement could turn your world upside down. Try to stand back and take an objective view. It is possible that the person who has uttered the words is simply trying to startle you into taking action and does not really mean what has been said. Youngsters need a firm hand; otherwise they will be up to all kinds of tricks. Be extra careful that they do not play around with electrical equipment while you are not present to supervise them. Calls are likely to be interrupted; making arrangements can be problematic. Keep a pen and paper handy to jot down notes so that you can keep track of the content of important phone conversations.

29. SATURDAY. Mixed. Sometimes you may doubt your creative ability, but these moods only reinforce an unrealistically low view of your natural talent. Have the confidence to pursue your artistic aims wholeheartedly and you will begin to make real progress. Libra parents are probably well aware of how expensive it can be to bring up youngsters. Now is a good time to sit down with them and explain that money does not grow on trees, and that they cannot automatically have everything they want. The day will go better if you knuckle down to household tasks this morning. Put some muscle power into getting chores out of the way and you can then enjoy your real leisure time all the more.

30. SUNDAY. Easygoing. Relax today. Do not make hard-and-fast plans because they are not likely to come off. The best way to cope is simply to go with the flow. Let what happens happen, and determine to enjoy it all. A leisurely trip will soothe and calm your nerves, leaving you with pleasant memories to which you can return whenever you need some inner peace. Romance is in the air, but you might slip into a relationship without even realizing that you are getting emotionally involved. Love does not always arrive with fireworks; sometimes it can just creep up on you. Find time for some quiet thought and meditation this evening to refresh your soul and clear your mind.

31. MONDAY. Frustrating. What seemed like a good plan to make a fast buck may turn out to be more complicated than you had bargained for. It may be that you just do not have what it takes to be a ruthless entrepreneur. For one thing, as a Libra you are naturally considerate of other people. There could be something of a mystery surrounding an older person to whom you are attracted. A sense of hidden knowledge is likely to fascinate you, but cultivating a true friendship may not be easy. If you are on the road, be prepared for delays or problems to develop. Difficulties may keep you from arriving on time for a meeting, or even from getting there at all.

FEBRUARY

1. TUESDAY. Successful. For once you have the chance to enjoy almost total freedom of thought at work and at home. Original ideas should be welcomed, even if they seem a bit extreme at first. An unexpected call from an old flame could set your heart fluttering. Consider meeting, even if you feel a few qualms. Getting together will give you a chance to measure how much you have moved on since you were a twosome. If there is paperwork to be completed, do not put it off. A ruthless approach to work will enable you to eliminate unnecessary jobs and concentrate on what is most essential. There should be no big problems with local travel; plan on mixing business with pleasure if at all possible.

2. WEDNESDAY. Rewarding. Libras looking for a sound investment could do worse than to put money into property. Seek expert advice, then see what you can afford; significant long-term gains could be made. Older relatives are likely to be supportive in a crisis. Because their life experience is richer than yours, they are able to understand and give you tips on how to turn the situation to your advantage. You can foster a warmer atmosphere at home if you let loved ones know how much you appreciate them. Do not take friends and family members for granted; just imagine what life would be like without them. Antique collectors may find a bargain at an auction or thrift shop.

3. THURSDAY. Manageable. Roll up your sleeves for a practical day. With an early start you can achieve a lot. This is not the time to focus on the big picture; instead, concentrate on getting details of current projects sorted out to your satisfaction. A family gathering may be more low-key than you expect. If the burden of organizing the get-together has fallen on you, you will probably be glad of a comparatively quiet time that still produces happy memories to cherish. Pay a little extra attention to your health and overall well-being. More exercise would probably be beneficial. Find a physical-fitness program that you can comfortably do in the privacy of your home.

4. FRIDAY. Cautious. This is one of those days when you are likely to be all fingers and thumbs. It is best to postpone intricate work for the moment; otherwise you might ruin an otherwise good start. Compassion for other people can mislead you into taking inappropriate action. Sometimes it is hard to judge just who is truly in need of help. Giving assistance in the wrong place at the wrong time can do more harm than good. Communications between you and your mate or partner should be clearer than usual, enabling you to tackle questions that are usually avoided. The goodwill and trust you both feel will only deepen your mutual bond of love. An evening out with friends should be fun for everyone.

5. SATURDAY. Variable. Libras who recently suffered the end of a special relationship can look forward to a fresh start. You need other people to mirror your own self-development, and right now a new attachment is right around the corner. Youngsters are likely to be in a negative mood, unwilling to do what you ask. They may seem to be testing their power against yours. You need to find the fine balance between allowing them their independence and asserting your adult authority. Money may be in such short supply that you cannot splurge as much as you would like for a special occasion. Use your ingenuity to make the best of it.

6. SUNDAY. Unsettling. An older acquaintance who has been a role model to you may suddenly be revealed in a less than flattering light. Because of this you may be faced with the need to reassess their influence and true worth as well as your own judgment. Sports and physical exercise can be a bit dangerous if you do not have a clear sense of the risks that are involved. Try to play it safe, otherwise there is danger of a minor accident. A romantic partner could be keeping you at an emotional distance. They may not feel as confident as you that the relationship is moving toward commitment. Discuss this openly, revealing your hopes for the future.

7. MONDAY. Mixed. You will probably work up to your best if other people leave you alone to complete private projects. The financial aspects of current concerns should be absorbing most of your energy right now. Efforts to save even small sums will be worthwhile. Sometimes you can be your own worst enemy, undermining your achievements through self-doubt. It may not be your role to make world-shattering discoveries, but every contribution you make that is well-done can be of special value. Neighbors may be more intrusive into your private life than you like, especially if you have invited their confidence in the past and given them a false sense of intimacy.

8. TUESDAY. Uncertain. As a Libra you are often not at your best when asked to make a decision. However, an organizational problem now requires your special skills of tact and diplomacy. Sooner or later you are going to have to choose one side or the other. Burning the candle at both ends will only wear you out. Being unable to work as steadily as usual could be a sign that you have been overdoing. A harmonious home environment is essential for you to feel truly relaxed; even small changes to your decor can make a big difference. Consider different ideas, such as rearranging furniture. There is no need to spend a great deal of money on redecorating.

9. WEDNESDAY. Favorable. At last romance is going your way. For single Libras, it may even be that wedding bells will ring out before long. This is not the time to worry; focus on what you have and enjoy the dream of happiness. Business communications can be improved by taking quite drastic measures. Mull over with your associates whether the current chain of command is really suitable to your long-term purposes. Legal papers should be signed without delay in order to wrap up the case as soon as possible. However, do not be in such a hurry that you fail to check over details or you could lose a vital advantage. Heed advice from an expert.

10. THURSDAY. Fair. You are likely to wake up with bright ideas that could fade out of consciousness unless you jot them down quickly. Do not let inspiration get away. Libra home buyers are apt to find the process more expensive than expected. With any major purchase, there are bound to be costs you had not budgeted for, but as long as you are fairly careful there is little chance of getting into financial difficulties. Sometimes you just cannot please your mate or partner, no matter how hard you try. At that point it might be wise to ask what other problem is upsetting them so much. A mutual acquaintance could introduce you to someone who is romantically very appealing.

11. FRIDAY. Sensitive. Think before you speak or act. There is no point making promises you probably cannot or will not keep. Other people will remember what you pledged even if it escapes your memory. It may be necessary to defuse your mate or partner in regard to inflated ideas of what you might be able to achieve together. One of you needs to keep both feet firmly on the ground or you may both lose sight of reality. A romantic affair that has been going on for some time might not be all that you hope. If the other person is rather elusive, they may well have something to hide. It is definitely to your advantage to find out what that is and how long it has been going on.

12. SATURDAY. Helpful. The day should get off to a good start if all the family pulls together to get household chores out of the way. Even youngsters can do their share in small ways, so do not leave them out of it. Lost items may be more obvious than you think. In fact, they could turn up in places you have already searched several times. It is unlikely that you feel in a particularly sociable mood; quiet entertainment with your nearest and dearest will be most satisfying. Where romance is concerned, your relationship is apt to be up in the air. You simply need to hang on and wait to see how the situation is going to develop, rather than forcing change.

13. SUNDAY. Difficult. The stage is set for tempers to flare unless all family members are willing to be a bit more flexible. It is often true that you cannot please all the people all the time; some compromise is always necessary. There could be a misunderstanding with a neighbor whose pet is not kept under as much control as you would like. Your viewpoints on the matter may just not be compatible. If you feel really strongly about the matter, it may be worth checking to see if they are committing a legal offense. Arrange to go out with your mate or partner on a special trip together. Time spent alone can revitalize even a flagging relationship.

14. MONDAY. Confusing. It may be difficult to keep your mind on what needs to be done. Your Libra tendency to drift off into daydreams is stronger than usual. Unfortunately other people will have little sympathy, so try to focus your thoughts and concentrate. Final details of a long trip may take some time to sort out. Although you are impatient to be off, it is vital to make sure all arrangements are in place if the trip is to go smoothly. Annoyed loved ones are likely to respond better to a thoughtful action than to a verbal apology. Make up for a small unkindness by planning an evening out with no expense spared to show that you really care and regret your words.

15. TUESDAY. Expansive. This is an ideal time to take up a new course of study. You are never too old to learn; fresh horizons could energize you. Libra business people may be put in contact with an exciting young talent. Your powers to charm and persuade can set a lucrative deal in motion. Rumors about a change of management at work might give you the impression that possibilities for promotion are opening up. It is probably best to keep what you know to yourself for the time being. However, there is no reason not to lay some plans so that you will be ready to act when the time is right. Try to keep your temper in check when dealing with angry loved ones.

16. WEDNESDAY. Harmonious. As a Libra you are fond of a quiet life. As long as you play your cards right, that is exactly what you should enjoy today. The secret is to wear your sense of responsibility lightly, trusting that everything will work out for the best. If you have been hesitant about buying a pet, try to come to a decision now. Even if you have children, remember that you will probably end up taking a lot of responsibility for the pet after their initial enthusiasm. Libras who are looking for work might receive a useful tip from a former colleague. Do not delay in following through by sending or faxing your resume.

17. THURSDAY. Disquieting. The tension between claims of home and your career are reaching a peak and can no longer be ignored. Much as you would like to devote more time to family affairs, for now you will have to convince loved ones that work must take priority. The outcome of a legal case may have left you with heavy costs. This might make you wonder whether it was worth pursuing; if there is a next time, an out-of-court settlement may be a more sensible choice. When it comes to romance, you could be courting heartache. There is nothing to be gained from falling for someone who already is engaged in a serious relationship.

18. FRIDAY. Variable. A selfless action on your part can do much to smooth over difficulties in a long-term relationship. It will not hurt you to make a small sacrifice, especially if it gives a loved one pleasure. Find a quiet moment to review your spending habits. Although occasional extravagance can do no harm, beware of letting this become a habit. Friends might pressure you into taking part in a social event that is not your cup of tea. Naturally you want to be a willing participant, but not if there is little pleasure for you. Insisting on always getting your own way with loved ones will only cause disruptions; be willing to give in now and then.

19. SATURDAY. Demanding. Unless you take good care of yourself, you run the risk of damaging your health. It is important to make sure your stamina is sufficient to fend off irritating coughs and colds. Focus on eating right and getting enough sleep and physical exercise. Getting through weekend tasks can seem a trial because your real desire is to slip away into a world of your own. It could help to sort out some old letters and photos that enable you to indulge in fond memories. Family demands may be greater than usual. You probably have to resign yourself to putting off some of your favorite leisure pursuits until you have more time to call your own.

20. SUNDAY. Sensitive. Sometimes it can seem all but impossible to make family members understand what you mean. It is all too easy for you and your loved ones to slip into the habit of not listening closely to what is being said. Also try harder to read between the lines. A trip may be subject to so many delays and problems that it hardly seems worth making the effort. Arrange an outing closer to home instead, which should be less stressful and more successful. Neighbors cannot always be relied upon to look after pets and plants when you go on a long trip. You will probably only find out who is trustworthy by trial and error, but a couple of days away can do no significant harm.

21. MONDAY. Quiet. The workweek begins rather slowly. Mail is likely to be lighter than usual. If you feel unwilling to get back into the swing of things, you can probably ease in gently and at your own pace. Make sure you are clear about arrangements for meetings and appointments so that you do not turn up at the wrong time. These quiet conditions are an excellent chance to catch up on work that needs finishing. Organize tasks so that the most overdue gets done first. Soon you will again be able to enjoy a clear conscience. Going over and over past mistakes in a relationship will only make you feel negative; resolve to learn from your errors and not to repeat them again.

22. TUESDAY. Unsettling. A new acquaintance seems to have you under a spell of fascination, so that you hardly know where you are. It could be that they are creating an air of mystery and glamour quite deliberately, hoping to be able to pull the wool over your eyes as to their true motives. Even though you may have been watching your finances closely, it still appears that leisure pursuits have swallowed up a fair amount of cash. Perhaps it's time to consider taking up a less expensive hobby. Youngsters will be able to twist you round their little finger if you let them. Be indulgent by all means, but don't allow this to become your habitual response.

23. WEDNESDAY. Challenging. A new look would give you the feeling of making a break with old and unwanted habits. Be bold—try a more avant garde image and carry it off with confidence! Those of you on the lookout for romance may have to be a bit more pushy than usual when a likely person enters your life. It's probable that they will be expecting a less conventional relationship than you are used to, but it will be stimulating all the same. Make a resolution now not to let work get on top of you. Don't let your social life slip. All work and no play makes for a dull Libra! If a competition appeals to you, then enter it; there is a good chance of winning.

24. THURSDAY. Frustrating. A promise of a pay raise may have raised your hopes, but do not go out on a spending spree just yet. The final sum may be less than expected, so a little caution is advised. Where deep-seated problems are concerned, it is often helpful to get expert advice. In trying to help an acquaintance with a personal problem, there is only so much you can do. It would probably be helpful if you could tactfully suggest that they talk to someone who can be professionally objective. Keeping up with practical tasks can make you feel more secure, with nothing to nag at you when you have the chance to concentrate on a more interesting creative project. Do not stay up too late tonight.

25. FRIDAY. Manageable. Although you and your mate or partner may have made good resolutions to save for the future, at the moment it is probably impossible to put away any significant sum. Instead of blaming each other, concentrate on pooling resources so that regular small savings can still be made. Do not let older relatives erode your self-confidence with their criticism of how you run your life. Keep in mind that they made mistakes in their time, although it is unlikely they will willingly admit to doing so. Give youngsters small tasks to perform around the house and they will be pleased with what they see as an adult sense of responsibility. However, try to keep a close eye on them if they are using anything electrical.

26. SATURDAY. Mixed. Your dreams can be so real that it is hard to wake up into the everyday world. There may be a message about your immediate problems concealed in dream imagery, so jot down the main fragments that stick in your mind. Romance is highlighted, with an interesting invitation coming from an unexpected quarter. It is not altogether clear, however, what sort of a relationship you would be getting into; it may be less straightforward than it first appears. Youngsters can be amused with games that keep them guessing, especially any kind of quiz or puzzle that engages their imagination. Eat out tonight with the whole family.

27. SUNDAY. Happy. Give your long-term romantic partnership a new lease on life by escaping from present commitments to a place that was a favorite when you first knew each other. Once you are free to indulge in memories, old feelings will doubtless come flooding back. Socially this should be quite a busy day, with invitations coming from several sources. You are in the right mood to be with people, so relax and enjoy the company. There is no point losing your temper with family members just because they do things their own way. It is not possible to constantly impose your will on others unless you want to cause a buildup of resentment.

28. MONDAY. Buoyant. If you have plans to propose, your good Libra powers to persuade should win the day. You should have no trouble finding ready words as long as the enthusiasm is there in the first place. When it comes to romance, it does not pay to hang back bashfully. You have to proceed full-steam ahead and make your intentions plain if you want to impress the other person with the strength of your feelings. There are small financial gains to be made by investing in the field of information technology, although you should be careful not to invest more than you can afford. Keep all business dealings open and aboveboard or you are asking for future trouble.

29. TUESDAY. Exciting. A tip from a friend or colleague could make all the difference to your long-term financial prospects. Take what they say seriously if they appear genuinely eager to pass on the benefit of their experience. It will not do you any good to listen to idle gossip; most of it is bound to be malicious or wildly inaccurate. Neither pass on nor act on rumors. Youngsters can be surprisingly destructive if left to their own devices, so channel their energy into activities that will tire them out before bedtime. If you are hoping to sell your home, you could get a good offer. Do not be greedy; if it is reasonable and without contingencies, accept it.

MARCH

1. WEDNESDAY. Fair. Your good eye for detail should help you complete an important project to everyone's satisfaction. Do not hide your light under a bushel; if you are proud of a job well done, make sure your superiors know about it. Pet care may take up more time than usual. If others in the family are not sharing the responsibility, point this out. As a Libra you have a tendency to live on your nerves when the going gets rough, which can affect your sleep and your overall health. Learning a relaxation technique would be beneficial. Consider treating yourself to a soothing massage; your Libra love of beautiful scents should find aromatherapy extremely calming.

2. THURSDAY. Helpful. If a colleague tips you off that important changes are imminent, you will be in a position to plan a course of action so that you are not too negatively affected. A distinct advantage can be gained by looking out for yourself just this once. Search for a lost item in the kitchen or bathroom; you probably put it away in an odd place in a moment of absentmindedness. A romantic entanglement may be making you feel out of your depth, but you do not have to remain passive. Although it can be all too easy to let the other person have most of the power, in the end that will not be satisfactory for either of you. Take a more active role in guiding all of your affairs.

3. FRIDAY. Cautious. Someone may be working against your best interests, making it hard to advance your career. Their motive is probably jealousy. No matter how sympathetic you may feel toward them, it is necessary to put a stop to their interference. There is a chance of mechanical problems with your car; it would be unwise to set out on a long trip without first having it thoroughly checked. Even a short journey could be interrupted, so make sure you allow plenty of time to reach your destination. Do not let youngsters get away with talking back to you. A certain amount of total honesty can be charming, but they have to learn good manners sooner or later.

4. SATURDAY. Sensitive. Current conditions indicate a bumpy ride ahead for Libra lovers. Although you are romantic by nature, you value a relationship based first and foremost on friendship. Sometimes it can be difficult to explain to your mate or partner that open communication is as important as passion. Criticism of your recent creative work may hit you on a tender spot. However, if it is meant in a positive way, try to keep a sense of perspective and judge for yourself how much truth there is in it. Although there may be a strong temptation to risk money on a gamble, it would be unwise to do so because you are more likely to lose than win. If you must bet, bet on yourself.

5. SUNDAY. Favorable. A long-term problem can be solved if you take a commonsense approach. There is no point worrying about all the world's problems. Focus on the immediate situation and concentrate on how it could be changed for the better. A slightly less indulgent diet would do wonders for your physical well-being. To get that glow of health back in your skin, cut down on sweets and eat more fruit and vegetables. Youngsters may need some extra loving as they confide their bad dreams and fears. You can give the most helpful support by taking them very seriously even if their troubles seem silly or amusing. Just remember how you felt when you were their age.

6. MONDAY. Promising. The workweek begins in a mood of hopefulness as a new project gives you something to sink your teeth into. Your mind is apt to be whizzing with ideas; the only problem might be deciding which one to try first. Your health should be good, especially if you have been exercising sufficiently. However, this is no time to rest on your laurels; build on the foundation of fitness that you have established. Libras who are looking for a new job opportunity might want to broaden the search. For instance, there may be jobs for which you could retrain, or an opening overseas could be just right for you.

7. TUESDAY. Exciting. If you are in the market for a new relationship, then spruce yourself up and keep your eyes open. A new acquaintance could enter your life quite unexpectedly, bringing an electric charge of mutual attraction that is absolutely unmistakable. Where a dispute with a neighbor is concerned, you might feel tempted to take the law into your own hands. However, it would be far wiser to try and talk out the problem; this will almost certainly help you find a mutually agreeable solution much more quickly. Sporting activities are highlighted, with the opportunity for you to lead or inspire team effort. You appear to be in top form and determined to win.

8. WEDNESDAY. Fair. Libras who are involved in imminent wedding celebrations should be finding the excitement very stimulating. Fortunately your organizational powers are appreciated, and the more original ideas you can come up with the better. Business associates appear eager to develop links with the communications industry. They consider that this segment could be very profitable, and they may well be right. Plan to get away for a few days soon with your mate or partner. It will do you both a world of good to have a complete break and change of scene. Hasty words could spoil an otherwise idyllic evening, so keep your temper in check and think before you speak.

9. THURSDAY. Expansive. Sometimes it is necessary to use your gift of gab to persuade higher-ups at work that your ideas are worth listening to. Right now you should not hold back; you can even exaggerate if need be to catch the attention of colleagues and bosses. A more optimistic outlook can help you reorganize your savings to bring in more interest. There is nothing to be gained from an attitude of fear; take a small risk or two and you will see there are gains to be made. Romantically all seems to be well, with a sense of growing harmony between you and your mate or partner. If your mind is turning to thoughts of long-term commitment, this is the day to broach the subject.

10. FRIDAY. Slow. Allow your responsibilities to weigh heavily on you and you are almost bound to feel overwhelmed. Instead, try to take a practical view. Delegate as much work as possible; it will seem much more manageable that way. It may be necessary to tighten the purse strings in order to save for a special occasion. Without the cooperation of your mate or partner, all your efforts to save may go to waste, so make sure your wishes are compatible. Handling money on behalf of others can be worrisome. However, as long as you are scrupulous in keeping good records there is no need for anxiety, and there may even be a small reward if you perform well.

11. SATURDAY. Disconcerting. The sense that a lover is not being absolutely honest with you is bound to cause some sleepless nights. You will only work yourself into an emotional state if you do not confront your mate or partner with your suspicions. It would be best to bite the bullet and get it over with. Celebrations for a youngster's birthday may have gotten a bit out of hand financially. Still, it is nice to be able to provide a thorough treat; just make it clear that this party is the exception rather than the rule. Libras trying to pursue studies are likely to find the demands of everyday living very distracting. Try scheduling a realistic timetable, then stick to it no matter what.

12. SUNDAY. Fair. This is an ideal day for getting out to some peaceful spot. The sight of lakes or rivers can be soothing and therapeutic to jangled nerves; even a water garden would refresh and delight. Arguing with friends over a point of principle can sour an otherwise good relationship. In the end, it is the person and not their particular beliefs that matters most. Vacation plans may have to be rethought if there is news of political problems at your intended destination. It would probably be wiser to alter arrangements now rather than wait to see if the situation calms down. Common interests can form the basis of a new and very valuable friendship.

13. MONDAY. Pleasant. Negotiations for overseas business are looking hopeful. Because you have put in the groundwork, your thoroughness is now paying off. The results of an aptitude test should give you the confidence to believe that you can achieve more in your career than you had hoped. Impatience with other people's narrow outlook could cause a breach between you and them. On the other hand, it is also probably a sign that you are hungering to develop a broader and more philosophical understanding of life. A decision concerning a close relationship seems to have formed in your mind without conscious thought or deliberation. Act on it without delay.

14. TUESDAY. Excellent. All systems are go, as work that has been held up for a couple of weeks finally begins to make progress. This should give your enthusiasm a boost and encourage you on to greater things. A check for which you have been waiting should finally turn up. Although it may take time for the check to clear, a special purchase you have been promising yourself is finally within reach. Libras who work from home will probably find the phone hardly stops ringing. It might be better to give up on the idea of getting routine work done, and instead devote yourself to dealing with the new business that is coming your way. Invite a loved one to go out somewhere special tonight.

15. WEDNESDAY. Manageable. Even though youngsters seem to be doing well at school, there are probably questions you would like to ask. You may have become more ambitious for them, and want to check that they truly are getting every opportunity to make the most of their education. A colleague finally seems to be on the point of declaring an attraction for you. This could put you in a quandary if you would prefer to regard them as a casual acquaintance. In any event, it will be necessary to keep on good terms if you are to continue working together. Tasks around the home can be soothing if you have a problem to mull over in your mind.

16. THURSDAY. Misleading. Finally you are able to face the fact that a loved one has been hiding an important truth from you. All the same, you have not yet gotten to the bottom of just why they have been doing so. Do not try to impress a new acquaintance with exaggerated ideas of your financial status. They are bound to find out your real situation sooner or later, and that will be embarrassing for both of you. If you are going out this evening, it might be best not to touch alcohol. A convivial atmosphere could make it easy to drink too much without realizing it. Unrealistic hopes of a romantic relationship will only lead to final disappointment.

17. FRIDAY. Variable. A friendship may take a sudden and unexpected turn into a romantic affair. This is apt to come as something of a surprise to you both, although mutual acquaintances will doubtless laugh and tell you they saw it coming. Do not be persuaded to engage in risky sporting pursuits against your better judgment. You know your own limitations, so stick to what you feel comfortable doing. Your mate or partner will almost certainly be eager to support you in bringing about a dearly held wish. However, they can only do so if you are open about exactly what is so important to you. A lively social evening will recharge your batteries.

18. SATURDAY. Liberating. Today's more expansive mood enables you to be truly generous to loved ones. Your nearest and dearest will be touched and moved by acts of kindness, promoting a harmony that affects the whole family. Sometimes your financial situation seems to be more affected by your perception of it than the actual reality. If you feel impoverished, you act accordingly. However, if you convince yourself that you have all you need, it is much easier to enjoy what you have. Memories of past relationships may be alluring, but they should not blind you to the virtues of your present connections. It is better to make a clean break with the past than to hang on.

19. SUNDAY. Tranquil. Your pleasures today will probably be quiet ones. Ideally you should spend time alone. This is a perfect opportunity to mull over your life and make sense of your hopes and dreams. The faith you have put in relatives' support has not been misplaced. Family members are glad to rally to your side when needed, and doubtless you will be in a position to return the favor someday soon. Relationships within the home can be improved if you are all willing to face up to problems that have been swept under the rug. Once difficulties are brought out into the open, they should seem much less upsetting than if you try to ignore them.

20. MONDAY. Useful. Once and for all you have to make up your mind not to let personal concerns get in the way of your work. You need to draw a distinct line between your private feelings and your more public obligations. Health matters may come to the fore as you realize that your energy level is not as high as it should be. You cannot afford to take good health for granted; your body needs to be cared for just as much as you look after your car. The ending of a relationship may cause some pain, but in the long run you will be able to see that it was all for the good. Allow yourself a period of recuperation before looking for a fresh romance.

21. TUESDAY. Rewarding. Greater involvement in community affairs could bring you into contact with some unusually interesting people. There may also be the satisfaction of seeing that individuals can wield power if they unite into a pressure group. News of an old friend is likely to stir up memories and lead you to review your life. Consider how you have changed since you previously knew the other person. Libras who sell for a living should be able to have a very profitable day. As long as you believe in what you are selling, you can convince others. If you are preparing for a test, try to cultivate a calm approach. Your thorough preparation will pay off.

22. WEDNESDAY. Tense. Arguments with your mate or partner are almost inevitable if you continue on the way you are going. You both have to back down and apologize; insisting on blaming each other will do no good at all. A business association is likely to get off to a rocky start unless you both are open and honest with each other. Unless this is established as a partnership of equals, there is bound to be trouble when it comes to making decisions. There may be a chance to make some extra cash by exploiting a talent developed through your leisure pursuits. Have confidence in your creative resources and this could become quite a lucrative sideline. Relax by spending a quiet evening at home.

23. THURSDAY. Difficult. Be careful if you are wearing favorite or expensive jewelry. A loose clasp could lead to losing a piece for good, so give it a thorough check before going out. Romance may be causing a few problems because one of you is more emotionally involved than the other. Unfortunately in this situation there is no point beating your head against a brick wall; the other person cannot be forced to change their feelings. A windfall could tempt you into a spending spree, but there is a distinct danger of digging into long-term savings if you get too carried away. Keep in mind just how much spare money you have to play around with.

24. FRIDAY. Relaxing. Concentrate on developing your personal talents and inner resources. There should be time today for some quiet meditation that might illuminate how best you can use your special skills to get more satisfaction out of life. This is a good time to check up on home security. Locks may need replacing or changing, or you might even consider getting a more elaborate security system if you have precious possessions to protect. As the day goes on, mental stimulation becomes increasingly important. Keep your wits sharp with word games or crossword puzzles, and make a habit of learning new words to increase your vocabulary. Youngsters can be kept amused with riddles.

25. SATURDAY. Positive. Sometimes a word in the right place can be worth a thousand that are spoken out of turn. Right now you have the chance to do a friend a real favor just by describing a situation in their life as you see it. Move ahead with plans for kitchen refurbishments, although they might be quite costly. However, the increase in comfort and efficiency will be well worth it. A friendship with an older person has much to teach you as you benefit from their life experience while they enjoy the freshness of your outlook. It is important to place a higher value on security these days, whether financial or emotional.

26. SUNDAY. Sensitive. It may be difficult to gather your thoughts together, but in fact there may be some value in letting them wander. Creative ideas could spring up from your unconscious if you shut out the outside world for a while. This is not the best day for getting practical work done; your talents simply do not lie in that direction. The most useful activity you can do is to listen to another person's problems and difficulties, then offer all the advice and sympathy that you can. The promise of a day spent solely with a loved one may not turn out quite as you planned. Small incidents could cause irritation unless you are both prepared to laugh them off.

27. MONDAY. Stimulating. Property speculation may seem beyond your means, but for once there might be the chance to make a small investment that could prove useful. Seek advice before you commit your funds, however. If you collect antiques, you could find just the piece you have been looking for tucked away in an obscure shop. You may have to pay a little over the going price, but it should be a valuable addition to your growing collection. Family gatherings can bring out unusual information about relatives who belonged to a former generation. You may be surprised to hear just what a colorful past you have inherited. Try to get some extra exercise during the day.

28. TUESDAY. Tricky. Although the day may not get off to a good start, try to keep your temper. Losing your cool will only set up a chain of negativity that might be hard to break. If your mate or partner's family is taking up a lot of your free time, it is understandable if you feel a measure of resentment. However, this is just a passing phase; soon you will have more time alone together. This may be the right time to check that your insurance is adequate; it is easy to lose track of the value of possessions as they accumulate over the course of years. Spend some time tidying up around your home, and try to create a brighter environment.

29. WEDNESDAY. Quiet. If you have not been spending a great deal of time with your family recently, due to pressure in other areas of your life, now there is a chance to make up for it. Relax and take advantage of some enjoyable hours together. Sometimes you feel nostalgic for places you have visited at happy times during your life. However, these memories should not make you feel dissatisfied with your current situation even if it does seem less romantic than those holidays in the sun. Where romance is concerned, it will probably pay to keep a low profile for now. The other person is not yet ready to respond to emotional demands, so be prepared to bide your time.

30. THURSDAY. Difficult. As a Libra you usually are not tactless, but now there is a chance of putting your foot in your mouth without meaning to do so. There is probably no graceful way out of the situation once the words escape from your mouth, other than to apologize sincerely. If youngsters are not doing as well as expected at school, look into the possible reason. They may be suffering from bullying and unable to concentrate even on subjects that they enjoy. Rumors about a romantic partner may appear at first to be nothing more than malicious gossip, but there might be a grain of truth in them. You may not want to believe it, but keep in mind that no one is without some faults.

31. FRIDAY. Deceptive. If underhand dealings at work are revealed, there is little you can do other than distance yourself from the affair as far as possible. Even the slightest involvement on your part could backfire at some future date. You may be short of funds right now, but taking a risk with what money you have is not the way out of trouble. Do not let anyone persuade you against your better judgment; be cautious and all will be well in the end. Even though you are currently enjoying a good relationship with a loved one, the need for some measure of freedom will soon begin to assert itself. Togetherness must not be allowed to become stifling.

APRIL

1. SATURDAY. Challenging. You should be buzzing with energy this morning. It would be a waste to spend the day on shopping and other chores, so make sure you get some enjoyable exercise. Old friends may get back in touch after a long absence; this could mark the start of a new phase in your life. If you are asked to take some responsibility for the care of elderly relatives, do so willingly. The burden is unlikely to be heavy, and their appreciation will make it all worthwhile. When a friend confides a personal problem, your Libra powers of tact may be stretched to the limit. In fact, you might be the only person who can tell them they are caught in an impossible situation.

2. SUNDAY. Enjoyable. This can be an excellent day for getting away from the rat race with your loved ones. During the course of your time together it should be possible to rebuild bridges that have been ignored in the hurly-burly of everyday life. Help is at hand if you need a quick injection of cash. A friend who owes you a favor is now more than happy to help you out, but make sure the terms of the loan are clear between you. You will only upset yourself by brooding on past losses and sadnesses. Sometimes it is necessary to let go of pain so that you can enjoy the present. Do not lose touch with distant family members; write to them or give them a call.

3. MONDAY. Pleasant. Even if you are prone to Monday morning blues, today you should get off to a more positive start than usual. Because your Libra love of a harmonious atmosphere can be satisfied by better work relations, do your best to keep things on an even keel. Work around the home can be immensely satisfying, particularly if you notice little details of decor that can easily be changed for the better. Small touches can make all the difference. There is no point making yourself suffer with a restrictive diet. In fact, it is more likely that you will overindulge to compensate for it, so find a diet that is enjoyable and satisfying rather than unduly punitive. Also be sure to get sufficient exercise.

4. TUESDAY. Useful. Where one-to-one relationships are concerned, you now have the chance to forgive and forget. Do not miss this opportunity to wipe the slate clean and begin again with a fresh sense of how much you mean to each other. As a legal case begins, you may feel somewhat nervous about the outcome. However, as long as you are convinced that you are in the right, there is little to fear. Plans to improve team efforts and cooperation at work should get off to a promising start. Your ability to coordinate is coming to the fore, making you an essential player in the plan or project. A romantic evening out on the town can round off the day quite nicely, but do not stay out too late.

5. WEDNESDAY. Sensitive. Some Libras may just be finding out how having children changes a partnership. Even though there is an element of strain, there is also the chance to bond closer together in mutual understanding. An unusual business proposition might attract you, despite the element of risk. Consult with your associates before making a decision whether to move; they may have a more objective view. This is a starred time to take up a new leisure pursuit that offers more of a challenge than your current activities. A healthy mind in a healthy body should be your aim, so find a way to give both some daily exercise.

6. THURSDAY. Mixed. Your motto should be to look before you leap. Although as a Libra you do not normally jump into a situation feetfirst, there is some danger of doing so now and getting out of your depth. Libra women may be attracted to men who have an aura of danger. In such a situation you need to be very careful and keep a cool head; such people may be very exciting but are not usually renowned for their sensitivity. A close acquaintance may seem determined to undermine your growing confidence in your creative power. Try not to take to heart their criticisms; turn to friends who have a more positive outlook.

7. FRIDAY. Variable. Because there may be problems with computer equipment, it would be wise to back up all important data at regular intervals. Lines of communication between you and a loved one may not be very clear at the moment. In fact, there is danger of a complete breakdown unless you both make a real effort to listen to what the other is saying and, even more important, what you both are feeling. Youngsters may show signs of wanting more independence. This can leave you in an awkward position, since you feel protective but realize they must learn to stand on their own two feet. A financial tip from a colleague can come in handy for raising extra cash.

8. SATURDAY. Fair. Developing a common interest can bring you and a loved one closer together. It is important to have a basic similarity in your understanding of life; otherwise you will be looking at many situations from differing perspectives. The prospect of an exotic vacation can do much to brighten up life. Right now you should have enough money for a real treat, so do not hold back. Even a day trip will allow you to unwind from the week's tensions. You may have to make a conscious effort to put problems out of your mind, but do not feel guilty about enjoying yourself. Romance can prosper if you take it at face value and do not try to analyze too much.

9. SUNDAY. Rewarding. Open your mind to all sorts of possibilities, and do not make any definite plans. Friends could phone out of the blue with unusual suggestions for spending the day, so keep yourself free to accept any offer that comes along. Where romance is concerned, a relationship that has a strong element of physical attraction may be deepening into something more solid. As time passes, you are apt to find out that you have more and more in common. If you are trying to study a subject with exams in view, enlist the help of a loved one to test your knowledge; make sure they are ruthless in quizzing you. Get youngsters to bed early so that you can enjoy a quiet evening.

10. MONDAY. Lucky. There should be good news in the mail if you are looking for a new job. An application you have actually forgotten about may have struck the right note with a prospective employer. Money is not likely to be a problem at the moment; in fact, the main question might be how best to invest a small surplus. This is a good time to ask the advice of a friend or an acquaintance who knows the financial markets better than you do. Sometimes you can be too conciliatory, even when it is against your own interests. If a colleague lets you down, do not hesitate to demand that they make up for it. And whatever you do, do not cover up for them.

11. TUESDAY. Exciting. Romance may be taking on an almost fairy-tale aura. Go with the flow; make the most of these enchanted days, and store up some special memories to share with your loved one in future times. You can do a friend some good by devoting a little time to listen to their troubles. They would do the same for you, so do not be stingy with your compassion. There may be career opportunities open to you that have not yet been widely advertised. Do not hesitate to push home your advantage; get your foot in the door right away. If you are being pressed to make a decision about whether to proceed with a legal matter, take your time doing so.

12. WEDNESDAY. Frustrating. You may find that a friend's word cannot always be relied upon, especially when it comes to making definite arrangements to meet. However, it is necessary to accept that different people have different standards of conduct. Not everyone shares your Libra view that punctuality is important. A romantic affair that has to be kept secret might seem exciting and glamorous at first, but the novelty will soon wear off. Once you begin to come up against the restrictions, you will begin to look at the other person in a more realistic way. Attention to detail can make or break an important work project, so be alert and thorough.

13. THURSDAY. Mixed. A business meeting should give you the opportunity to air matters that you consider important. Others will be impressed by your sincerity, so it may be a good chance to get action taken. A trip with friends can be a surprisingly serious affair as the talk turns to deep matters. Because you are probably in the mood for this, you will find it more satisfying than superficial social chat. Your energy level is not at its highest, making it foolish to push yourself too hard. Even if pressure is piled on at work, try to pass on some of it rather than taking on more than you can possibly do. Spend less on social activities for a while.

14. FRIDAY. Easygoing. The workweek winds down to a fairly trouble-free close. A long lunch with colleagues should give you time to get to know each other better outside the context of work, and to develop a personal relationship. Find time to write down what you want to achieve in your life during the course of the remainder of the year. Just putting it into words can focus your attention and your will to get results. Make sure you leave all unfinished tasks neatly organized so that you are ready to get off to a flying start after the weekend. You will feel all the better for having nothing nagging at the back of your mind. Let your mate or partner make arrangements for weekend entertaining.

15. SATURDAY. Useful. You and your mate or partner can come up with some sound plans for long-term savings if you put your heads together. There is no reason to feel that security is beyond your means; it is never too early or too late to start saving. The death of a close friend's relative could raise all kinds of issues. Naturally you want to be as supportive as possible. Also remember that the process of grieving takes longer than most people realize. The will to win could drive you to almost superhuman sporting feats, and you will probably prefer to claim the glory for yourself rather than for the team as a whole. Do not risk a physical strain or injury by overdoing it.

16. SUNDAY. Confusing. The possibilities for misunderstandings with your mate or partner are almost unlimited if you continue to wander about in a world of your own. They may be trying to tell you something of importance, which is far more urgent than your private dreams. Youngsters will respond better to a conciliatory attitude than to a show of authority. They need to be taught the value of reason, and in any case will resent it if you put your foot down. You cannot expect family members to give you emotional support if you do not do the same for them. Support should be mutual, not a one-way street. Social events are likely to bring out the sparkle in you.

17. MONDAY. Fortunate. Contract negotiations should be going well, thanks to your talent for diplomacy. Make sure your superiors fully appreciate just how much hard work you have put in and that the successful results are due largely to you. Libras who write for a living can find new means of self-expression by trying some experimental techniques. Do not be afraid of a few failures: eventually you will hit on just the right style for your unique voice. Try not to slip into the habit of taking your mate or partner for granted. Try to think back to the last time you told them you loved them. Relax in a hot bath tonight, with your favorite music playing or a good book to read.

18. TUESDAY. Stressful. You have come to the crunch where a long-term relationship is concerned. There is only one way forward, and it is up to you whether you want to continue on or bring it all to an undignified end. Youngsters can blurt out some refreshingly funny observations about adults; these, in fact, could give you insights about friends and relatives that are quite valuable. If a romantic involvement has swept you off your feet, it will probably do you good to place your fate in someone else's hands for once. Sometimes it is vital to put your trust in love, even if you then have to go through the inevitable ups and downs of a serious relationship.

19. WEDNESDAY. Deceptive. You do need to keep an eye on your finances in all respects. If you are trying to save money, it may be better to leave credit cards and cash at home. If you do carry them along when you go out shopping, make sure they are kept well hidden from any possibility of pickpocketing. Try not to get inflated ideas about making money from a leisure pursuit. There may be some profit to be earned, but it is likely to be quite modest. For this reason you should not fall into the trap of laying out a lot of capital for supplies. It will help if you keep personal issues on the back burner when doing any kind of research. Otherwise there is a danger of distorting whatever facts you discover.

20. THURSDAY. Unsettling. Sometimes it can be a case of two steps forward and one back when you are trying to put aside a sum of money for a special purpose. All kinds of emergencies tend to arise, forcing you to dig into funds. All you can do is keep on trying to save; you will get there in the end. The best that can be said of the Libra mood today is that you are able to express your feelings, although other people may not always want to listen. An ability to identify underlying issues beneath social chitchat can make you quite an uncomfortable companion as friends sense that you can see into their souls. It is necessary to be as supportive and sympathetic as possible.

21. FRIDAY. Helpful. If you are having difficulty getting paperwork finished by the week's end, do not hesitate to ask for assistance. People who owe you favors will be pleased to lend a hand.

Romance should be very enjoyable as long as you are honest about your emotions. Opening your heart can make you feel more tender toward your mate or partner. Take more pride in your creative work; do not be too modest to blow your own horn from time to time. As long as you show other people that you are serious, they will respond in a similar vein. An evening out locally with friends could lead to making a pleasant new acquaintance.

22. SATURDAY. Fair. You should not be short of mental stimulation as friends phone to gossip and catch up on the latest news. You could learn something to your advantage, so listen carefully and with an open mind. Youngsters can be kept busy with games that inspire their imagination; you might be surprised just how inventive they can be. A romantic involvement could come to an untimely end for the want of a few pertinent words expressing your emotions. Do not run the risk of losing a promising relationship just because you feel too shy to express your feelings. Shopping with your mate or partner can be enjoyable, especially if you are buying items for pure pleasure. Treat yourselves as royally as possible.

23. SUNDAY. Exciting. Today's electrical atmosphere may make it difficult for you to relax because you will be anticipating something wonderful to happen all day. In fact, as long as you keep an open mind, there may be encounters with interesting and creative people that light up your life. Socializing with neighbors can be more pleasant than usual. You will not have to make any major effort to get along even with those you usually find unsympathetic. Make the most of this chance to get to know some local people better; you can all find ways to help and support each other. You will probably be happiest at home this evening, so do not make any unusual social arrangements.

24. MONDAY. Reassuring. If you have been on tenterhooks waiting for a property deal to be finalized, you should be able to relax at last. Once it is all wrapped up, take a breather before looking ahead to the next stage of the proceedings. The answer to a question that has been bothering you is probably right under your nose. Ask family members if they can shed any light on your problem; they are almost bound to be able to help. Joint savings with your mate or partner should be accumulating nicely. This could be the time to treat yourselves rather than just continue to squirrel money away. Shop for something you both want to beautify your home.

25. TUESDAY. Challenging. Make the most of today by putting your good Libra powers of intuition to work. There is no need to focus on an obstacle to your wishes. Look at the situation from another angle and you should soon be able to figure out how to go ahead. Your mate or partner may come up with an interesting plan for a vacation. Even if it is not the kind of trip you usually enjoy, it might be worth giving it a whirl. Libras looking for a new home may feel somewhat constricted by a tight budget. It may not be possible to buy as large a place as you would like, but that does not mean you cannot find an attractive, livable home. Try to maintain the peace between family members of different generations.

26. WEDNESDAY. Misleading. If you have gotten yourself into a financial muddle, good advice unfortunately may not be available. Those you consult may have their own interests at heart more than yours. You will just have to cut your spending a bit. Your romantic partner may have put you on a pedestal, which can be rather disconcerting when you are only too aware of your own faults. It may be necessary to point out gently that they are being unrealistic, and that no one is perfect. Be ambitious for youngsters by all means, but if they sometimes fail to live up to your expectations, it would be wrong to punish them for it. Get to bed early tonight.

27. THURSDAY. Disquieting. As a Libra you are normally mild-mannered, but when someone disturbs your sense of harmony there is a strong temptation to lash out. However, words said in a moment of anger can return to haunt you, so try to keep a rein on your temper. If you expect too much of a romantic situation, you are bound to be disappointed. A current relationship may actually be quite a pedestrian affair, only really becoming glamorous in your own imagination. As far as money is concerned, it could be a case of easy come, easy go. If you are happy with this it is fine, but your mate or partner may take a different view. Try a new restaurant tonight offering special taste sensations.

28. FRIDAY. Satisfactory. Little rifts between you and your loved one can be healed with a few well-chosen words. Just the fact that you are taking the initiative to patch things up should help bring you closer together. Youngsters may want some special loving; for once you should not hesitate to spoil them a little. It is important for all family members to feel secure and cared for at all times. If you are looking for romance, turn on the Libra charm. You can get what you want if you are prepared to go all out for it; sincerity comes later on in the game. A legal case is turning in your favor, so you can wait for the result with high hopes.

29. SATURDAY. Fair. Either clear weekend tasks out of the way early this morning or forget them altogether. It will not hurt for once if you concentrate on more urgent matters than cleaning and shopping. A friend with some financial insight could give you a hand organizing your savings. Even if you do not have much money, someone who is in the know can help you make the best use of your funds. Do not delay taking your car in for servicing if it is due. There are likely to be small faults which can be nipped in the bud if you act right away. Be sure to check your tires also. Youngsters seem to be developing a habit of answering back, which cannot be allowed to go unchecked.

30. SUNDAY. Good. Organize yourself and you will be surprised how much activity you can fit into a single day. The trick is to find the pace you are comfortable with, then not allow yourself to be hurried by anyone. A less indulgent diet will soon get rid of extra pounds, and you are sure to be flattered by the comments that friends make. Begin now and there is more chance of sticking to your resolutions. A regular regime of exercise can benefit the whole family, but do not try anything too strenuous until you get in better shape. Youngsters may find items that you thought were long lost; for once you will be grateful for them poking around in drawers and closets.

MAY

1. MONDAY. Auspicious. There is no need to adopt an aggressive approach to get a new plan or project off the ground at work. You should be able to sneak it in by the back door; colleagues will find themselves cooperating before they know what has happened. You should receive a great sense of pleasure from treating a loved one to a special concert or theatrical performance. Everyone needs beauty in their lives, and it is important that you maintain a balance between everyday reality and your long-term dreams. You can enlarge your circle of friends by being a bit more outgoing. Do not be shy about introducing yourself to new people whenever you have the opportunity to do so.

2. TUESDAY. Productive. Today's more impulsive mood can free up your creative imagination. Problem solving may become a positive pleasure once you find the knack of tackling challenges with a determination not to be beaten. Libras who are hesitating about proposing cannot afford to wait much longer. Even if the ideal occasion does not present itself, pluck up your courage and go ahead. A small gamble may pay off, but it would be wise to go by instinct, only taking the risk if you feel entirely happy with it. Youngsters' talents need developing from an early age if they are to fulfill their potential, so think about signing them up for classes.

3. WEDNESDAY. Deceptive. Superiors who claimed they would be supportive may just not seem willing to live up to their promise when the crunch comes. You are likely to be thrown back on your own resources to get out of an awkward situation at work. Money may be flowing through your hands like water at the moment. Unfortunately there is little point searching for advice; the answer lies with your own attitude. The result of a research project may be deceptive because all the facts are not yet available. You may think you have the whole picture, but a little more digging around is apt to unearth information that can throw fresh light on the situation.

4. THURSDAY. Variable. Focus on a fresh attempt to improve your future security. With the support of your mate or partner you should be able to make significant advances, although some sacrifices will have to be made. A new romance may have you in a whirl; the excitement of the physical attraction is bound to be undeniable. However, if you want the relationship to last you will have to work on other levels of sharing. Every family has a skeleton in the closet, so do not be shocked when you find out something about an ancestor that seems out of character. It is far better that all aspects of family history, even negative ones, be brought to light rather than kept as a deep, dark secret.

5. FRIDAY. Mixed. You will probably have to bite your tongue if you are to avoid an argument with a loved one. There are likely to be fundamental differences of opinion between you, which can only be ironed out if you are both willing to sit down and talk them over at length. This is a good time to take up a new course of study. You have the mental energy and will to make a success even of a subject that you would normally consider beyond your grasp. Libra teachers are probably well aware that students look up to those in charge as ideal, attractive figures. However, any temptation on your part to play on their vulnerable emotions must be strenuously resisted.

6. SATURDAY. Misleading. There are all kinds of motives for getting into a relationship, but a feeling of pity for someone is not the best or most positive one. You run the risk of being pulled down into the other person's negative feelings if you allow your compassion to get the better of you. Financially you may not really have much of a grasp of your current situation. It might help to go through your assets and obligations with a loved one who has a more a realistic approach. Organizing a social evening can be rather tricky because it seems impossible to please everyone. Guests may be focusing on their own problems and find it hard to leave them behind in order to have fun.

7. SUNDAY. Pleasant. Try to spend this day away from the house. Forget your sense of duty for once. This should be a day dedicated to pure pleasure and enjoyment. A close romantic relationship is at a turning point. You both need to decide just how you perceive future developments. Fortunately it appears you should be basically in harmony but, all the same, do not take this for granted. A more conciliatory approach will win over family members who have been keeping their distance. Although your Libra pride may suffer a bit, you should soon forget all that once a good atmosphere has been reestablished. A generous gesture is sure to be appreciated.

8. MONDAY. Successful. A small but useful legacy may enable you to put down a deposit on an expensive item you have wanted for a long time. This purchase should give your mate or partner just as much pleasure as it gives you, so make sure you share all stages of its acquisition. You are in a position to help out a colleague with a quiet word in the right place. There is no reason not to be as generous in your assessment as you can be. Youngsters are probably bounding with energy, and will really keep you on your toes. Make sure they are kept fully occupied, and do not lose your sense of humor. A job interview should go well just as long as you radiate confidence.

9. TUESDAY. Satisfactory. If you are trying to meet new people, it might be a good idea to join a club where everyone shares a common interest. This will ensure you have a certain level of sympathy with everyone you meet. Keeping a secret is never easy, especially if you are aware that your knowledge gives you a measure of power over someone. Consider the consequences if you reveal what you know; decide whether you would really want to take the responsibility for ensuing events. Mistakes in a bank statement could cause a few problems. It will probably take you some time and effort to get it all sorted out, but you must make sure that you do not lose out as a result.

10. WEDNESDAY. Volatile. A superior could come down on you hard for a small error. You may well feel you have been unfairly treated, but unfortunately there is nothing to be done but correct your mistake and accept the blame. Your romantic situation is rather volatile, with both you and the other person in your life flinging accusations that are meant to hurt. Stop this before you get into a spiral of increasing anger. Once you both calm down, you should be able to see that the disagreement blew up over almost nothing at all. There may be problems getting the information you need to complete a work project. This is likely to be a simple case of crossed wires, so try to keep a sense of perspective.

11. THURSDAY. Confusing. When loved ones suddenly fly off the handle and accuse you of trying to control them, you are apt to be at a loss regarding how to react. If you take a more objective view, however, it may become clearer how your behavior has been irritating them. There may be a strong temptation to move funds around in the hope of making a quick profit. However, unless you know exactly what you are doing, it would be far better to leave well enough alone. A romantic attraction may have you all in a spin, but this could just be a flash in the pan. If the two of you have very little in common, after the first thrill of excitement you will probably lose interest.

12. FRIDAY. Fair. Making a regular donation to a favorite charity can do a lot of good, so arrange to do so even if you can only afford small sums. An old friendship can be revived when someone you knew long ago moves into your neighborhood. You will probably start talking as if you had never been separated. Try to round off the workweek neatly by getting all financial matters in order. This is especially important if you have responsibility for someone else's funds. Local traffic conditions may be very congested as people leave town for the weekend. However, losing your temper will not get you to your destination any quicker than if you keep calm and in control.

13. SATURDAY. Variable. If you are going on a vacation you should be able to get off to a good start. However, it is almost certain that you will leave something behind, so make sure you have enough cash or credit to replace essential items. Although as a Libra you do not usually relish the idea of exercising, there are pleasant ways to do so. A gentle and rhythmical discipline such as yoga can be soothing and calming to your mind as well as good for your body. A romantic affair that looked promising only a short while ago seems to be coming to an abrupt end. The other person may simply cut off from you. Although this is bound to hurt, you may actually be better off in another relationship.

14. SUNDAY. Good. Cultivate a more glamorous image, then see how your confidence improves as a result. A different hairstyle and classic clothes should suit your Libra taste for the romantic. Libras with children need to focus on their needs and wishes. At this point you should be doing all you can to instill a sense of compassion and idealism in them; otherwise there is a danger of them becoming desensitized through the pressures of school and society. You can overcome a self-imposed limit if you believe in yourself. Early conditioning may be responsible for a feeling that you can achieve only modest aims, but this is definitely not true.

15. MONDAY. Challenging. Start the workweek with a resolution to break a bad habit, and tell others that you are doing so. In this way, loved ones and colleagues will help keep you to the mark. For once you should not let your romantic partner have things all their own way. It is time to put your foot down and make your own desires clear. If your mate or partner is a bit surprised, that is all to the good. If you rely on your creative work for a living, you can come up with bright new ideas about marketing yourself. You need a strategy that makes you stand out from the crowd. Do not let childhood slip by without making a photographic record of youngsters' activities.

16. TUESDAY. Tricky. You will not do yourself any favors by agreeing to work extra hours for nothing. Even if a superior tries to flatter you, it is not a good idea to give in because this is bound to be the thin end of the wedge. It is time to get practical with home security; you can no longer rely on trusting to luck. Consult with friends or neighbors as to the best means to adopt in order to protect valued possessions. Physically you may be a little under the weather, probably due to neglecting to eat properly. Right now you need to build up your stamina or you could come down with a series of irritating minor ailments. Spend a quiet night in the comfort of your home.

17. WEDNESDAY. Rewarding. A financial bonus may come as a pleasant surprise, even though you richly deserve it. What probably will mean even more to you is that it is a token of appreciation for your conscientious, diligent work. Romantically all seems in good order. A deeper emotional bond forming between you and your loved one will not be disturbed by any surface disagreements. This is the time to develop a greater interest in the spiritual content of life. Finding meaning in your existence should now be taking up more of your attention. Be generous, but do not overspend on a gift for a friend or a contribution of time or money to a charity.

18. THURSDAY. Demanding. It just may not be possible to put off any longer a decision concerning your finances. You cannot afford to keep on muddling through; it is time to get properly organized. A critical remark might cause a crisis in confidence but will serve to show just how dependent you are on the approval of other people. This is an area of your personality that needs working on; you must develop the courage of your convictions. Do not punish a loved one by withholding affection. If they have done something to upset you, then tell them so, but in a kindly way and with tact. Be careful if you are working in the kitchen when youngsters are around.

19. FRIDAY. Unsettling. Sometimes words come out of your mouth before you have had time to think, which could be a recipe for disaster. As a Libra you have an uncanny knack of homing in on loved ones' weak spots and revealing them in a way that can be quite hurtful. Quick thinking can save the day where an overseas business deal is concerned. If you hesitate you could be lost, but today you just have to accept the element of risk. Travel is likely to be frustrating, with long delays on public transportation. Make sure you have plenty of reading matter to occupy yourself, especially if you are going on a long trip. Enlist the help of a friend or neighbor for a heavy task around the house.

20. SATURDAY. Changeable. There is not much point making definite plans because they are almost bound to be overturned by events. You need to hang on to your sense of humor if things begin to get out of hand. Friends may turn to you for help as a last resource when other people have failed them. You can hardly fail to respond to their pleas, even though you may not have much sympathy for their plight. Libras who are looking for love will almost certainly be able to find a relationship of some kind, but it is not likely to be ideal by any means. You would be unwise to pin your hopes for future security on a new liaison. Physically demanding sports should be avoided.

21. SUNDAY. Easygoing. Stay close to home as much as you can. Trips out are best confined to the immediate locality; there may be areas quite near you that deserve further exploration. This is a good time to catch up on letter writing. It can be all too easy to drift out of touch with friends who have moved away, and as time goes by the value of old friendships becomes clearer. If you have to keep youngsters amused, occupy them with games that have an educational content. Learning should be fun, for you as well as for them. Libra gardeners can do some useful work. You will probably find it soothing rather than tiring to dig and plant.

22. MONDAY. Favorable. Libras who are searching for a new home may be able to afford a larger place than expected. A stroke of luck could lead you to a spacious house that is relatively cheap. This is one of those times when you can trust your hunch that an unlikely investment is a good risk. All the same, it would be wise to play it fairly safe and not overextend your financial resources. Family heirlooms might not mean much to you now, but it can be comforting to have pieces that link you to your family history. Even if the items are not really your taste, they should be cherished for the memory they contain. Be prepared for a surprise visit.

23. TUESDAY. Manageable. If you are having money troubles, family members will probably be pleased to help you out with a loan. Those who have suffered shortages themselves will be most sympathetic. You might recoil from the disruption caused by extensive redecoration in your home, but in the long run it will be worth the inconvenience. Once everything is just as you have always wanted it, you will wonder why you waited so long. Libras preparing for exams must try not to overdo it. Too much studying can make you stale and tired on test day, so try to relax a little. A romance based on mental rapport offers the tranquillity you desire and deserve.

24. WEDNESDAY. Fortunate. Flashes of inspiration can come to you if you cease trying to use logic to solve a problem. In fact, you might surprise yourself with the knowledge that has been hidden away in your mind. Plan an outing or a vacation that will enable you to develop a talent. There are plenty of organizations that cater to special interests, and you should be able to find something that suits you with no difficulty. Libras who need to travel in the course of work may be at the point when it is tiring rather than stimulating. However, making a new contact can renew all your enthusiasm and make you realize how fortunate you are to be paid for such variety.

25. THURSDAY. Difficult. A romantic affair for which you have great hope may not be as stable as you think it is. In fact, the other person may turn out to be so wayward that you begin to wonder whether it is a good idea to take the relationship any further. Your social life may be rather humdrum, making you long for more exciting companions. Ultimately, however, it is up to you to find new ways of introducing stimulation into your leisure activities. No matter how careful you are with money, it still seems a problematic issue. Blaming your mate or partner for overspending is no solution; you need to work together to create a balanced budget.

26. FRIDAY. Disquieting. Make sure that pets are securely indoors before you go out; otherwise there is a possibility of their wandering off for long distances. No matter how much you do to assist a superior at work, they may seem to just continue to take you for granted. In fact, they might even take credit for work that you have done on their behalf. Perhaps it is time to start looking out for yourself a bit more. Travel plans might be held up due to bureaucratic regulations. Unfortunately there is no way around this particular red tape; you will just have to be patient. Keep an eye on youngsters' health if they seem a bit low in energy and always tired.

27. SATURDAY. Happy. Normal reality is unlikely to hold many charms for you because you will be much more interested in pursuing your dreams. Thinking big is exactly what you should do. The higher you aspire, the more you are bound to achieve. A romance with someone who is artistically inclined should be extremely pleasing to your Libra sense of beauty. However, you may soon find that you also have to deal with their absentmindedness and unreliability; if your affections are true, that will not seem important. Do not let petty problems spoil a day out. There will still be much to enjoy as long as you maintain a positive mood.

28. SUNDAY. Sensitive. Most people feel a conflict from time to time between the need for security and the desire for freedom. Coming down on one side or the other is not really a long-term solution; you need to somehow find room for both in your life. Where money is concerned, you may not know whether you are coming or going. Try to find time to get your accounts up to date so that you have a clear picture of exactly where you stand. You may have to go along with the plans of other people to a great extent. Although doing so usually does not bother you, it can get irritating if you begin to feel loved ones are not willing to be equally as flexible.

29. MONDAY. Rewarding. There is nothing like an ambitious project to draw together colleagues and superiors. Right now almost everyone has the opportunity to pool resources and ideas. Just make sure that all contributions are valued and acknowledged. Libras who have entered on a legal action may be having second thoughts. In fact, it is not too late to try to reach an amicable agreement, so see if something can be worked out. Arguments within the family can be settled as long as everyone is willing to take their fair share of the blame. Papering over the cracks is not enough; get to the bottom of the problem and sort it out once and for all.

30. TUESDAY. Buoyant. It is said that you cannot hurry love, but after a long wait it appears that just the right person has come along. You may feel a little nervous about getting emotionally involved after a difficult experience, but this person is almost certain to have your best interests at heart. The results of an exam or test may come as a surprise after a long delay. You have probably done better than you expected, so try not to worry. Travel for pleasure is highlighted; you and your mate or partner deserve a romantic break in a different climate. Do not just dream about it, get it organized. A career opportunity could come up in a field outside your usual sphere of paid activity.

31. WEDNESDAY. Confusing. Money is not coming your way right now, and it may be hard to see how your expenditure can be so high. There is no sense in feeling helpless, however; it is not impossible to cut costs right now. You will not do yourself any favors by being overly modest about your talents. There is no use expecting others to appreciate you for your true worth unless you are able to do so yourself. Youngsters can slip out of sight in the wink of an eye, so make sure you are extra vigilant. Unfortunately a romantic attachment seems doomed to disappoint. The other person is not really in a position to give their heart to you and may be simply playing with your feelings.

JUNE

1. THURSDAY. Frustrating. Prospects for travel do not look good, especially if you are going a longer distance than usual. Libra drivers need to be extra careful to keep calm and not let any discourtesy on the part of others on the road upset you. Small incidents can have a profound impact and make you question your overall understanding of life, which somehow has to include all the baffling mistakes and accidents that occur. If you are on the lookout for romance, realize that you cannot adopt a hardheaded approach. Love often comes out of the blue; you cannot expect to just pick on someone at random and decide that they are the one to make you happy for life.

2. FRIDAY. Stimulating. A little extra persistence should pay off, with all obstacles standing between you and a specially enjoyable weekend break falling away. This is one of those times when you can be absolutely clear about what you truly want, then go all out to get it. A romantic partner may open your eyes to new opportunities for self-development. It is necessary to grow together in order to stay together, so do not hesitate to focus on expanding your horizons. You can make a fresh start on a work project involving overseas connections if you apply your particular expertise. Even though your present contribution might be modest, there is room for change.

3. SATURDAY. Disruptive. A lot of time could be wasted looking for an object that is actually unlikely to turn up. Of course this will be frustrating, but sometimes you just have to accept that precious things are gone. Trips are almost certain to be less comfortable than you hope. Once family members are away from home and their own responsibilities, all kinds of petty grievances can come to the fore. A romantic affair is in danger of foundering unless you can patch up your differences. If you are honest with yourself, you should realize that there is a power struggle going on between the two of you, each wanting to prove that the other is more emotionally dependent.

4. SUNDAY. Pleasant. A breath of fresh air would do you a world of good, so do not mope at home even if you have private work to sort out. Letters can be written in the open air, and even more serious paperwork can be completed as long as the surroundings are peaceful. This is a starred time to begin giving youngsters some more responsibility around the home. Having small tasks that are designated as theirs alone can foster a lifelong habit of reliability. Calls from distant relatives may come as a pleasant surprise, strengthening emotional ties that you had all but forgotten about. Make a resolution to keep in touch with them from now on. Wind down this evening with a favorite novel.

5. MONDAY. Useful. Libras who are currently looking for a new job should begin the workweek with a positive outlook. Make the most of all of your contacts, even unlikely ones. There is almost bound to be an opening that can lead to better opportunities even if it does not seem tempting at first. Financially your situation is looking up, thanks to some sound advice from an expert. As long as you are prepared to tighten your belt for a while, there are worthwhile profits to be made on a long-term investment. Your job may require you to assume extra responsibilities for a period of time. This should be taken seriously; a good performance will count strongly in your favor.

6. TUESDAY. Fair. For once you need have no qualms about speaking your mind in a meeting. As long as you have a sound point to make, other people will listen to you with respect and will probably act on your suggestions. Libras who are politically inclined may decide that this is the time to become more actively involved. There is no need to feel that one person cannot make a difference. Every voice counts, and your input can improve a favorite cause's chance of success. If you have recently ended a relationship, a good pick-me-up might be to plan an indulgent vacation with friends. Once you are in a beautiful location and have good company, you will soon be your old self again.

7. WEDNESDAY. Disquieting. There is every danger of throwing out the baby with the bathwater if you are tempted to break your ties with a group of like-minded people. Differences of opinion can be accommodated if you are only willing to see reason. It would be a real pity to end your association and lose the companionship of friends with whom you have a lot in common. A romantic relationship may be almost too hot to handle. It might be wise for both of you to back off and not see each other for a while. This will give you a chance to calm down and take a more objective view. In addition, time apart will make you realize that you actually miss and need each other.

8. THURSDAY. Variable. Begin to wind the week down by finishing off pressing tasks. If there are difficult phone calls you have been avoiding, you will feel far better after making them. A decision to break free of an old attachment should be comparatively easy once you have definitely made up your mind. Your present life is rich enough for you not to need clinging memories of the past. It is important right now to be very supportive of youngsters; any adverse criticism could make a deeper impression on them than you suspect. Do all you can to make all family members feel special and valued. Local journeys could be delayed due to road repairs and long detours.

9. FRIDAY. Changeable. Time spent caring for elderly relatives will not be wasted. Even if you feel you have not done much to improve their situation, just the fact that you are offering help means a great deal. The results of a legal decision may return to haunt you after a long period. However, it is vital that you put past unhappiness behind you and do not allow yourself to feel guilty. There might be some extra money to be made by working at home. Consult with loved ones before making a decision, since this will affect them too. Some slightly shady dealing could snarl up an overseas business deal unless you bring it out into the open.

10. SATURDAY. Favorable. You have every reason to be proud of yourself when it comes to your creative work. Take this opportunity to shake off your shyness and accept the praise that is due you. Loved ones will be more willing to cater to your desires if you make it clear that your plans are going to benefit them as well. Mutual cooperation can sweeten the atmosphere at home even if it has been a bit difficult lately. Romance should go your way as long as you relax. This is not the time to be pushy; just enjoy the attention you are already receiving. Shopping trips can turn up exciting new ideas for changing your style of clothes and even your whole image.

11. SUNDAY. Exciting. At the moment you need some mental stimulation, which is exactly what loved ones can give you. A whole new facet of your relationship could open up as you develop more shared interests. Libras who feel ready for romance should be sure to look fashionable and smart. Social events are almost bound to bring you into contact with a like-minded person who finds you attractive. All leisure activities are favored, especially if you are trying something new. You do not need to indulge in risky sports to get a sense of excitement out of life; new ideas can be just as thrilling. Make sure you give loved ones your full attention this evening.

12. MONDAY. Mixed. Make the most of the morning hours to get important work out of the way. In addition to firing on all cylinders, you have a valuable personal viewpoint that can put plans in a different light. Sometimes it is enough simply to dream about travel rather than undergo the stresses and strains of the real thing. If you feel you need a break, a good book about exotic locales could actually be more relaxing. Because your finances may be a little shaky, it would be a good idea to keep a sharp eye on how much you are spending on everyday items. Savings can be made if you are prepared to sacrifice the convenience of buying all goods locally and shop further afield.

13. TUESDAY. Challenging. If the chance comes along to improve your career prospects, do not hesitate to take it. You might have to be a bit persuasive, but as long as you are enthusiastic that should not be any problem. The results of your recent efforts to save should be obvious at last, allowing you to build up a useful lump sum for emergencies. The danger, of course, is that it is tempting to spend it right away, but try and restrain yourself. Unfortunately you cannot rely on loved ones to run errands for you, even though they may be simple ones. You are bound to be annoyed by this, but bear in mind that you have moments of forgetfulness yourself, and have let loved ones down occasionally.

14. WEDNESDAY. Difficult. There is no point relying on receiving funds that have not yet materialized, especially if there is some confusion over when you are likely to get the money. It would be far better to restrict yourself to current funds; then the extra money will seem to be a windfall. It is not always possible to second-guess decisions made at work that affect you directly. The best you can do is plan for every possible eventuality you can think of. A problem that could be solved by an injection of cash may just have to wait until the tide turns. Patience is a lesson that comes easily to few people, but in this case you have no choice. Put a plan on hold until conditions improve.

15. THURSDAY. Sensitive. Sometimes getting a loved one to talk can be like getting blood out of a stone. However, when there is obviously something on their mind, it is almost your duty to try to find out what is wrong. Be prepared for travel chaos, with public services being cut and jams on the roads. Walking to your destination, if that is possible, might be preferable than a slow car or bus journey. Youngsters may seem less willing than usual to tell you about school, which should alert you to the possibility that they are hiding something. Perhaps they feel they are not doing as well as you would like in some subject, and are afraid that you will criticize their effort and their abilities.

16. FRIDAY. Demanding. A period is now beginning when you will be doing some deep questioning about your direction in life. Perhaps your aims no longer satisfy you, causing you to begin wondering how you can get a sense of personal satisfaction by contributing to the greater good. Now more than ever it is important to keep all your relations at work totally aboveboard. Nothing is to be gained by trying to get an advantage through the use of dubious methods. Some tension between the demands of daily living and the search for a more profound meaning is inevitable for every thinking person. An effective way for you to reconcile this is by gaining greater trust in your special creative powers.

17. SATURDAY. Disquieting. Although you are probably doing your best to please other people, your efforts may not be having the desired effect. Loved ones are unlikely to point out to you the obvious truth that you cannot decide what others want without first consulting them. Shopping is likely to take you to many stores; because of this you will probably end up spending more than expected. Make sure you keep all receipts because the gift you select may not be exactly what was wanted and might need to be returned. Even though you are happiest when others are happy, there are times when you need to put your own interests first. Try to explain this to loved ones without getting angry or annoyed.

18. SUNDAY. Cautious. Today's more restless mood impels you to get away from home. You are apt to be in something of an inner turmoil. Spending some time at a scene of beauty is bound to calm your emotions. If you are planning to entertain at home, do not let nerves get the better of you. There is no need to go over the top with arrangements; if you prepare too elaborate an occasion, your guests are apt to feel uncomfortable. If you are working on your house, beware of being overly ambitious about what you can achieve. Every job needs to be finished; keep in mind that you have a certain tendency to start projects that can be rather far beyond your current capabilities.

19. MONDAY. Productive. Even if you do not feel like getting back into the swing of work, there should be an interesting project assigned to you that will fire your enthusiasm. Some prudent financial planning can do much to ensure your future security; a trained, professional adviser should be more approachable than usual and able to give you some sound advice. A little extra research into a problem that has been baffling you can yield the answer. You need persistence along with the imagination to look at unlikely sources of information. A superior may test your organizational abilities; there could be a promotion ahead, so do your best to make a good impression.

20. TUESDAY. Uncertain. It is difficult to explain your feelings to loved ones when you are not even sure yourself what they are. However, it would be better to go away and do some thinking rather than give a wrong impression of your emotions when so much is hanging on your words. Double-check all social engagements; friends are apt to be rather forgetful at the moment and could unwittingly let you down. The promise of a romantic holiday can do wonders for your relationship with your mate or partner. The only problem might be in actually getting past the stage of dreaming and on to practical action; check with a travel agent without delay.

21. WEDNESDAY. Disruptive. Although you may not see eye-to-eye with higher-ups on certain matters, remember that they are in a position of power which you cannot reasonably challenge. If their decisions are wrong, then the results will inevitably reveal that the mistake is theirs. A moment of rash action could lose you savings that have taken a long time to accumulate. It is said that fools rush in where angels fear to tread; rarely is a profit made by doing so. Where romance is concerned, you are in for some surprises. That special person in your life might actually be more frank than you are comfortable with, revealing details of their past that will take some time for you to digest.

22. THURSDAY. Fair. Take a deep breath and resolve not to be rattled by events in the early part of the day; things will calm down later. However, you do need to beware of making rash promises that you have no means of keeping. An eye for the immediate problem can be of immense assistance in keeping a sense of perspective on a long-term project. The secret is to prioritize so that the whole effort will become manageable. A long-held wish can begin to come true if you are prepared to do some groundwork. The early stages of your plan may be tedious, but that is the price you pay for attaining an important goal. Treat a loved one to a good evening out on the town.

23. FRIDAY. Variable. If you are hoping to get through a lot of work today, you may be disappointed. It is likely you will be tripped up by poor communications with others, as well as the natural tendency to slow down as the weekend approaches. Health matters should be receiving some extra attention. Efforts made now to give up an unhealthy habit should be successful; your willpower is strong, and you know you will feel all the better for adopting a more sensible lifestyle. An eagerly awaited letter from a loved one may have been delayed, putting you on tenterhooks as you wonder what the contents might be. You only have to be patient a little longer.

24. SATURDAY. Manageable. At last a pet that has been causing you some concern seems to be in bouncing good health again. As both you and youngsters begin to relax, it is obvious how animals can become an important part of the family. This would be a good time to go through savings and pension plans in detail with your mate or partner. You may find that your needs have changed, or even that it is possible to save larger sums regularly. An older relative may have useful advice to offer where a close relationship of yours is concerned. Their view is likely to be less romantic and more pragmatic than yours, so what they say might not at first be welcome until you really think about it.

25. SUNDAY. Enjoyable. Try to share the day's activities with loved ones; this can bring you closer together. Trips to special places of interest in the locality might be more exciting than you suppose. Even if you have lived in the same area for a long time, there are almost always new places to be discovered. Youngsters are likely to be more cooperative than usual. Make the most of their pliable mood to persuade them to learn something new. Even quite little children can have an amazing grasp of ideas that are considered deep by most adults. Libras playing sports may feel an uncharacteristic urge to lead the team. Just be careful not to be too forceful or you may raise hackles.

26. MONDAY. Changeable. Romance can take you by surprise. You might even find yourself being pulled out of your depth if you are not careful. It would certainly be unwise to make any commitment yet to someone who you hardly know, even if your future together seems fairly certain. Business associates appear more willing than usual to seriously consider your creative input. Make the most of this by being as professional as possible in your presentation. You could find yourself handicapped in the search for a new job by lack of relevant training. It is no use assuming you can pick up new skills as you go; employers want to see proof of your present abilities.

27. TUESDAY. Tricky. Being vague about your finances may work as a ploy to get your mate or partner to take more responsibility, but that is not really fair. In the end, you should both be working in tandem to improve your situation. A disagreement with a family member during the morning should not be allowed to upset you unduly. Because you both dislike arguing so much, you will make up before the day is out. Even if you are involved in work that is not high profile, your boss or another superior is well aware of the worth of what you are doing; there is likely to be a reward when the time is right. A more tolerant attitude to your mate or partner's ambitions will do their self-confidence a world of good.

28. WEDNESDAY. Disconcerting. This is the time to admit that an ongoing difficulty with a loved one could benefit from some outside help. There are some problems you cannot be expected to sort out without an objective view from someone who can stand outside the situation. If you have been careless dealing with the tax office, you could find yourself in trouble even though your conscience is clear. It is necessary to be absolutely meticulous when filling in forms. A meeting at which you are called upon to speak in front of others is likely to be far less of an ordeal than you expect. In fact, you might even find that you enjoy being in the limelight.

29. THURSDAY. Satisfactory. At long last things seem to be looking up financially, thanks more to a bonus than to your long-term planning. This should give you the incentive to get better organized and to capitalize on the funds you have. Romantic Libras could meet someone interesting at an art gallery or concert. Do not be afraid to strike up a conversation; there is every possibility of a mutual attraction springing up. Plans for long-distance travel may have to be shelved for the time being. The time simply does not seem right, as you will probably realize if you rely on your intuition. In-laws can be very supportive in a time of financial or emotional need.

30. FRIDAY. Lucky. A whole new area of life could open up if you allow your natural curiosity to lead you onward. Life will be enriched by taking up a new course of study that can give you insight into an area that is of particular interest to you. Libras who are working in the media may come into contact with unusual new ideas for marketing that at first seem a little bizarre. However, if something about them sticks in your mind, that is proof that they have worth and should be snapped up. A more open atmosphere at work enables you to finish the workweek with a friendly drink or meal with associates. Valuable insights can be swapped with them in informal surroundings.

JULY

1. SATURDAY. Stressful. There appears to be conflict brewing between you and a loved one. If you allow this to develop into a battle of wills, long-term damage could be done to the relationship. To prevent this, swallow your pride and back down. Sometimes it seems parents are taking up more of your emotional energy than you like; you may even begin to wonder just who is caring for whom. Naturally you have obligations toward them as well as a strong bond of affection, but as an adult your first concerns should be for the life you have created for yourself. It is important to find ways of working off your excess energy; working in the garden or participating in team sports would do you good.

2. SUNDAY. Favorable. You might be surprised when someone for whom you have great respect asks you to attend a social occasion with them. Obviously they regard you as an equal, so there is no reason for you to do otherwise. Romance promises to be happy, with expressions of affection on both sides. Just for once there is no harm in being a bit sentimental, even if you feel slightly embarrassed about it. Entertaining at home can turn into quite a formal occasion, with guests on their best behavior. You are likely to enjoy this for a change, and there is every chance of making a favorable impression on someone special. Be open with loved ones; they will appreciate it.

3. MONDAY. Fair. If you need to make trips as part of your work, try to get as much traveling as possible done today. There should be no delays, and you can free up the rest of the week to work without further interruption. Youngsters may be doing better than expected at school, and teachers' reports should be good. However, there is always the question of further education to be considered; this might be a good time to consult with school officials as to what may be appropriate. A friend who is a little overdue repaying a loan may finally come up with the money; their expression of appreciation will probably be so sincere that you are glad you were able to help.

4. TUESDAY. Disappointing. If you have been nursing a broken heart for quite some time, you cannot really hope any longer that there is a chance of getting back together again. For this reason it is time to put on a brave face and start looking for a better relationship. Although the ideals of a group you have recently joined seem very worthy on paper, the reality may not be quite so attractive. Every organization has to contend with personality clashes, and you should try to keep in mind the inspiration that drew you all together in the first place. The profit from a small business venture may be meager, but you should gain some useful experience along the way.

5. WEDNESDAY. Disconcerting. Misplaced trust in some expert advice may have landed you in a difficult spot. Right now you can appeal to loved ones, who are bound to rally to your side. Self-development always involves an element of effort, and it is easy to become discouraged if you feel you are not making any real progress. However, a moment's reflection should remind you how far you have come and give you faith to carry on. Your attempt to work in private will probably be interrupted by colleagues who want assistance. If you try and spread yourself too thin, however, there is very little help you will be able to give.

6. THURSDAY. Auspicious. More ambitious Libras may be considering starting a business. Naturally this will involve a lot of planning before you can really decide if it is feasible, but with determination and hard work there is a good chance of success. As a Libra you are not usually inarticulate, but there are some subjects that normally are difficult to discuss. However, right now you have a flow of eloquence that enables you to impress a loved one with carefully considered thoughts on a matter that is important to both of you. Sometimes it is both safe and satisfying to be the power behind the throne, so do not worry about your input being overlooked.

7. FRIDAY. Mixed. If loved ones rub you the wrong way, the natural reaction is to lash out. Today, however, there is a real possibility of causing hurt with hastily spoken words, so try to restrain yourself. There could be well-deserved praise coming your way for recent written work. The secret seems to be that you have managed to be direct and clear in making essential points.

Youngsters could display alarming temper tantrums, which test your patience. The best way to cope is probably to let the storm blow itself out while making sure that you are available to contain the worst of it. Do not be too hasty to agree to an unusual financial or business proposition.

8. SATURDAY. Variable. Although you may not often make your voice heard in local affairs, when you feel strongly about an issue it is time to speak out. Neighbors will probably be impressed enough to agree on definite action. Past attempts to get yourself more organized may not have resulted in much. Perhaps it is more comfortable for you to muddle through chores while dreaming of more inspiring subjects. When loved ones try to push you to make a decision before you are ready, it can be tempting to say anything on the spur of the moment. However, a rash choice is not likely to work out in the long run, so explain that it is not appropriate for them to put the pressure on you.

9. SUNDAY. Unsettling. No matter how happy you are with your own appearance, it is still rewarding to receive compliments from loved ones. Today, however, a less than kind remark could be more hurtful than it was meant to be; you should strive to remember that it was probably said in a moment of thoughtlessness. There may not be time for you to get in the practice you need at a creative leisure pursuit because friends demand your presence at a special occasion. You are bound to feel rather frustrated, but if you are able to socialize wholeheartedly you will doubtless end up having a good time. Let your mate or partner choose what the evening entertainment is to be.

10. MONDAY. Fair. Get an early start. Spend some time polishing up a written report; your extra effort is bound to pay dividends. In fact, it may draw the attention of a superior to your undeveloped potential as a skillful communicator. Personal savings are of concern right now. Do not overlook any opportunity to put away some extra money. There will almost certainly be an occasion soon when cash in the bank will make a vital difference. It is especially important for Libras to be surrounded by beautiful possessions. A special gift from a friend can be a delightful addition to your collection; bear in mind that you owe them a return favor at some future date.

11. TUESDAY. Fortunate. There may be some assistance in the form of a glowing reference if you are looking for a new job. That this is being offered by a superior you did not get along with makes it all the more valuable. Financially there might be an opportunity to invest in a new venture, but go into it with great care. As long as you trust the people involved, it should be a fairly safe bet for the long haul. At last you are able to tell friends about a romantic attachment which previously had to be kept secret. Now that circumstances have changed, you may become aware of the strain you have been under all this time. As a Libra you welcome open honesty from yourself as well as other people.

12. WEDNESDAY. Frustrating. If you try to manipulate youngsters to do what you want, you will only regret it. Children have an instinct for correct behavior and will only respond wholeheartedly to honest demands openly made. If a declaration of romantic interest comes out of the blue, you may feel that the ground has been swept from under your feet. However, ask yourself whether you truly want to get involved with this person, or would you be happier keeping them as a fantasy figure. Be prepared for travel to be disrupted. It might be best to leave the car at home if that is possible and use public transportation. Long-term plans may have to be sacrificed to more immediate needs.

13. THURSDAY. Happy. A more social period begins today as friends urge you to go out more often. This will do you a world of good, so put aside some money to cover extra expenses and determine to enjoy yourself to the full. There should be few problems with travel; do not get uptight if you think you are going to be late for an appointment. At the last minute there will probably be a chance to make up for lost time, although that is no excuse for reckless driving. A romantic relationship is on the point of reaching a whole new level, with an unexpected sense of communion between you. In time you may take this for granted, but right now it should be very enlightening and exciting.

14. FRIDAY. Calm. If a useful chance comes along to finish up paperwork that has been piling up, instead of sitting back make the most of the quiet hour or two. Libras who are feeling a financial pinch could try looking at classified advertisements in the local paper to see if there are any bargains. It is often possible to pick up secondhand household and electrical goods at a very reasonable price. Try to get some of your weekend chores out of the way this evening; you should not feel too tired after this fairly relaxed day. It might be nice to go out with a few friends to while away the evening, or invite them to your home if you want to talk privately.

15. SATURDAY. Challenging. It is said that hope springs eternal, and where romance is concerned it seems that your Libra instincts are right on target. An involvement that friends told you would not work out seems now to be giving both of you a great deal of quiet pleasure. There is no reason to suppose the relationship will not develop further. When an acquaintance appeals to you for help, it may be money that they are thinking of. However, in fact you might be of more value to them just by listening to their problems and offering the best advice you can muster. Plans for a more elaborate garden may turn out to be more labor-intensive than you bargain for.

16. SUNDAY. Variable. As a Libra you are known as a peacemaker, and that skill certainly is in demand today. Older children seem ready to break away from parental authority, and it will take a lot of tact and diplomacy to recognize their need for independence while persuading them that those with more experience really do know best. There is no point flinging yourself into redecoration plans without doing some thorough preparation. Shortcuts rarely ever are satisfactory, and shoddy work always shows up sooner or later. A family gathering should increase a sense of solidarity between the generations. After all, everyone was young once and, with luck, will grow old.

17. MONDAY. Sensitive. No matter how delicately you tread, you may just not be able to avoid jangling a loved one's nerves. Nor will it help to point out that they are making a mountain out of a molehill. In fact, the best you can do is keep as quiet as possible until their mood improves. Everyone's ideals take a knock from time to time. Although it is by no means pleasant to find that an idol has feet of clay, you are better off recognizing that all humans are fallible. There is some money to be made from a leisure pursuit if you are prepared to be extroverted enough to sell your special skills. The support of a friend in this endeavor is sure to be of enormous help.

18. TUESDAY. Unsettling. Sometimes you are apt to feel so out of sync with the rest of the world that it can be easy to think you are all alone. Although other people do not understand you from time to time, it is almost certain that they too have moments of feeling equally as isolated. Where romance is concerned, you may have no idea what is going to happen next. Your present relationship is probably not ideal, but that is not sufficient reason to break it off when there is no alternative currently on the horizon. Problems with electrical equipment are likely; be especially careful if there are youngsters around. Do not attempt to do any repairs unless you are fully qualified; get them done professionally.

19. WEDNESDAY. Demanding. The result of a recent financial gamble may leave you wishing you had not taken a chance. However, everyone learns by their mistakes, and all experience can be turned to the good. A romantic involvement between two people of widely differing ages may seem exciting and refreshing at first. However, after a while differences in outlook are bound to surface, and it will be necessary to work seriously to keep the relationship on an even keel. If you are taking one or more courses you are probably hoping for good marks even though you may not have put in as much reading as you should. There is no substitute for thorough study, as you will find out.

20. THURSDAY. Mixed. The apparent loss of some important papers is likely to panic you. Fortunately they are probably just mislaid, so try to keep calm. Also make a mental note to keep your paperwork in better order from now on. Libras caring for youngsters will be hard put to get daily chores done with little ones underfoot. The best way to keep them occupied is by giving them games and puzzles that engage all their mental agility. You may be asked to help out a colleague who is overburdened with urgent communications. Cooperate with a will; you should get real satisfaction from doing an efficient team job.

21. FRIDAY. Excellent. Someone you met through friends may have had quite a profound effect on you, and happily the impression is likely to be mutual. If they show interest in meeting you again, arrange to spend time talking rather than being entertainment; there is probably much for you to discuss. At last you have the opportunity to put into action your ideas for improving the long-term future for you and your children. Getting involved in a local activity can be a first and modest step toward bigger and more ambitious plans. A superior will be pleased to give you the recognition you deserve, even if it means they have to take a back seat.

22. SATURDAY. Fair. Be prepared for the phone to ring with a surprise invitation to quite a classy event. A friend may want your company to bolster their confidence, knowing that you will feel at ease even among people who are strangers to you. Youngsters may need help solving a problem. Even if you think they should figure it out themselves, this is one occasion when you can really be of help. Your teaching style may not be the same as they are used to at school, but with a little patience you should be able to clarify their problem. Do not let romance slip out of a long-term emotional partnership; surprise your mate or partner with a generous gesture of affection.

23. SUNDAY. Cautious. Romantic affairs augur well providing you are prepared to take the rough along with the smooth. Getting involved with an individualistic person may never be boring, but you will learn that neither does it rarely feel secure. Proceed with arrangements for a family celebration. This is the right time to enlist help from your loved ones. After all, the whole point of such an occasion is to get pleasure from sharing. There may be angry words spoken if you fail to take seriously your mate or partner's ambitions for the future. They have just as much right to respect as you, and just think how you would feel if they failed to support your aims.

24. MONDAY. Deceptive. While you might have been vaguely aware that not all of your colleagues were pulling together on an important project, it is unlikely you realized the full impact of what was going on. If someone appeals to you for help it might be better to turn them down, since they have gotten into trouble entirely by their own fault. It is said that love is blind, and nothing could be truer of your condition at the moment. Friends may be trying to warn you that the person to whom you are attracted has a less than stellar reputation, but you may be determined to find out the hard way. Do not trust funds or anything of value to anyone you do not know well.

25. TUESDAY. Difficult. As the truth about a friend's mate or partner comes out into the open, they are likely to turn to you for comfort. The news may actually catch you by surprise or even shock you, but your first duty is to conceal your feelings and provide all the support possible. There is no pleasure to be gained from attending a social event simply to impress other people, to see and be seen. Unless you are truly interested, it will be fairly obvious that your mind is elsewhere. Do not be backward in airing views for improved work efficiency to a superior. As long as you have thought through your proposed plans, they will probably be taken very seriously. Some overtime could bring in useful extra money.

26. WEDNESDAY. Sensitive. If you let a mood of pessimism take over, you will be in no position to make the most of this day. There are some reasons for looking on the bleak side, but just as many for taking a more optimistic view. Take care of the pennies and the dollars will take care of themselves. See if you can make some small savings; they will soon add up to a substantial sum. If you are preparing for job interviews you may not realize your best points. It might be a good idea to consult with a colleague and see what they think are your particular strengths. Then you will have a better idea of what to play up on your resume and in person.

27. THURSDAY. Tricky. Even the most reliable friends can turn their back on you from time to time. At the moment you may not quite know who to turn to for support, as everyone appears to be preoccupied with their own problems. Romantically speaking, this is a time when you should let your head rule your heart. Difficult though this may be when a particularly attractive person comes along, the situation is probably not what you imagine it to be, and there is every possibility of being hurt. Vacation plans could be ruined by illness, but do not despair. It is not too late to make other arrangements, and you could even wind up with a better holiday.

28. FRIDAY. Successful. The prospect of fulfilling a dream is likely to make you feel as if nothing can get in your way. Now you need to get loved ones on your side, so that if you run out of steam they will be there to encourage you to continue. The results of an examination or test are likely to to vindicate your confidence that you would do well. This could indicate that you can pursue your studies further, perhaps even to the professional level. You may feel rather frustrated in your present job, but it would not be wise to make a move for that reason alone. Look around and see how you can better your prospects by taking a step up the career ladder.

29. SATURDAY. Enjoyable. An invitation to go out may not get you very excited, but you will probably be surprised at the mixture of people you meet. There is bound to be at least one with whom you strike up an instant friendship, which may well last for years. A marked disinclination to settle down to routine tasks can make it difficult to get anything done that lacks an element of pleasure. In fact, it will not hurt to forget the housework and gardening and treat yourself to a day off. Youngsters may ask some awkward questions. If they are at an age to be told the facts of life, this may be the moment to do so; just remember to keep your explanations as simple as possible.

30. SUNDAY. Variable. Your main aim should be to keep from losing your temper no matter how much you are provoked. Loved ones seem determined to try the limits of your patience, and it will be a challenge not to rise to the bait. Sporting activities can be more enjoyable than usual because you are in the mood to test your skills against the opposition. Just be sure not to get carried away, especially if you do not exercise regularly. The prospect on the romantic front is not bright; in fact, it might be hard to see the way ahead. A relationship based on physical fascination can go only so far, but once you begin to see the real person things should look very different.

31. MONDAY. Satisfactory. Begin the workweek resolving to get more involved in social occasions that are linked with a favorite leisure pursuit. The old saying that you can choose your friends but not your lovers is true, and you have plenty of scope for getting together with like-minded people. Focusing your mind on achieving a long-term ambition is a big step toward doing so. Where there is a will, there is a way; it is really up to you. The ending of a relationship may come as a shock, but you will also be surprised how quickly you get over it. It may be that you were just using the other person to fill a gap in your life, and now you have the courage to stand on your own two feet for a while.

AUGUST

1. TUESDAY. Slow. You are apt to have some difficulty concentrating on work matters since social events are on your mind. As long as you do not drift off totally into a dream world, there should be no major problems since you do not have to cope with anything urgent. A dream can come true, with a little help from your friends. What is impossible for one person to achieve can easily be managed by several working in unison. Libras attending a conference should be able to make useful contacts. Jot down names and contact numbers; it would be a shame to lose the chance to expand your circle of friends and business acquaintances.

2. WEDNESDAY. Manageable. Fortune favors the bold; if you act with determination, a romantic attachment should work out just as you want. Do not wait for the other person to guess your feelings. Let them know just how important they are to you, and then it is up to them to respond. All kinds of communication are highlighted. If you have been putting off a difficult phone call, you need to get it over with. Using your good Libra tact should allow you to present even unpalatable truths gently. Make good use of an hour or so of solitude to finish up odds and ends of business that have been hanging fire, then resolve to keep up-to-date from now on.

3. THURSDAY. Fortunate. If you recently retired you are probably wondering now how you ever found time to work. This is a period when you can experiment with all kinds of activities which you have dreamed about for years. When an insurance policy matures, there may be the temptation to blow it all on a special vacation or other expensive treat. It might be a better idea, however, to allow yourself to splurge with just part of the money, and put the rest away for a rainy day since that was the original aim of saving in the first place. The day should come to an energetic close as you catch up with back work. Round off the day with an enjoyable social evening.

4. FRIDAY. Harmonious. It can be fairly easy to drift through part of the day without making too much effort; you will probably find out the truth of the saying that when you smile, the world smiles with you. However, do not relax so much that you miss an opportunity to expand your mental horizons by paying attention to those who know more than you do about a subject of mutual interest. Other people will cooperate on an important project if they feel you are an appropriate leader, so do your best to be firm and authoritative. Romantically this may be a pleasant day, although you would be unwise to try to push for a long-term decision. Just enjoy your beloved's company.

5. SATURDAY. Fair. The urge to break away from convention comes over you from time to time, and suppressing the feeling will not make it go away. Allow yourself to go with the flow for once, proving that you can be a true individual. Make sure you have a camera handy on social occasions; there is bound to be much that you want on record. Do not aim to take formal, posed pictures; snapshots that catch the spontaneity of loved ones will be far more enjoyable. Youngsters may be less than inclined to toe the line, and will probably not respond to reason. The best you can do is let them have a certain amount of freedom and then learn the lessons that will result.

6. SUNDAY. Frustrating. If you are going to be entertaining at home, it may seem harder work than usual to get everything as you want it to be. However, you will enjoy the occasion more if you just lighten up a bit and take things a little more casually. For Libras involved in a romance, this is not likely to be the easiest of times. That special person seems determined not to give you the assurance you want that their affections are yours alone; trying to force the issue will probably only make matters worse. You might be reluctant to spend money on a day out organized by friends if you are not sure it will be much fun. It will not do any harm to make your excuses and skip the get-together.

7. MONDAY. Variable. There is every chance of hearing about an interesting career opening if you keep your ear to the ground. The position is likely to offer more responsibility, but the financial reward should make it attractive. Libras who have been involved in research on behalf of someone else may be able to wrap up efforts with a sense of satisfaction. You can be assured that your work has been of use and that you have also learned useful points for future projects. It seems futile to rely on a lover for a sense of security when they seem very clear that they do not want to be tied down. It is up to you to decide if you are fond enough of them to continue the relationship on their terms.

8. TUESDAY. Tricky. If you are feeling less full of bounce than usual, keep in mind that you cannot expect to keep up a busy social life and work long and hard as well. Something has to give if your health is not to suffer. A new acquaintance may be turning on the charm; there is a strong likelihood that you will find it irresistible. At the same time, there should be warning bells going off in your head, alerting you to the fact that they do not have only your happiness at heart. Involvement in a group committed to certain ideals can be immensely satisfying, but inevitably there will be periods of doubt when you need faith to continue. Work for the change you envision.

9. WEDNESDAY. Misleading. It is almost certain that loved ones do not intend to give you the wrong impression, but that is just what seems to be happening. Before you get carried away with delight, stop and listen to your intuition to see if anything seems to be amiss. Keep a close eye on youngsters; they may slip out of view in no time. Keep them away from water if possible. Ideas for new creative ventures may seem immensely inspiring at first, but there are probably flaws you cannot yet see. Be prepared to spend considerable time and money working out the practical details to achieve a dream; put your whole heart into it. Allow extra time for every new project.

10. THURSDAY. Unsettling. Business meetings and seminars are not likely to go smoothly because everyone seems to have an ax to grind. It appears likely that other people will appeal to you as a Libra to arbitrate, but you will have to tread carefully in order to avoid the firing line yourself. Friends may try to bully you into complying with their wishes, and you may be tempted to do so in the interests of peace. However, there is little point in giving in if you are really reluctant. Take action now to support an altruistic aim; you will achieve deep satisfaction from knowing you have played your part. Exam results might be disappointing, but you must admit you could have worked harder.

11. FRIDAY. Productive. You cannot afford to miss any chance for improving your job prospects. Right now there is an excellent opportunity just waiting to be grasped. Improve your skills and many new horizons can open up. Romance may blossom through casual conversation at an evening class. What begins as a casual relationship based on mutual interests might soon deepen into a profound liaison as physical attraction is added to mental rapport. Youngsters may be getting bored with summer vacation from school. It is vital that you find ways for them to develop their special talents to the fullest. Even for little ones it is not too soon to start thinking about their future.

12. SATURDAY. Good. Current conditions offer a fine chance to pick up bargains in unexpected places. Libras who are attracted by period furnishings could find a really special piece. However, you will probably have to bargain hard to get it at a decent price. Conversations with friends may veer toward subjects that are normally taboo. It is a mark of how close you have become that you can trust each other with your deepest fears and secrets. Airing them can be immensely healing. You are unlikely to find idle socializing satisfying today; what you need is food for your soul and stimulation toward self-development. Plan on visiting a special place that will awaken your mind.

13. SUNDAY. Variable. You really need to get in better shape and are probably eager to do so. Team sports can be a good way of beginning to tone yourself up; they tend to be less demanding than one-on-one games. You will not do yourself any good by nursing a broken heart and feeling that a recent lover has let you down. Persistently playing the victim can become such a habit that it will be difficult to look to the future, so try to accept your share of the blame and put the affair behind you. Libra students who have studies to pursue should be able to get some valuable work done. For once family members will respect your need for privacy and give you some peace and quiet.

14. MONDAY. Uncertain. You probably are not prepared to walk into a minefield this morning, but that is likely to happen. There are passions and jealousies seething beneath the surface of what should be an ordinary working day. You would be wise to stay out of it and keep your head down. The possibilities for misunderstanding a lover are all too obvious when you only hear what you want them to say. In fact, they are probably frustrated because no matter how clearly they tell you their feelings, you keep on refusing to acknowledge the truth. Find time to shop locally; you are likely to pick up an item you have been hunting for a long time, and at a bargain price.

15. TUESDAY. Frustrating. A longed-for getaway may not have lived up to the promise of the travel brochure. Even though you doubtless made the best of it, a let-down feeling is inevitable; rather than shrugging it off, make a written complaint. It may be quite a struggle to get colleagues' assistance on an important project. There is apt to be some bad feeling concerning the way authority has been shared. This will have to be addressed before everyone is willing to do their best. If a romantic affair develops unexpectedly, you may be left wondering whether what began as a light flirtation can really be satisfying on a deeper emotional level. Advice about your love life may not be useful.

16. WEDNESDAY. Changeable. You can get new ideas adopted as long as you are not too aggressive in putting them forward. There is a fine line between enthusiasm and being domineering, so try to err on the side of caution. Travel should be fairly easy; even if there are delays you should be able to make it to your appointments on time. The results of recent indulgence in exotic cuisine may begin to show on your waistline and will do nothing positive for your sense of fitness. Make a resolution now to stick to a less rich diet until you are once again trim and able to run upstairs without getting out of breath. Beware of imposing your ideology on friends or co-workers.

17. THURSDAY. Calm. This should be a very useful day for clearing up work that needs finishing off. For once there is enough time to concentrate on details that might usually be overlooked or rushed. It would be a good idea to give some thought to your health and your family's. Even if you do not often have to visit a doctor, it is sometimes useful to consult an alternative practitioner such as a homeopath just to ensure that you are not a little below par. Because pets can give elderly relatives a lot of satisfaction as long as they are able to care for them, you might want to ask if a family member would enjoy the companionship of a cat or dog. Let your mind float free tonight.

18. FRIDAY. Happy. A legal case should be going quite well, although the outcome is not absolutely certain. However, as long as you feel you have a case worth fighting, there should be nothing to fear. A long weekend break with your mate or partner would give you an opportunity to catch up on discussions that often get shoved aside in favor of daily concerns. Treat yourselves to some real peace and quiet in the country. If you are looking for romance try to get back in contact with friends you drifted out of touch with during the year. They might well have new acquaintances to whom you could be introduced, with happy results for a new romantic relationship.

19. SATURDAY. Favorable. Go with your mate or partner when buying gifts for others; their taste should be a sure guide. This is not the time to talk about superficial aspects of your relationship. There are deeper issues that both of you may have been shying away from, but if you have the courage for an open discussion much can be cleared up for once and for all. Libras contemplating marriage and children need to be quite sure that you both have a similar mental picture of the future. It is not possible to expect all your plans to work out effortlessly, but at the very least you need to start life together with similar expectations. Go out as a twosome tonight rather than with friends.

20. SUNDAY. Fair. A social occasion can bring you into contact with like-minded people, sparking some interesting exchanges of views. There are long-term friendships to be enjoyed, so make sure you have the means of staying in touch. Helping your mate or partner make strides toward achieving a personal dream will bring you that much closer together. Their pleasure is sure to light up your own life. Try to include youngsters in whatever activities you plan for the day; they will love being treated as honorary adults. If you are involved in a romance, beware of letting the other person take advantage of your compassionate Libra nature.

21. MONDAY. Disquieting. You are apt to begin the workweek in a prickly mood, all too ready to jump down the throat of the first person who annoys you. Give in to this tendency and you can expect a difficult day. Instead, take a deep breath and practice a little tolerance. Impulse spending tends to be a Libra weakness, but right now you cannot really afford to let down your guard. There are serious needs that must be addressed, rather than splurging on pure pleasure. As one door shuts, another one is bound to open. Bear this in mind as a romantic attachment comes to a somewhat abrupt end. You deserve a better relationship, and next time may be the answer.

22. TUESDAY. Disconcerting. There is no use expecting other people to guess that you have a problem. Mope around and you will probably find them avoiding you rather than asking what is wrong. Difficult though it may be, it is vital to confront the person who you feel is responsible for making your life unpleasant. Libras who are taking correspondence courses are likely to find it an isolating method of study. However, the other side of the coin is that this encourages you to be very disciplined. If you can make yourself sit down regularly to work without the stimulation of a class, you need have no fear that the exams will be beyond you. Do not fall for charm and compliments.

23. WEDNESDAY. Difficult. There may be a real difference of opinion between you and a superior at work. You probably will not be able to concentrate on what you should be doing until this is sorted out. Self-doubt can be very undermining, especially when you are trying to expand the boundaries of your abilities. This might be a good time to practice some meditation techniques to put you in touch with the part of yourself that knows you can achieve whatever you put your mind to. Your parents' philosophy of life is probably very different from yours; there are times when this causes arguments that could easily be avoided if you refuse to argue.

24. THURSDAY. Variable. At last you are able to look to the future with confidence when it comes to romance. You and that special person in your life have already been through enough to test your faith in each other, and you have discovered enough to be sure that you have the foundations of a solid and lasting relationship. Libras who have been trying to get a book published may feel that the trends are negative. No matter how excellent your work, it needs to have a certain element that fits in with the current fashions in publishing. You could be in for a shock when someone you met on vacation last year gets in touch with you. Decide whether you want this relationship to be more than just a memory.

25. FRIDAY. Favorable. There should be no need to push yourself forward at work; the recognition that is due to you will not be denied. If a colleague asks you to keep a confidence, you must act honorably; the time will come when you can reveal what you know, but not yet. The decision to break long-outworn habits can be deeply refreshing. If you take a long, hard look at yourself you will doubtless find that you still indulge in behaviors that are no longer appropriate or even enjoyable. You have the willpower to change. Libras who are searching for a new job could receive an offer that comes as something of a surprise. Mull it over before making a final decision.

26. SATURDAY. Pleasant. Try to find time to spend quietly alone. There is much going on in your mind at the moment that can best be sorted out in solitary meditation. It might help to write down your thoughts; otherwise you may have some difficulty getting them in order. Look for romance where you would least expect it. A new relationship has much to teach you, although it may not be your idea of a perfect liaison. Family members who have some problems getting out and about are sure to appreciate a visit, especially if you can take them out for the day. Help given to others is never wasted, and you will probably enjoy your relatives' company.

27. SUNDAY. Mixed. The best-laid plans often go awry, and it is all too possible that this will happen to you today. Although you are eager to put into action ambitious schemes for more exciting activities than usual, they do not appear destined to come off. If you are trying to work around the home, youngsters may distract you to such an extent that it is very difficult to get anything done. If there are small jobs they can do to help, that might be the best way of keeping them occupied. Do not let an argument with a neighbor drag on; unless you make overtures of peace, a promising friendship could be ruined. Spend a quiet evening at home rather than going out with friends.

28. MONDAY. Unsettling. You may think you have done well not to start an argument at home this morning, but nothing has been gained if you let off steam at some innocent colleague instead. A moment's reflection will make you see your own responsibility, and that should be a sobering thought. Romance is unlikely to settle down into a long-term relationship, and there is little you can do to force the issue. Your romantic partner needs a lot of freedom; unless you are able to freely grant it to them they will simply find it by leaving you. Creative ideas that seem brilliant to you may not go over too well with superiors. If you can tone down your plans you will be more successful.

29. TUESDAY. Stressful. This can be an upsetting day for playing sports of any kind. You may have lost a clear idea of your own physical limits. As a result, you run the risk of a nasty sprain if you take things too far. All financial matters need to be approached with extreme caution. Commit funds without thoroughly investigating the credentials of your favored scheme and there is the chance of heavy loss. Libras who are studying in the hope of improving future career prospects need to summon up reserves of patience. All worthwhile knowledge takes time to absorb. A long-term health problem could benefit from professional treatment; do not rely for too long on home remedies.

30. WEDNESDAY. Quiet. Sometimes your peaceable Libra nature longs to retreat from the hustle and bustle of the world. Periods of solitude can be immensely refreshing. There are many places offering facilities for a peaceful weekend retreat away from mundane reality. Libras who work from home may be feeling a little restless. It can be restricting to your imagination to spend too much time indoors. Try to plan your days so that you take in plenty of impressions to stimulate your mental processes. Although it is never easy to let go of a romantic attachment, right now you probably cannot deny that a current relationship just is not working anymore.

31. THURSDAY. Satisfactory. Take a critical look at your wardrobe, and have the courage to start weeding out some of the older items. Charity shops always welcome secondhand clothes. It is time for you to cultivate a more business-like image. There may be a chance to apply knowledge you have picked up through reading to make a bit of extra money. It is not necessary to be an expert on any subject as long as you can apply common sense and act responsibly. All you have to do to attract romance is be your usual charming self. The only question is whether the right person will be around to respond. You need to use some discrimination in a crowd.

SEPTEMBER

1. FRIDAY. Stimulating. As a Libra you are sometimes prone to indecisiveness, but today there is little doubt that you will be able to come to swift and accurate decisions. Your intuitive powers are stronger than usual, giving your judgments the weight of authority. Creatively this can be an exciting time. It is vital that you have some means of self-expression since you have much to offer as an individual. Romance can bring an edge of excitement to your life as an independent yet magnetic person comes to occupy center stage. Just make sure you do not bore your friends by telling them too often how wonderful this person is. Keep your feet on the ground even if your heart is soaring.

2. SATURDAY. Challenging. There is no point going out shopping if you are trying to save money; temptations are likely to come thick and fast. Even if you intend to restrict yourself to buying essentials, it can be all too easy to let luxury items catch your eye. A romantic affair may have lost direction, perhaps because lack of a goal has led to stagnation. You can only avoid commitment for so long before the other person begins to lose interest; this point may now have been reached. A friend from overseas may get back in touch, and be very full of their exotic lifestyle. Before you become too envious, consider whether they are trying to impress you with some exaggerations.

3. SUNDAY. Buoyant. This could be the day you have been waiting for, as a romantic partner says the words you have been longing to hear. Impress this moment on your memory so that you can treasure it for years to come. Artistic Libras who have been searching for a distinctive style are on the way to achieving this aim. At last you are marrying your creative skills and vision to produce a truly individual type of art. Be careful if you are working on or with electrical equipment at home; repairs need careful and expert handling. Friends may seem more eager than usual to make you see their point of view, but do not allow yourself to be bullied into agreeing with them against your better judgment.

4. MONDAY. Difficult. High hopes for a business trip may have to be put on hold because the situation is becoming less favorable than it was. You are apt to be sorry to miss the moment, and it will be hard to recapture your original enthusiasm. There is money to be made from travel memoirs if you have amusing or amazing tales to tell. You will probably find several magazines willing to accept short articles, which may encourage you to write at greater length. Do not become disheartened if a retraining course does not turn out to be as useful as expected. Even if it does not qualify you for a better job at the moment, keep in mind that you have still gained valuable experience.

5. TUESDAY. Disquieting. It is likely that all is not as it should be between you and a loved one. Feelings are simmering away, with both of you afraid to take the lid off for fear of an explosion. Be careful on the roads; tempers are apt to be shorter than usual, so keep alert for hasty and careless driving. Do nothing that might encourage road rage. A friend's support can mean a great deal when you are going through difficult times in a romantic affair. Even a shoulder to cry on can be a great comfort until the situation improves. If youngsters seem rather withdrawn, try to find out what is bothering them. It is not a good sign for them to be too quiet.

6. WEDNESDAY. Profitable. If you are involved in advertising of any kind, this should be a creative and exciting time. New ideas make it possible to break away from usual selling tactics, and you will benefit by pursuing them as far as they can be developed. A letter from an old lover could stir up powerful memories. However, you should also be aware of how much you have both changed. You might also reflect on how difficult life would have been if you had stayed together. Encourage youngsters' imagination as much as you can. They can lose their vividness all too quickly in the process of growing up, unless you foster and value their fresh outlook. Be sparing with your words at work.

7. THURSDAY. Mixed. You can only go so far in trying to please a loved one before the situation begins to tip off balance. If you are not careful they are apt to slip into the habit of ordering you around, but still without really being happy. Property negotiations may be a struggle because neither side appears content with the offer price. If the deal is to be finalized, some compromise must be reached. A family gathering might start off with a slightly strained atmosphere, but before long everyone will loosen up and old feuds can be forgotten. You are bound to be fascinated to see the different generations getting along well together. Take photos to save today's memories.

8. FRIDAY. Lucky. At last your hard work seems to be paying off and you have come through with flying colors. Do yourself justice and celebrate to the full. After all, you have put in a lot of effort and deserve a fitting reward. An older colleague who appears to be taking an almost parental interest in you may have very sound advice to offer. Push away any suspicion that you are being patronized, and store up their words of wisdom for future reference. As one project is wrapped up, there is the chance of a breathing space before another begins. This can be a useful opportunity to take stock and decide whether you can make better use of your outstanding talents.

9. SATURDAY. Deceptive. Sometimes it may seem that you cannot even trust yourself because you are so willing to fall for the wiles of other people. Although your friends can see that you are being led up the garden path, you may refuse to listen to them. Social events are likely to be rather unorganized, even chaotic. All the same, there is no reason not to enjoy yourself; there should be unusual people from different walks of life for you to meet.

This is an excellent time to get some thorough exercise. Even a gentle swim can do a surprising amount of good, as well as being deeply relaxing. A romantic movie can help you shake off the day's tension and get a good night's sleep.

10. SUNDAY. Favorable. If you feel the need to charm a prospective lover, you should have no difficulty doing so. Adopting a more romantic persona can be very effective, especially if you act a little mysterious and elusive. Creatively, this should be a fruitful day, even if you only jot down ideas for future projects; there will be time later in the year to bring them to reality. If you listen closely to what youngsters have to say, their intuition can teach you a lot. Trips can be successful as long as you are not afraid to look beneath the surface of reality to find out where the truth lies. Do not believe everything you read or even what you are told by a friend.

11. MONDAY. Unsettling. As a Libra you normally have no problems getting along with people, but today they may seem determined to try your patience. It is tempting to react by being autocratic, but you should be aiming for greater cooperation rather than control. Do not be surprised if youngsters get into trouble during the course of the day; their natural curiosity is likely to lead them into all sorts of odd corners. A business meeting can be immensely stimulating as long as you keep an open mind. However, if you challenge a colleague on the validity of their ideas, it is apt to be a different story. Work off some of your excess energy in physical exercise if possible this evening.

12. TUESDAY. Frustrating. If you are hoping to set off on a journey you may have to hang around a long time before getting under way. Flights delays are all too likely. If youngsters are traveling with you, they will need plenty to occupy themselves. A course of study may not seem to be as easy as you expected. If the workload is fairly demanding, you may even be wondering whether to give up. However, persevere to the end and the reward will be more than adequate for the hard work you have put in. There is little point imposing a strict health regime on yourself if it just means you spend more time longing for an easy life. Lighten up a bit and try to enjoy each and every part of the day.

13. WEDNESDAY. Demanding. You have reached something of a crunch point when it comes to deciding how much of your time to devote to other people. Everyone needs some private moments for themselves. You cannot go on sacrificing your own needs for the sake of loved ones. Youngsters' health may be causing you a little concern. It is important to make sure they are eating properly and getting enough sleep; growing is a demanding business. A visit from a relative who requires quite a lot of care and attention will place heavy demands on you. Do not shoulder the full burden yourself; make sure your mate or partner or other family members take an equal share of the responsibility.

14. THURSDAY. Satisfactory. Compliments on your appearance should be coming your way, and a show of modesty might make you even more attractive. Do not brush off what other people say; allow yourself to feel good and you will glow even more. Even if you do not usually socialize with your workmates, this could be a good time to give it a try. A quiet lunch together or drink after work can help you get to know each other better. An inquiring turn of mind may lead you into unusual areas of study. Spend some time browsing in a local bookshop to see what subjects particularly strike your fancy. Allow romance to take its natural course; the pace will soon begin to speed up.

15. FRIDAY. Variable. Local gossip can have some insights as long as you treat it with caution. Although there are bound to be distortions from the truth, you might pick up information about developments that could affect you and your loved ones. You need have no fear of failing to express yourself well when it comes to written work. An ability to cut through unnecessary detail and get right to the point will make your work both pointed and powerful. There is apt to be trouble brewing with your mate or partner, as neither of you is willing to give in to the other's point of view. Do not allow this difference of opinion to get to the stage where thoughtless words are blurted out.

16. SATURDAY. Pleasant. Even less active Libras may be cajoled into taking more exercise in the company of friends. It will be hard to resist their enthusiasm for a new sporting activity, so go along with them and enjoy yourself. Even a long-term romantic partnership can take on a new lease on life when one of you develops a fresh interest in an ideological issue. Instead of feeling that the other person is growing apart, you can take this chance to follow them toward their goals. There is great pleasure in beginning to make a dream come true. What once appeared impossible is now within your grasp, so fire on all cylinders and go for it.

17. SUNDAY. Uncertain. So much in your emotional life seems unclear at the moment that it may be difficult to know where to start sorting it out. Your heart is apt to be pulling you in several directions. Although making a decision is painful, it has to be done for the sake of your loved ones. Financially you may be a little shaky, your accounts in a muddle. This is a good moment to buckle down and try to make sense of the situation before it gets out of control. Social events are best kept simple and low-key; no one seems to be in a very extroverted mood. A friend may need some emotional support in going through a crisis situation; be sure you are there to help.

18. MONDAY. Stressful. No matter how hard you work, there always seems to be someone doing their best to undermine your efforts. You can choose to go on regardless, or face the fact that there is little you can achieve right now and turn your attention to less demanding work. Travel is apt to be somewhat grueling, with unexplained detours and delays. There is no point working yourself into a lather; just take a philosophical view and practice detachment. A romantic affair could be so exciting that you fail to realize that all is not quite as it seems. The other person may have very different ideas from yours about what constitutes an enduring relationship.

19. TUESDAY. Fair. The key to success lies in self-expression. If you are stuck in a situation that is frustrating, now is your chance to break free through your own efforts. Youngsters can provide a great deal of unconscious humor, but it would be humiliating for them to be laughed at. Enjoy the joke by all means, but be sensitive to their feelings. A lawsuit that seems to have been dragging on for a long time shows no sign of coming to an end just yet. However, patience will bring its own rewards. This is a better moment for discussing travel plans than for actually making arrangements; do not hurry matters. Be honest and do not try to deceive yourself.

20. WEDNESDAY. Promising. All of a sudden a romantic difficulty is likely to disappear as if it had never existed, leaving the way open for the relationship to develop in a whole new direction. There is no need to analyze what has happened; the heart has reasons beyond the comprehension of the intellect. At last an opening in the jobs market offers the chance of using your talents more creatively. Do not put off applying for an opening; there is bound to be considerable competition. A deeper understanding of yourself can spring from developing a habit of mulling over the day's events each evening. You will soon begin to recognize patterns of behavior and unconscious reactions to events.

21. THURSDAY. Variable. If it seems that a superior is blocking your advancement, pluck up your courage and ask what is going on. It could be that they do not intend to get in your way but, at the same time, are unwilling to lose your assistance. Although memories of past holidays are pleasant to dream about, do not let them make you feel that your life is lacking in romance now. Life is what you make it: dull or exciting, enjoyable or problematic. Make a decision now to really clear out your closets, attic and basement. The extra space will be useful, and there is no knowing what you might come across among the accumulations.

22. FRIDAY. Disconcerting. Sometimes you feel the need to balk against authority just for the sake of asserting yourself. However, you can get into all kinds of trouble by doing so. It would be prudent to stop and consider whether you really feel strongly enough to make a major fuss. You may have to learn the hard way that it is not always possible to rely on people's promises. Offers to help you through a busy time at work may just not materialize into practical action. It appears that if you want a job done, you must do it yourself. At this time of year you should be feeling ready for a fresh start; instead of stagnating, make some changes.

23. SATURDAY. Manageable. You will probably feel in the mood to get out of the house. Light socializing is not going to fulfill all of your emotional and mental needs. You require some artistic inspiration, so arrange to visit a gallery or attend a concert of favorite music; this is bound to refresh you. Parents are apt to be more understanding than usual, willing to support you in a creative project. They will undoubtedly feel very proud if you are able to achieve your goals. If you are hoping to move you could find a beautiful place, but it is apt to be beyond your means. Still, it should give you good ideas for looking elsewhere.

24. SUNDAY. Stimulating. Social events promise lively communication and no lack of mental stimulation. Libras on the lookout for a new relationship can make an impression by initiating sparkling conversation on a favorite subject. Trips will go better if you form a group; everyone can contribute to making the day go well. Even a family gathering can be enhanced by the presence of a couple of friends. You and your romantic partner may not seem able to agree about certain fundamental issues. If the relationship means a lot to you, make a pact not to discuss these matters, but be aware that disagreements are not going to go away just because they are unvoiced.

25. MONDAY. Changeable. The week gets off to a good start with you full of ideas and willing to work hard to get them put into practice. For once you have the courage to stand up and be counted, which should give you greater confidence for the future. Try to organize an evening's entertainment for yourself and your friends. It is unlikely you will feel like staying quietly at home.

Unfortunately, suspicion on your part may be endangering a close relationship. If you get into the habit of sneaking around trying to find out about your mate or partner behind their back, they will very soon realize you do not trust them; at that point, you can consider the relationship over.

26. TUESDAY. Mixed. You have probably made quite an impression on someone who is now taking a romantic interest in you. However, their image of you may not really match up to reality very well, giving you the choice of playing along or trying to get the person to see your real self. Praise for some creative work might encourage you to realize that your talents are salable. There is nothing to be lost by having a go at making a little extra cash from a leisure pursuit. Short journeys are likely to be plagued by problems that you could not have predicted. Unless your car is in good shape, leave it at home and use public transportation.

27. WEDNESDAY. Sensitive. As a Libra you like to be surrounded by beautiful possessions, and this is part of your charm. There comes a point, however, when your mate or partner may begin to resent your spending money on ornamental items when you need to buy basic practicalities. Where romance is concerned, some extra tact is necessary. Say the wrong thing and you risk hurting a lover's pride to such an extent that they will take a long time to forget it. Do not hesitate to flex your muscles at work by taking on more responsibility. Happily, you have a light touch when it comes to exerting authority over others; make sure you do not lose this very valuable talent.

28. THURSDAY. Favorable. It will pay to go through the mail carefully, no matter how busy you might be. There is almost certain to be something of interest. If you are alert, you will realize that here is an opportunity to make big changes in your life. Sometimes when you are faced with an important decision it can be wise to pay attention to your dreams. Even if you do not usually remember them clearly, making an effort to write down the bits that stick in your memory will bring them into focus; after a week or so the oddest images may begin to make sense. Romantically, do not hesitate to strike while the iron is hot, or you are apt to lose your chance.

29. FRIDAY. Variable. Put on your thinking cap and try to figure out some plans to improve your personal finances. It may not be so easy to increase your income, but that does not mean you have to keep spending everything you earn. Even small savings come in useful from time to time. Your self-confidence is bound to be improved by becoming knowledgeable about a practical subject. If you are able to be self-sufficient in an area where most people rely on professionals, it will be a great boost to your self-esteem. Recent hard work appears to have affected your nerves, with the result that a period of relaxation is now essential; spoil yourself this evening.

30. SATURDAY. Good. Treat a loved one to a surprise gift and see how delighted they are. Be as generous as you can; after all, it is impossible to really repay all that they have done for you in the course of your relationship. A long, hard look in the mirror will show you exactly where you need to work a little on your appearance. Generally you are in good shape, but there is always room for improvement. Do not expect to be able to spend the whole day pleasing yourself; family demands are likely to intrude after a while. However, as long as you keep some time free, there should be pleasure in doing a good turn for someone who is sure to be appreciative.

OCTOBER

1. SUNDAY. Confusing. There is little point in trying to convince your mate or partner that you are in control of your finances when the opposite is probably true. It would be a far more positive move to own up to being in a muddle and ask for help with straightening out your checkbook and bills. Romance is suffering from your reluctance to be honest about your feelings. That special person in your life needs to know where they stand, so do not try to keep them at arm's length any longer. Make the most of a quiet hour to finish off writing a letter you began and then abandoned. You do not have to worry about producing a literary masterpiece; just write as you would speak.

2. MONDAY. Satisfactory. Be prepared to jump in at the deep end if you are given responsibility for a new work project. At first the workload might appear impossible, but if you settle down and figure out a plan of action, you will soon see that you can manage it with a little help from colleagues. Some measure of shyness in regard to romantic matters can be very attractive, but play too hard to get and the other person is apt to lose interest. For this reason, make your intentions plain. Do not force your loved one to do all the running. Communications within the family are not at their best at the moment, but keep in mind that nothing is to be gained by refusing to discuss a problem with your loved ones.

3. TUESDAY. Sensitive. There is a real danger of rubbing someone the wrong way to such an extent that they determine to get back at you. As a Libra you hate to make enemies, but that will happen if you continue on the current collision course. A friend who can pull some strings on your behalf could get you an introduction to a more interesting social circle. Even though you might feel out of your depth at first, in no time you will be quite at home among these new acquaintances. Make a lightning raid on the stores at some point during the day; there is every chance of picking up an unusual and beautiful gift for a loved one, or even for yourself.

4. WEDNESDAY. Difficult. Working behind the scenes may suit you sometimes, but everyone needs acknowledgment and praise, which you may feel is lacking. It is not easy to see others being praised when you have worked just as hard and efficiently. Give in to self-doubt and it will be that much more difficult to expand your abilities and free your mind. What you need right now is for loved ones to back you up in all your creative efforts; make sure they know you want their support. If travel for pure pleasure is on your mind, it will not hurt to indulge yourself for once. Even poring over travel brochures and losing yourself in dreams can be beneficial.

5. THURSDAY. Profitable. Libras who are selling the family home can ask and get a good price for it. As long as you find the right buyer, there should be no problem with negotiations. This is a good time for looking around antique and junk shops in the hopes of finding a bargain. Be alert for less obvious items. For example, you may find a picture that is of little interest but beautifully framed. Clear out your desk drawers; most of the old papers can probably be thrown away. Try to keep things more tidy from now on, or at least in enough order that you can find what you are looking for even if other people cannot. Read a good book tonight rather than going out.

6. FRIDAY. Reassuring. Once you have sorted out youngsters' schooling, you should feel a great deal more confident about their future. Finding the right school is not always easy, but you will know which is best as soon as you come across it. Often it is comforting to consult an expert on a problem, even if you think you know the answer. Having your opinion confirmed can give you confidence that you are taking the right step. A relationship that begins from a shared sense of idealism can be heady stuff. At first you will probably feel as if it were meant to be. After a while, however, realism will bring you back to earth, and that is no bad thing.

7. SATURDAY. Productive. It could be quite a struggle to pull yourself out of the dream world this morning because your nighttime musings were so vivid. Try not to forget what you were dreaming; it is important. Where romance is concerned, be happy to take things day by day. Neither you nor your romantic partner appears to know how you want the relationship to develop, so there is no hurry to press for commitment. This can be a productive day for creative Libras since your inspiration is on the rise. Although your sense of perfectionism makes you eternally dissatisfied with your work, other people will take a more positive view. Do not expect family members to guess you have a problem without telling them.

8. SUNDAY. Disconcerting. From time to time a mood of contrariness gets into Libras, making it impossible for other people to know how to cope. If you can go off by yourself today, it will spare loved ones a frustrating time. Social events are unusually exciting, although they are unlikely to go as planned. A good mixture of guests will guarantee some lively exchanges of opinion; it might even be difficult to bring the occasion to an end. You need to tread on eggshells if your mate or partner is being supersensitive to the slightest criticism. A loved one appears to have lost their sense of humor at least for a while. Try not to take their words or actions to heart.

9. MONDAY. Disquieting. Libras who are working for charities could be shocked to find out that there have been some shady dealings going on. This might shake your faith in human nature, until you stop to reflect that the culprits are few and the rest of the people with whom you are involved, without exception, are well-meaning. Disappointing marks for written work can either depress you or make you determined to do better; it is obvious which of the two is preferable. A close relationship could be doomed unless you can both grow and change together. When one is satisfied with their lot and the other restless for change, it is very hard to accommodate both. Compromise is the best answer.

10. TUESDAY. Buoyant. It's time to stop hiding your special light under a bushel; come out and show the world just what you can do in the way of creativity. It might even be possible to take a hobby to the professional level providing you have the drive to do so. You can twist a romantic partner around your little finger because they are so fond of you. However, if you are honest, you realize there is no pleasure to be gained from taking advantage of someone's emotional vulnerability. Getting household chores done can seem almost impossible when the phone keeps ringing. It is up to you to decide which is more important: a tidy house or communicating with your friends. Choose your evening companions wisely.

11. WEDNESDAY. Good. You may feel that you cannot put a foot wrong. The main problem today might simply be relaxing too much. News of an imminent pay raise should brighten the morning, but do not use this as an excuse to splurge. Bide your time; if you spend the money now you will feel you have earned nothing extra. Efforts to improve your working environment can be worthwhile. As a Libra it is particularly important for you to be comfortable in order to do your best. A more serious attitude toward a one-to-one relationship can be rewarding. You have gone way past the stage of flirtation and casual friendship. Now is the time to consider long-term commitment.

12. THURSDAY. Favorable. Entering a competition may not always appeal, but when there is a prize worth winning you really have nothing to lose. Consult your mate or partner and see if you can come up with an entry that will stand out from all the rest. Libras involved in a legal case should be feeling quite optimistic. The weight of evidence seems to be on your side, and hopefully there will be a judgment in your favor without much more delay. Where romance is concerned, you can no longer afford to sit on the fence. You should be clear enough by now about your level of involvement to make a firm decision. Try a new local restaurant with friends or a loved one tonight.

13. FRIDAY. Difficult. This particular date usually makes an impression even on those who do not consider themselves superstitious. However, if events do not seem to be going your way, you still have freedom of choice. There is no need to be a passive victim and blame bad luck. You may be pulling in a different direction from a business associate; until you can get back in harmony, work is likely to suffer. Because the difference is not profound, if you both abandon your pride it can soon be sorted out amicably. Libras who have been going through the divorce process will undoubtedly have mixed feelings when it is over, but at least you can face a more promising future.

14. SATURDAY. Deceptive. It may be rather hard to know who is fooling whom on the romantic front. If neither you nor your loved one has entered the relationship with entirely honest motives, you may now find yourselves in deeper than expected, your original expectations a thing of the past. Although you probably cannot refuse to give a friend a loan, you can and should make it absolutely clear that there is a time limit on it. Otherwise this could turn into one of those stories that run and run. When a loved one confides in you, you are apt to feel a little uneasy being cast in the role of counselor. It could be more helpful to suggest they get professional advice from someone who is neutral.

15. SUNDAY. Complicated. You may have gotten yourself into a pickle by dipping into what should be shared savings on your own behalf. You of course intend to pay back the money, but doing so is never easy. Now it is necessary to confess your actions. Information about a romantic partner revealed to you by a third party may be tempting to use against them in an argument. However, to do so would be unfair; the only decent course of action is to let them know what you have been told. This is an excellent time to finish off jobs around the house that you have been avoiding. You can get a lot of odd tasks done in practically no time at all.

16. MONDAY. Variable. Recent research may not yet seem to be yielding very interesting results, but you do not know what is just around the corner. With a little perseverance you could discover a really useful item of information. Family obligations are apt to be weighing rather heavily on you at the moment. Partly this is due to your attitude; if you could worry less, everyone would be able to relax more. Rumors of a merger are likely to be making the rounds at work. However, the truth is far from clear, and there is no cause for panic. Falling in love with someone you respect means that a partnership of equals is now possible. Focus strongly on this relationship.

17. TUESDAY. Mixed. Beware of trying to run before you can walk. Overoptimism can annoy or anger other people who know more than you do. Libras who are planning a holiday break should think big. You may want to pull out all the stops for once and choose an exotic long-haul destination. It may seem to you that your recent work has been unfairly criticized. Although this may be the case, that is no reason not to make the improvements suggested. If you are studying for exams, do not rely on being able to pull out facts from your memory bank without having learned them thoroughly first. It is possible to leave a certain amount to chance, but hard work is bound to pay off.

18. WEDNESDAY. Fair. As long as you believe in yourself, there is little that can stop you from reaching a longed-for goal. The higher you aim, the more likely you are to hit the jackpot. If you are waiting for a special friend to get in touch, take the initiative and contact them instead. There is nothing worse than waiting around on tenterhooks, and you do not need to do so. Self-employed Libras occasionally have difficulty getting prompt payment. All you can do is be persistent, and perhaps hope to embarrass the client into treating you fairly. A good travel book can do a lot to calm your restless urge to escape from the everyday world. Consider an exotic cruise or a tramp-steamer adventure.

19. THURSDAY. Stressful. A recent bout of spending may have left you short of ready cash at an inconvenient time. There may be nothing to do but take out a loan, although a relative might be able to help you out. If you persist in looking for romance in the wrong places, you are going to keep on suffering disappointment. Try to stay away from the type of people who are obviously unable to commit their emotions to you. Instead, look for someone who is in circumstances similar to yours. A timely word with higher-ups at work could alert them to factors of which they are ignorant. You are naturally more in touch with events because you are in the thick of them.

20. FRIDAY. Sensitive. Usually you do not order other people around, but from time to time you like to be in the driver's seat. Remember that people usually react far more positively to a request than to a command. Information passed along by a colleague in the know could put you onto the scent of a promising new job. However, it might be wise to do a bit of research on your own before putting in an application. A more realistic attitude toward money may take a certain thrill out of life but will also enable you to make useful savings. Spontaneous spending can get out of hand, as you well know. An evening out with friends could put the sparkle back into your eyes.

21. SATURDAY. Satisfactory. Make the most of an invitation to a formal occasion. Dress well, as only you know how. You are bound to make a great impression since your Libra taste is good. There may even be a special person present who will be very attracted to you. The realization of a long-term plan may be more expensive than you bargained for. However, it is not a good idea to try to cut corners; doing so may only spoil the end result. Although youngsters can be bothersome when you are trying to have fun with friends, do not allow yourself to get annoyed with them. They probably just want to be part of the fun, so make an effort to include them in whatever you are doing.

22. SUNDAY. Tricky. You may have to use your good Libra powers of intuition to guess what loved ones are driving at. They may be too emotional to be articulate, but a misunderstanding at this point can make matters even worse. Arrange a day out for the family, but keep the destination secret. Even if it is somewhere you have visited before, the extra excitement will lift the day out of the ordinary. A chance remark could bring back memories of a past love affair. You are bound to have happy recollections, but it would be unfair to your present mate or partner to lose yourself in them. When socializing, be less reluctant than usual to be the center of attention.

23. MONDAY. Challenging. Your sixth sense may tell you that someone is working against you, and that they may have enough influence to do you some harm. The best plan of action is probably to confront them outright, preferably in the presence of colleagues so that everyone can see what the situation is. Ambitious plans for self-improvement may have to be scaled down somewhat; otherwise you run the risk of failure. Do not bite off more than you can chew; there is no need to hurry. Much goes unsaid in even the best of relationships, but this is one time you cannot afford to shut your eyes when things are going wrong. Take steps now to sort out your problems together.

24. TUESDAY. Slow. There is more than one way to get over a relationship. If you can brace yourself to feel angry, that will at least keep you from moping. Just resolve that you will never put yourself in such a position again. Work done in seclusion will be most satisfying, since you need solitude to concentrate properly. Do not refuse to take on some tasks to help out a colleague; they are bound to return the favor when you need assistance. A small sum of money from a legacy can come in handy to get some repairs done which your house has needed for a long time. The longer you put them off, the more expensive the work will become.

25. WEDNESDAY. Fortunate. Float through the early part of the day. You should be on a creative roll, and you need make little effort to get things going your way. A more glamorous image could do wonders for your self-confidence, which always proves attractive to other people. Go for a more classic look rather than anything daring. Romantically you are likely to be on cloud nine as a new person enters your life just when you are beginning to tire of being alone. Take each day as it comes, and enjoy them all. There should be few travel problems. Bring a friend with you on a short trip, if possible; you will both get pleasure from having good company on the road.

26. THURSDAY. Deceptive. Promises of overtime that would enable you to boost your income may not come about. Once again your financial situation can only be improved if you tighten your belt and make some savings. An exercise program you have been trying out may not actually be doing much for you. It is important to find a keep-fit activity that is enjoyable, since that is half the battle. Sometimes friends are all too eager to give advice about romantic matters, even if you do not ask for their opinion. On this occasion even people who know you very well are not really impartial or objective, and you should take what they say with a grain of salt.

27. FRIDAY. Frustrating. If you have been getting excited about the prospect of a luxurious break from routine, it will come as a letdown when a loved one has to postpone it. Unfortunately the pressure of work must be given priority. You will just have to arrange your treat for a future date. A business trip offers the hope of good profits, but the reality may turn out to be somewhat different because there is bound to be a catch. You are likely to return home with a less exciting deal than you expected. Make a resolution now to take better care of your health. You know how good it feels to be in peak condition, and there is no reason not to maintain your vim and vigor.

28. SATURDAY. Disconcerting. Libra lovers are rather allergic to discord, but that is exactly what you may have to face right now. Your mate or partner may have been brewing up discontent for some time without you realizing it, and now the lid is about to blow. Be prepared for an expensive shopping trip. You have a weakness for good quality, which is economical in the long run but expensive when you are making the purchase. Be extra careful of your money and credit cards when out in public. There is a strong chance of losing one or the other through sheer carelessness, which can be more upsetting than you may think. Loved ones need to be handled with kid gloves.

29. SUNDAY. Fair. Some extra effort put into clearing up less attractive areas of the house and garden will be both satisfying and good for your general fitness. You may be surprised at the long-term results; a beautiful environment is necessary to your Libra sensibility. It can be all too easy to slip into old arguments with parents or other relatives. Because you know exactly where you disagree, there is little point going over and over the same old ground. Attempts to get your financial accounts into shape might be futile, since you are not really in the mood. Postpone it for another time, and concentrate on doing something you enjoy instead. Do not forget to tell your mate or partner you love them.

30. MONDAY. Manageable. Finally you have reached the point where you are ready to accept your responsibilities instead of trying to evade them. There is no doubt that you like an easy life, but it is also necessary to be realistic about your obligations. A good idea for making a little extra cash could be passed on to you by a friend who has already tested it out. With this good recommendation, do not waste any time having a go yourself. Youngsters' demands for new clothing and sports equipment may seem endless. This is an excellent moment to explain to them that money does not grow on tree but must be worked for, by them as well as you.

31. TUESDAY. Demanding. Naturally it is upsetting to rely on colleagues, only to be let down. They may have actually tried to pass off some of your work as their own, but you must not let them get away with it. Travel conditions may not be good. Watch out for children playing near the road or crossing without due caution. Angry words could be exchanged with a loved one who you feel is taking you for granted. You must admit, however, that some of the blame is yours; if you made more demands they might take you a bit more seriously. Resolve to think only positive thoughts, and refuse to let yourself get angry. It is vital for you to stay in control.

NOVEMBER

1. WEDNESDAY. Tricky. Unless you avoid idle daydreaming, you are not going to hear what is being said to you. There is no use guessing at the meaning; that will only lead to trouble later. The temptation to take a financial risk may be strong, but it would be unwise to give in to it. Because your judgment is not at its best, there is every chance of falling prey to those who are more astute and ruthless than you are. Work on your home can be done more economically than you might suppose; make sure you get more than one price quote and you will probably be surprised at the difference. There may be some home repairs or redecorating that you can manage yourself providing you are careful and thorough.

2. THURSDAY. Excellent. As long as you are happy to take a back seat at work, this can be a very satisfying day. The most important work is often done behind the scenes, and you should have the satisfaction of knowing your efforts have been crucial in getting a big project off the ground. Some extra money could come from an unusual source; be alert for opportunities that are out of the ordinary. Since your willpower is particularly strong right now, do not hesitate to make a resolution to give up a habit which has been troubling you for some time. It will be easier than you think to leave it behind. Explore new local leisure facilities with a loved one this evening.

3. FRIDAY. Variable. All property negotiations are promising, although you may have to make some concessions in the asking price. This is a promising chance to lay down foundations for a more secure future. Investing in a home is a big step, but a sound one. Look for mislaid items in the bedroom; they could be closer at hand than you think. As a distant relative passes away after a long illness, the family can come closer together than usual. Even sad occasions can be the means of reviving shared memories and giving positive support to each other. High hopes of winning a competition may be dashed, but there will be other chances.

4. SATURDAY. Promising. If you are romantically inclined, put your best foot forward and make the most of any chance encounter. The best way to make an impression on someone who attracts you is by engaging in conversation; just make some excuse to talk and see where it takes you. Socially this should be an enjoyable time, as friends invite you to a cultural event designed to stimulate the mind. As a Libra you enjoy elegance and sophistication, so you will undoubtedly be in your element. Shopping for pleasure can turn up some surprises. Make sure you have enough cash with you, or take a credit card; you may have no time to hesitate before buying.

5. SUNDAY. Mixed. There is no point denying yourself pleasure because you feel it is self-indulgent. Put aside your inhibitions and let go; there is nothing to lose but your shyness. You may be rather worried about money at the moment and feel you have made a wrong decision concerning a recent investment. To set your mind at ease, make an appointment with an expert who can spell out the options that are now available to you. Try to find some time to fix small items around the house, especially latches that do not work or locks that need replacing. A deeper sense of inner worth can come from knowing you have fulfilled all of your obligations.

6. MONDAY. Disquieting. Your efforts to get ahead in the job market may not be making much of a difference to your career prospects, at least not yet. The problem could be that you are simply not being confident enough. Aim higher and there may be more chance of making an impact. Long-distance travel can be subject to delays. There are times when it is possible to get around bureaucratic red tape, but this is not one of them; do not even think of trying it or you could make matters worse. Youngsters' schooling is apt to pose a few problems. If you do not feel sure that they are receiving enough basic teaching, a discussion with their teacher or principal could be in order.

7. TUESDAY. Changeable. There are ways of making yourself indispensable at work, and one of them is to master a task that no one else can manage. This should not be beyond your capabilities and can be an invaluable skill, especially if it is helpful to your colleagues. Lovers' quarrels may not always be taken seriously by onlookers, but all the same they can be extremely painful. You probably have realized by now that it is usually best to let small differences of opinion go by the board; otherwise you can cause unnecessary hurt. If eating at a local restaurant seems to have had an unfortunate effect on your digestion, stick to a plain at-home diet for a while. Also avoid caffeine and sugar.

8. WEDNESDAY. Manageable. Once a communication for which you have been waiting arrives, you should at last have the go-ahead to put a personal plan into action. This is apt to definitely improve your personal finances as long as you are prudent. There is no longer any way of ignoring a mistake you made during the past few weeks. Own up to it now and get it over with; probably no real harm has been done, so the worst you are likely to face is a sense of embarrassment. Research into family history can turn up some fascinating information. Probably most of your relatives will be interested to learn more about their ancestry, and this can form a stronger bond between you.

9. THURSDAY. Stressful. You are likely to be more tense than usual. Little things can make you lose your temper. Loved ones may not seem to know just how to cope with your moods. Take a deep breath and vow not to take out your moodiness on others. Hopes of settling down with a romantic partner could be fading fast. You will not get anywhere by issuing ultimatums; the only effect will be to drive the other person more and more to assert their independence. An impulsive purchase is likely to set you back a pretty penny, and probably will not be really worth it. Too late you may regret being so extravagant. Clear the air with a loved one concerning a problem that has been troubling both of you.

10. FRIDAY. Exciting. Intuition can lead you into a relationship that may not seem obvious to your friends. Instinctively you know when someone has a lot to offer, even if it is not apparent at first. Libras who make a living from creative work have every reason to be more confident than usual. A recent sale should have gone well and is likely to lead to others. A close friend who is down in the dumps will be immensely cheered by a special gift from you. It does not have to be expensive; just give something spontaneously to let them know you care. Guard against falling for the ploys of people or organizations who appeal to your compassion. Use common sense before parting with your hard-earned money.

11. SATURDAY. Disconcerting. Disagreements with your mate or partner over money can get out of hand if you allow them to escalate. The easy route is to blame each other, but a more realistic way of dealing with the problem is to sit down and discuss what savings can be made. Where romance is concerned, this is definitely not a good moment to bring up emotional issues. You are both far too fragile and should avoid any topic that is likely to stir up problem areas of your relationship. A friend may press you for a decision concerning a project in which they want to involve you. However, it is too soon to say whether this would be a positive move, so bide your time for a while.

12. SUNDAY. Sensitive. You can get out of an unwelcome social engagement by pleading poverty, but it might be a shame to do so. There is a chance of meeting someone influential who could put you on the path to career development. Do not let parents or other older relatives upset you. They really have your best interests at heart, although sometimes their way of expressing concern leaves much to be desired. Romance with someone whose outlook on life is more balanced than yours can be quite transformative. You will find the mixture of attraction and mental stimulation a heady brew. This is one time when it is important to make your own needs clear to loved ones; you deserve respect as well as affection.

13. MONDAY. Fair. The workweek begins on a note of domestic harmony, as you and your mate or partner agree on alterations to be made to your home. Working together to make these changes can do wonders for your relationship providing you are careful to maintain the atmosphere of goodwill. If travel is on your mind, you are unlikely to be satisfied with a local destination. Instead, you need a complete change of culture and a chance to see a different way of life. As the autumn evenings close in, this is an ideal time to begin studying a new subject. With the world such a vast and complicated place, you could go on learning about it forever! Get to bed early to refresh yourself.

14. TUESDAY. Variable. Although you may be longing to spend more time at home, the demands of your work make this all but impossible. If you are worried about missing out on youngsters growing up, this may be the time to consider your other career options. An appraisal of your house might come as a shock because you were expecting it to be worth more. This could mean rethinking plans to move, if that is no longer such an attractive proposition. You can talk to a superior at work almost as if you were their equal, as long as you have an air of confidence. After all, you have skills that they lack, which is why they need you. You might even want to ask for a pay raise.

15. WEDNESDAY. Confusing. A feeling of having been there and done that could plague you when a problem you thought had been solved resurfaces. At least you have a better idea now of how to tackle it. The demands of your romantic partner may be difficult to interpret, probably because they do not seem to know themselves what they want from you. All that is clear is that you are failing in some way to please them, and it is up to you to discover how to resolve this problem. It will be difficult to get a loan repaid if you do not keep a record of all the details. You may not really be on the ball where money is concerned, so it would be all too easy as time goes by for the repayment arrangements to slip your mind.

16. THURSDAY. Buoyant. Right now you are best at putting ideas into action. Let others come up with a plan and then pass it on for you to work out the practical details. Efforts toward self-improvement can be very rewarding. You have the enthusiasm to push out the boundaries of your talents in an entirely new direction, which could open up all kinds of possibilities. Libras engaged in studies probably have done enough groundwork to allow a little time for relaxation. You should be able to draw on your resources now to write or speak more spontaneously. Job interviews can go well; summon up all your confidence and you are bound to shine.

17. FRIDAY. Mixed. There is apt to be some confusion over the nature of your relationship with a close friend of the opposite sex. A strong element of attraction is obviously present, yet neither of you may be quite willing to admit to a romantic interest. Do not let your savings dribble away on social events that are your friends' choice rather than yours. Unless you envision pleasure from the activity, there is little point spending money on it. A snap decision to get away from it all for the weekend could pep you up. Sometimes activities done on the spur of the moment turn out more successfully than the most carefully planned venture.

18. SATURDAY. Disquieting. If you are hoping for a day without interruptions, you are going to be disappointed. No sooner will you settle down to work around the house than friends may call wanting you to accompany them to a special occasion. You can either risk upsetting them by refusing or sacrifice your peace; ask loved ones how they feel about it. It can be difficult to get to the bottom of a financial arrangement between friends which you got involved in some time ago. You may be called upon to arbitrate, but the situation is by no means clear-cut. Problems with a loved one cannot be solved by avoiding them. Face the music now and clear up the matter.

19. SUNDAY. Sensitive. Sometimes the obligations to your family tend to get you down and fill you with the desire for more personal freedom. However, stop and consider just what life would be like without your loved ones; that should give you a different perspective on the matter. Recent financial demands may have eaten into your savings. Now is a good moment to consider how you can replace the loss. Doing so could be a bit of a struggle, but your future security must not be put in jeopardy due to current desires. Although a trip may be disappointing when the destination does not live up to your expectations, there is no reason you cannot still enjoy the day if you adopt a positive attitude.

20. MONDAY. Satisfactory. There is great pleasure being able to help out a friend who is in a tight spot. You will not even mind making a small sacrifice to assist someone who is close to your heart. A sense of responsibility weighs in your favor when it comes to finishing work started by someone else. You are probably aware of details that need attention, which could easily have been overlooked by someone who is less meticulous than you. Find time to visit a friend or relative who has been sick for a while. They will be glad to see you, and would undoubtedly welcome regular visits. A mislaid check or bill is probably somewhere among your papers; instead of panicking, search diligently.

21. TUESDAY. Variable. Someone who is fond of you can be persuaded to take the next step, as long as you are not too aggressive. You may appear most attractive by displaying a degree of bashfulness. If you have been requested to relocate for work purposes, you might be reluctant to pull up roots. However, your new locale shows every sign of being congenial, and you are sure to settle down and make new friends in no time. A sense of mystery may envelop a new acquaintance. This can be fascinating, but it could also be a deliberate pose to bolster the confidence of a rather shy person. Family quarrels must not be allowed to spoil the overall positive atmosphere.

22. WEDNESDAY. Unpredictable. You can put a brave face on it, but friends will soon pick up the truth that your love life is going through a difficult period. At the moment the very strength of your mutual attraction is probably causing problems. Just remind yourself that it is better to feel strong emotion than to feel nothing at all. A family event could reawaken old differences of opinions. Even though everyone realizes the get-together is neither the time nor the place to air grievances, there are bound to be a few sticky moments. If you start to feel a bit bored, youngsters can be immensely refreshing. It may be therapeutic for you to join in their games.

23. THURSDAY. Deceptive. If you live as if you have a bigger income than in fact you do, there is trouble ahead. You may persuade others, and even yourself, for a while. However, in truth you are just living on borrowed time. A romantic relationship may be maintaining a strong hold on you but not be satisfying your inner needs. You and your partner have much to learn from each other, but it can save some heartache if you do not presume that the affair will last forever. Get some physical exercise, but do not congratulate yourself on getting fit until you are properly tired. There is little danger of overdoing when you are in a lazy mood.

24. FRIDAY. Fair. Have the courage to speak out on an issue that concerns you. The confidence you gain can be quite amazing. Once you realize that you can make points clearly and with force, there is no need to be shy about making your opinion known in public. Hearing from an old friend can bring a ray of sunshine into your life. You will have much to talk about because both of you have gone through big changes since you last met. Do not skimp on spending money on your home; consider it an investment. It would be foolish to compromise when you can get exactly what you want by splurging a little. Youngsters need you to help them feel extra secure at the moment.

25. SATURDAY. Demanding. What appears to be a sudden flash of inspiration may in fact turn out to be misleading. Your financial problems are not going to be solved all in a stroke; you need to exert some persistent effort to see real results. If youngsters seem more willful than usual, it may be due to your own attitude, especially if you have been coming down rather hard recently on their minor misdemeanors. There is a chance to begin mending a quarrel with one of your neighbors. You may have to make concessions, but keep in mind that it is essential to live in harmony with people you see nearly every day. An evening out with loved ones can do much to restore your good humor.

26. SUNDAY. Useful. It might be most satisfactory to find your entertainment locally. There is bound to be something to keep youngsters amused, allowing you to relax with your mate or partner. A fresh romantic affair can be helped along by the tactful intervention of a mutual friend who will not be at all averse to playing Cupid just this once. You may have some problems finding time to pursue a course of study because more immediate concerns keep getting in the way. However, concentration and perseverance will win the day. If there is a problem on your mind, come right out with it. It is unfair to loved ones to keep them in the dark concerning what is troubling you.

27. MONDAY. Good. Libras who are in the business of public relations should start the workweek on a high note. There is no shortage of bright ideas that you can develop; so put your shoulder to the wheel and see if you can come up with something really exciting. Baring your soul to your romantic partner may seem like an unnerving prospect, but you will probably be delighted with their reaction. The sympathy between you is strong enough that your loved one probably had an inkling of what was up. Youngsters can make great strides forward if you add some extra tutoring to their usual schooling. Much can be gained just as long as you are not too ambitious for them.

28. TUESDAY. Disconcerting. It may be a waste of time urging caution since you may think you are invulnerable in certain areas. However, other people will soon tell you differently if you overstep the limits of acceptable behavior. An overseas business deal that appeared promising may now run into difficulties. Although there is probably little you can do without being on the spot, unless funds are freed up it is unlikely you will be able to travel to the scene in time. Tests of ability at work are usually something you take in stride; your confident attitude is certainly helpful. However, on this occasion it is important not to become careless or take anything for granted.

29. WEDNESDAY. Mixed. Libras with a garden should find it relaxing to spend some time on general cleaning up. At this time of year the work can be quite heavy, but your aim should be to get into a rhythm that will be enjoyable without tiring you. Business associates are apt to be less amenable than usual to you taking time off from work. Look back over the past year and you might be surprised at the total amount of time you have been away due to sickness or emergencies. Delight your mate or partner with a special item for the home that you have both wanted for a long time. Just for once it will not hurt to splurge. A meal at home with friends and loved ones should be ideal.

30. THURSDAY. Uncertain. Romance is a tricky business at the moment. Even if you have become extremely fond of someone, you need to consider whether you are prepared to keep on hoping for commitment when they seem so elusive about the subject. Youngsters need plenty of imaginative input to keep them from becoming bored and irritable. Search your memory to recall what used to amuse you at their age. If you are looking for a cheaper place to live, glance through the advertisements in the local paper. There are apt to be good opportunities if you are able to act quickly. End a family quarrel with a simple but sincere apology even if you were only partly to blame.

DECEMBER

1. FRIDAY. Variable. If it is hard at the moment to see your way ahead financially, just bear in mind that you have been through periods like this before. A solution will present itself in its own good time. Youngsters may need a little extra discipline. There is no need to be harsh; firmness will make the point that there are times when you definitely do know best. It can be a real tonic in the middle of winter to start thinking about a vacation in the sun. Early planning has the advantage of giving you longer to save for a really enjoyable break. A loved one may surprise you by organizing a special treat that brings back many shared memories of your early days together.

2. SATURDAY. Promising. Where romance is concerned, there is no need for you to hang back. The other person is probably hoping and waiting for you to make a move, so take your courage in both hands and go ahead. Creatively, this is a day when you get a lot of work done. Leisure projects may be pushed into a new phase as the inspiration strikes to solve a long-standing problem. If you are getting bored with your usual wardrobe, shop for something more eye-catching. You will have the confidence to carry off a designer outfit as soon as you see how good it looks on you. Do not lash out at youngsters without thinking; they may be more deeply hurt than you would suppose.

3. SUNDAY. Disquieting. Today may feel like an uphill battle as a series of incidents shake your usual Libra calm. A romantic involvement may be getting off on the wrong foot because you have misunderstood the other person and now feel let down. If you allow this to come between you, there is not much hope of further developments. Criticism of creative work can deal a blow to your sense of self-worth. However, try to stand back and see if the comments could have been inspired by simple jealousy. The day's entertainment may have to be postponed because it is necessary to finish off household chores first. This might not go over too well with family members, but get them to pitch in and tasks can be finished quickly.

4. MONDAY. Difficult. There is not much chance of being allowed to settle down quietly to your work this morning. You are due to be hauled over the coals by a superior who wants to blame all kinds of mistakes on you. It may be difficult for you to defend yourself. Problems on the home front cannot be allowed to develop any further. Even at the risk of provoking an explosion, you need to tackle the matter without further procrastinating. The last few weeks have been rather stressful, leaving your nerves in a decidedly shaky state. Wearing yourself to a frazzle is not the answer. Instead, carve out some quality relaxation time for yourself by delegating some of your easier responsibilities.

5. TUESDAY. Excellent. A legacy from a distant relative is apt to be surprisingly generous, making you almost wonder what you can do with it. Look for the answer in safe investment, unless there are items you need to buy urgently. Romance could be staring you in the face, although you may not recognize it as such. You may have known the person for so long that you simply have not realized how your feelings toward them have been developing. Helping out a colleague could lead to a better job opportunity; the more skills you learn, the better the range of employment for which you can apply. Some extra cleaning can make your home a showcase for your friends and family.

6. WEDNESDAY. Happy. All will be well between you and a loved one providing you communicate openly with each other. Do not be shy about putting your emotions into words: this is one of the best ways of drawing closer together. A helpful neighbor can come to your assistance if you are finding youngsters a bit of a handful. Keep in mind that you will then owe them a good turn; in fact, this might be the moment to consider setting up a barter system in the neighborhood. Libras whose job includes traveling are unlikely to encounter any major hitches. Use your initiative if it is not possible to get in touch with the office when a major decision needs to be made on the spot.

7. THURSDAY. Confusing. If a superior has been saying one thing while thinking another, you may now not quite know what your next move should be. Ultimately you can only rely on your own good Libra judgment. It is possible that you are making too much fuss regarding a disagreement within the family. Although a point of principle may be at stake, that is no excuse for being inflexible. Beware of taking yourself too seriously, and do not let a recent success go to your head. Friends and loved ones will soon bring you back down to earth if you become pompous. Make sure all travel connections check out ahead of time so that you can set off with no anxiety about reaching your destination.

8. FRIDAY. Unsettling. Since you have probably been slightly vague about money recently, it may come as a letdown when your bank statements arrive. Your accounts are rather depleted due to careless spending. At the moment you may have stars in your eyes thanks to a new romance. In time, however, you may become aware of what friends are trying to tell you now: that your current partner is not being entirely honest with you. Your interest in finding a deeper meaning in life is to be encouraged. However, without guidance from a reliable friend or counselor you run the risk of getting into some questionable areas that will turn out to be dead ends. Consider joining a group of like-minded searchers.

9. SATURDAY. Successful. If you have any interest in amateur dramatics, this is an excellent time to get involved. There are many ways you can contribute if you are not confident of your acting ability, and you can have some excellent fun along the way. Encourage youngsters and all family members to think for themselves. It can be tempting to tell them what you know, but sometimes it is more valuable for them to find out for themselves. A proposition from a close friend could take you by surprise. It would probably be rash to answer right away; tell them you need time to think it over. Come to an agreement with a loved one regarding money; there is really nothing to argue about.

10. SUNDAY. Mixed. You will probably wake up in a better mood than usual, raring to go. It would be a waste of your energy not to get out and do something special, so give yourself a real treat. Plans to better yourself by getting advanced training should not be allowed to go by the wayside. Of course there is a danger of running out of steam after the first flush of enthusiasm, but keep your long-term goal in mind and that should inspire you not to give up. If you are too shy to declare your love, write it in a letter. In that way your relationship can develop at a slower pace, which may suit you better. Check to see if your car is due for servicing; there might be problems now developing.

11. MONDAY. Exciting. The atmosphere this morning is electric with excitement. There is a sense of new opportunities opening up and ways to improve your future prospects. Do not miss this chance for self-development. A business deal could come to crisis point when it becomes clear that you cannot rely on overseas connections. Fortunately you have the energy and the know-how to sort out this problem, although it will probably necessitate putting in some overtime. Libras who are contemplating moving may be unsure of the best area to live in. Keep in mind that the move will be disruptive; try to spare yourself further stress by obtaining expert advice from a real estate professional.

12. TUESDAY. Cautious. Even if you do not usually listen to local gossip, there is an item of news making the rounds that may have some special relevance to you. In any case, it would be safest to pay close attention. As youngsters become more curious about the world at large, you are likely to be torn between a desire to protect them and the need to teach them caution. It can be challenging to instruct them to be careful without damaging their sense of trust. A new romance is about to blossom. You should find yourself able to relax into it more than previously because your sense of inner worth has grown to the point that you do not feel the need to impress a potential partner or anyone else.

13. WEDNESDAY. Variable. Your strong Libra sense of justice makes it hard for you to keep quiet when you witness any unfairness. However, it would pay to think twice before setting yourself up against someone who has more power than you. In particular, beware of entering into a personal vendetta. You need to get some hard physical exercise to tone yourself up, although you should be careful not to overdo it. Everyone has a competitive instinct, and yours can be surprisingly strong when it is aroused. A work project can be successful if you are willing to dig out a few facts which might not at first seem important but could turn out to be the knowledge that gives you the leading edge.

14. THURSDAY. Deceptive. A friend to whom you offered a great deal of support in a time of difficulty may not really appreciate it as much as you think they should. In fact, they may seem to think it is your duty to continue putting yourself out for them. However, this is the time to put your foot down. Where romance is concerned, you cannot afford to throw caution to the wind. Unless you are very careful, the other person could manipulate you into a position you later come to regret. A chance to attend a business conference some distance from home would be a sound career move as well as a stimulating experience; agree to it without delay or discussion.

15. FRIDAY. Changeable. Quick thinking can come to your rescue in a sticky situation. It should be possible for you to weigh your options and make a decision that might astonish colleagues. Do your best to encourage all creative activities on the part of youngsters, even if they involve making a mess. It is important that their imagination be fostered from an early age. A relationship could come to a sudden end unless you are prepared to be a little more forgiving. Naturally you have high standards, but you must also realize that other people will not always live up to your ideals. Begin the weekend with a night out in good company, and enjoy yourself.

16. SATURDAY. Uncertain. Do not be surprised if loved ones get irritated with you because you appear unable to join them in the real world this morning. Doing practical tasks is probably a waste of time because concentration is a real problem for you now. It would be better to allow yourself some space and let your mind wander until your mood changes. Ambitious plans for a day out might need to be pared down to a more realistic level. Not everyone is as enthusiastic as you, and it is important to take their feelings into account. Unfortunately anyone or any organization out to con you may have an easy time of it. Try to listen to hard-luck stories with a critical ear so that you are not taken for a ride.

17. SUNDAY. Slow. Current moods offer a good chance to finish off work inside the house since no one there is really enthusiastic to go out. Tidying up that you meant to complete ages ago can be satisfying, and will also delight your mate or partner. Take time to review your life up to now, then give yourself a pat on the back for your achievements. You are the only one who really knows what challenges you have faced and overcome; to an outsider, your progress might appear effortless. Disagreements with loved ones are no excuse for making snide remarks about them. It is always unfair to hit below the belt, and comments that are hurtful will be remembered for a very long time.

18. MONDAY. Rewarding. A colleague who can wield some influence on your behalf may be eager to push you into the limelight. This is not the moment to be bashful. If other people have confidence in your abilities, that should be enough to persuade you that you have something worthwhile to contribute. There is a strong possibility of getting buried under a mound of paperwork unless you make strenuous efforts to keep up-to-date. It is astonishing how quickly bills and letters can get out of hand, especially when you are reluctant to deal with them. Every opportunity to get ahead should be grasped, even if it is a long shot. Taking a well-calculated risk could lead to getting a few more strings in your bow.

19. TUESDAY. Favorable. An intense romantic involvement should be giving you the mixture of passion and friendship you have always wanted. Be sure your mate or partner knows just how much you appreciate them, and make them feel really loved and wanted. A money-making idea could be sparked off by a chance remark. As long as you are prepared to devote some of your leisure time to it, there is a real chance of getting a substantial sum of extra cash. Play up your good Libra skills of arbitration if you are aiming for a more fulfilling job. You will be happiest in a position where you can use your natural talents to the fullest. A change of image is bound to intrigue your loved ones.

20. WEDNESDAY. Mixed. It will probably be hard for other people to get a word in edgewise this morning as you get carried away by your own enthusiasm. Try to be objective enough to see if you are inspiring your listeners, or perhaps boring them. Usually you are the last person who needs to be reminded about putting loved ones first. Right now, however, a desire for independent action may lead you to forget the virtues of cooperation in a relationship. Written work should not be daunting. Set your mind to work and see how quickly you can complete it; just do not be too much of a perfectionist. Be extra careful with money; there is an especially expensive time ahead.

21. THURSDAY. Sensitive. Where love is concerned, you cannot do enough in taking the other person's feelings into account. No matter how considerate you are, they may seem to feel compelled to find fault. If possible, it is best just to shrug it off and not take it personally. Your financial fortunes are on a yo-yo string, up one moment and down the next. Unless you get a better grip on the situation, you could be headed for trouble before too long. Sometimes your longing for security simply cannot be satisfied. Times are changing so rapidly that it is necessary to ride the tide as much as possible. Spend an evening at home; you and your loved ones have a lot to discuss.

22. FRIDAY. Fair. Do your best to get all important calls out of the way as early in the day as possible. You will enjoy the holiday atmosphere all the more for having a clear conscience. Other people may be surprised at how decisive you can be when the need arises. Your hunches are usually correct, so you can afford to wait and reason out decisions once they have been made. There should be no difficulty getting your point of view across to family members, even if they have misunderstood you in the past. They are likely to be impressed by the directness of your speech. No one wants to admit that time is passing, but you cannot deny you are getting older and need to plan for the future.

23. SATURDAY. Satisfactory. You are likely to be in a last-minute rush to buy gifts since you are not quite as organized as you might be. Shopping is not going to be an easy experience, especially if you do not enjoy being in a crowd. However, with your eye for beauty it should not be difficult to choose some appropriate items fairly quickly. Libras who are hoping for romance might at last hear the words you have been waiting for. Even a simple invitation to go out can be the start of something big. If you are setting off on a trip you are almost bound to experience transportation delays. Just keeping a sense of humor you should be able to shake off the stress.

24. SUNDAY. Happy. An early gift from a loved one may be almost too exciting. This proof of their affection is revealed not so much in the cost of the present as in the thoughtfulness used in choosing and presenting it. Love may strike from a clear blue sky at a friend's party. At first you might not be sure what is happening, but there is every chance of turning this meeting into a stimulating long-term relationship. Do not keep your fears from loved ones; they are only too willing to lend you support just as long as you tell them what is on your mind and in your heart. They might even be feeling shut out at the moment, since it must be obvious to them that you are preoccupied.

25. MONDAY. Merry Christmas! Make this day really special by pulling out all the stops for a traditional family celebration. Hosting relatives for the day need not involve too much extra work because they will be pleased to lend a hand. The atmosphere will be all the warmer for having good company. Keep a camera at hand to record youngsters' delight, especially when opening their gifts. If your closest love relationships have been going through a difficult period, today's joyousness offers a fresh start. As you relax, remember all the positive things that keep you together. Do not neglect to let your mate or partner know just how much you care and appreciate them.

26. TUESDAY. Easygoing. Although there will be plenty to do, it helps to realize that there is really no hurry to clear up as long as your Libra sense of beauty is not offended by a bit of a mess. Stay close to home and relish the company of your loved ones. If you have domestic matters to talk over, this is an ideal time to discuss them. Even quite daunting home-related challenges can be overcome if you plan carefully. You will probably be grateful for the presence of parents, in-laws, or other older relatives who can keep youngsters amused. At this time of year it is common to feel nostalgic about the past and miss the presence of loved ones who are no longer with you. Indulging in happy memories can be very healing.

27. WEDNESDAY. Manageable. There is a sense that a cycle of your life has been completed, leaving you open to new developments. Your next move is not going to just happen: you need to decide what you want to do and then take steps to achieve your aims. Use a peaceful hour or so to go through accounts and all financial papers with your mate or partner to make sure that you both know where you stand. If you are considering moving in the near future, it is essential to agree on what assets can be used. Careful investigation of an incident in family history may reveal distant relatives you never knew existed; do not hesitate to get in touch with them as soon as possible.

28. THURSDAY. Demanding. You are not out of the woods yet, romantically speaking. A doubt in your own mind may have communicated itself to your loved one, so that now neither of you are entirely sure whether you want the relationship to develop further. Youngsters are likely to be in a rather secretive frame of mind; you would probably be wise to be a little suspicious of their requests. If they slip out of sight for periods of time, it is almost certain that they are up to no good. Recent expenses may have left you feeling rather shaky financially. It will take persistence to get back on an even keel. There is no time like the present to plan a better budget and vow to stick to it.

29. FRIDAY. Frustrating. If loved ones are keeping you guessing as to their real feelings about an action you propose taking together, there is no point trying to force a decision. Lose your patience and they are likely to dig in their heels and refuse to cooperate at all. If over the past few weeks you have developed a warm appreciation of a new acquaintance, you may now feel you would like to get to know them better. However, it can be difficult deciding just how to act if a romantic involvement would not be appropriate. Do not give in to the temptation to put your hard-earned savings at risk; you are almost bound to lose if you gamble in any way.

30. SATURDAY. Variable. Even if you wake up determined to get household chores out of the way quickly, it is unlikely you will be able to do so. Larger issues are apt to keep intruding and cannot be pushed away. This is the time to realize you should be paying more attention to the underlying patterns of your life. Today is excellent to start considering how you can increase your income. Some extra cash would certainly come in handy, and there may be ways to generate funds that do not necessitate changing jobs. Be sure to get some exercise, but be gentle with yourself and do not overdo it. Do not stay out too late tonight.

31. SUNDAY. Good. At last you should be able to devote some time to your home environment. It is very important for you to be surrounded by beauty. All plans for redecorating or remodeling should go really well. If you overindulged during the holiday season, make a resolution to get back in shape as quickly as possible. You will be glad when you can once again look in the mirror and enjoy what you see. A disagreement within the family circle may be rumbling below the surface, but you cannot afford to let it drag on any longer. It is time to get to the bottom of the matter so that you and your loved ones can look forward to the new year with a real sense of mutual optimism and excitement.

LIBRA
NOVEMBER–DECEMBER 1999

November 1999

1. MONDAY. Calm. Teamwork is strongly favored today, its excellent blend of skills enabling you to make good progress as part of a group. There is opportunity for you to do a job that is both personally fulfilling and financially rewarding. However, guard against a tendency to be too detail-oriented at work, especially if you have a deadline to meet; you have less time to finish than you may realize. This is a good day for community activity; your contributions can help bring about a much needed change. You may be asked to sign a petition for a local cause or be interviewed in connection with a political issue. Enjoy a lazy evening at home.

2. TUESDAY. Variable. This is a day to bring friends and loved ones together, especially if it is the first time. They are sure to hit it off well. In other situations you need some time to yourself to mull over possibilities and find a solution to a problem. Retreat from the hurly-burly of the workplace, especially if you are in an open plan office or on the shop floor. If possible, find a place to work where you are less likely to be distracted or interrupted. Use any lull in the day to catch up on neglected correspondence. Communication devices, especially fax machines, are apt to act up at just the wrong moment.

3. WEDNESDAY. Manageable. Clearing out the attic, bottom drawer, or a filing cabinet can be an eye-opener. At some point projects seemed to come to a standstill, but work has been going on quietly behind the scenes to ensure that it gets back on track. What you learn today is likely to put your mind at ease. This can be an opportunity to prove yourself to those who matter. Guard against giving in to other people's demands, particularly if they disregard your special personal talents and assets. Knowing your own worth is the key to your eventual success. Only back down if convinced you are wrong.

4. THURSDAY. Excellent. Even as conditions shift to more routine matters, you are likely to be looking at the world through rose-colored glasses. Libras in love are probably walking on cloud nine. If you are not in love, indications are that you soon will be. Guard against a tendency to dream away the day and waste your valuable skills. This is an excellent day for Libras who work in a creative trade. Your perseverance is sure to win you the respect of your co-workers and of higher-ups. If you are in the planning stages of a project, choose your options methodically and with extra care. Put more of yourself into everything you do.

5. FRIDAY. Stressful. Unexpected responsibility may be foisted on you. It could prove a little daunting at first, but this chance is likely to ensure the promotion you are seeking. Avoid saying anything out of turn. Be sure to keep any new information under wraps. It is too early to make your long-range intentions known. An older relative may express some extreme views but do not get drawn into an argument; you are unlikely to change their opinion. Letting your irritation show is likely to result in a serious disagreement. Make the most of any lull in the day to relax. Some physical exercise this evening can take away the stress of the day.

6. SATURDAY. Difficult. Although you know of a friend's special need, your generosity and help must be given voluntarily. If others try to compel you to assist them through appeals to your sense of duty and responsibility, you are not able to do so with a minimum of effort. This could lead to disputes about how much you feel restricted by the relationship. This is not a good time for investing or for trying to plan a budget for the coming holiday season. Although spendable income is coming in, you have a tendency to be pessimistic about your current financial situation. If you are feeling the pinch, you may be able to put in some overtime to make up for the shortfall.

7. SUNDAY. Uncertain. If you are involved in a creative hobby, ideas should be flowing thick and fast. However, most of them may be too unrealistic to be of much practical use. Try not to let any sense of discouragement tempt you to give up. Chances are you have a genuine talent, but present conditions do not favor creative activity. Take particular care if you go out with children. There is a strong possibility that one of them might wander off and get lost for a while. Bring along extra cash to cover any unexpected expense. Beware of pickpockets; you are apt to be too trusting. Keep your wits about you at all times.

8. MONDAY. Sensitive. Chances are you will feel the lack of spendable cash particularly keenly today. Any negative financial news you receive may well be the spur you need to take action. A completely new strategy is indicated. Consider ways in which you can put your special personal talents to good use; this does not have to be one you normally associate with your usual profession. If you are going to receive a pay raise or bonus, invest it in a retirement fund. Do not allow money worries to lead to a domestic dispute. Discuss any major new expenditure with your mate or partner in advance.

9. TUESDAY. Enjoyable. A short trip could be an ideal opportunity to mix business with pleasure. Consider taking your loved one along. Even if it is just a day trip, there should be enough time for a little shopping or sightseeing together. Be sure to keep a confidence to yourself; letting the cat out of the bag could lead to a loss of trust. Keep your checkbook and credit card separate to guard against loss or theft. Carry a significant amount of money only if you really need it. Someone close to you, probably a young person, is likely to ask for a small loan. If you decide to give it to them, do not expect repayment any time soon.

10. WEDNESDAY. Challenging. A difference of opinion with your loved one may reveal a previously unknown side of their character. This can be viewed as a positive revelation, offering an opportunity to put the relationship on a more realistic footing. You can rely on promises that have been made to you, but check your calendar before making any of your own. A letter that comes in today's mail may make you feel you are walking on air. Business communication, however, may arouse your suspicions. Try to keep an open mind and not jump to hasty conclusions. Stay as positive and upbeat as you can.

11. THURSDAY. Sensitive. If you look at recent work with fresh eyes you may discover a significant mistake. Seek the advice of an expert before starting anything new so that your relative inexperience does not result in confusion and disappointment. Spend some time with a friend who rarely makes demands on you. If you are in a position of authority at work, this is an ideal time for an informal discussion with employees. Their views could be a surprise to you but are likely to be instructive as well. An invitation to an impromptu party could be just what you need to help you wind down and relax tonight.

12. FRIDAY. Variable. Although you may be looking forward to a happy, relaxed day, personal relationships are unlikely to be as smooth as you hope. Resist any urge to retreat into yourself to avoid conflict. At the same time, refrain from raising your voice; others are apt to react unfavorably to any display of temper. A past mistake may be causing you remorse, but there is little to gain giving yourself too hard a time over it. A purchase you have set you heart on may be too expensive; consider buying a slightly damaged equivalent that can be easily repaired.

13. SATURDAY. Mixed. Old grudges may cause renewed tensions between you and your loved one. Guard against taking a stubborn line or you are certain to make matters worse. If you are depending on other people's help, indications are that they may have to change their plans at the last moment. Plan a family outing to a destination that offers something for everyone. However, do not attempt to organize everyone's day for them. The best approach is to live and let live so that you do not seem overbearing. Someone you thought you could depend on may let you down late in the day. A long soak in a hot bath should help soothe away the day's troubles.

14. SUNDAY. Unsettling. Make sure you have plenty of food and drink for unexpected guests who arrive at your door. Loved ones may be difficult to understand because of their uncharacteristic behavior. You may be at cross-purposes. Make your own needs known, especially if you want to relax this weekend; others are apt to have different activities in mind. Your emotions are ruling your head; beware of making a fool of yourself or wearing your heart on your sleeve, even with someone who is already close to you. Do not be tempted by what looks like a sure-fire winner; this is a day to expect upsets.

15. MONDAY. Fair. Keep a close tab on children and pets. Find a way to keep them out of your hair. Let a loved one do the talking in a tricky situation, especially if it involves disciplining or rebuking. Do not become impatient because of other people's reluctance to move forward. Your natural Libra enthusiasm to get ahead does not always translate into immediate action from others. Spend time on your favorite pastime, but first meet all your obligations. Doing someone a good turn without telling them about it can give you a boost as well as them. This is not a time to loan money or anything of value; you may never get it back.

16. TUESDAY. Cautious. An older person may try to disrupt your happy home, either intentionally or merely by inappropriate interference. Make it clear that you have no intention of giving way on issues that are important to you. Although you cannot expect to get everyone's support, those who matter most to you are likely to see things from your point of view. A well-calculated gamble is apt to pay off. Entertainment plans look promising. However, official confirmation is unlikely to reach you today. Do not let an overheated imagination make you fear the worst. There is not any need to fear moving forward and making changes.

17. WEDNESDAY. Slow. An unusually heavy workload could have a stressful effect on you. Although you are eager to get on with it, someone else's demands on your time and energy may prevent you from doing so. If you try to deal with everything right now, you could wind up running around in circles. Stay calm and stick to the priorities you have identified. It is often easier than you think to refuse someone's request. Take extra care if driving; your attention is not as good as usual. Try to find time for a leisurely lunch. Nothing is so important that you should eat on the run. Keep your caffeine intake to a minimum.

18. THURSDAY. Buoyant. This is a better day for emotional matters. Someone older than you is more than willing to share the benefit of their experience and wisdom in regard to affairs of the heart. You may be comforted to find that others have overcome your current dilemma. It can be equally reassuring to know that some things withstand the test of time. Creative ideas can be crystallized now and academic interests developed. If you have written something you would like to get published, have it reviewed by a professional. Reading about exotic, distant localities can broaden your interest in wanting to visit for yourself. Do all that you can to break with routine.

19. FRIDAY. Good. This is a good time to finish up a project and submit it for approval by higher-ups. Your work could win you the recognition you deserve, even fame. Conditions favor dealing with the heads of large institutions or corporations. An appeal for a grant or other financial backing can prove successful. This is also a good day for dealing with routine financial matters, especially filling out forms and requests. Good news is coming from a family member. Later, someone may offer to relieve you of a task or responsibility which you dislike having to do. Enjoy being with friends and loved ones tonight.

20. SATURDAY. Unpredictable. As a Libra you have a tendency to make mountains out of molehills. Guard against creating extensive plans based on flimsy ideas. Putting off doing something or meeting someone you have been avoiding recently is no longer the wise thing to do. Gather your courage; you may later wonder what you were shying away from. This is an auspicious day for partnerships and romance. Let your guard down a little to reveal how you really feel. Later in the day, an older person is unlikely to be available when you want to get together. Do not be tempted to go ahead with a plan without their blessing in advance.

21. SUNDAY. Rewarding. In small but significant ways, this day should start to bring about the fulfillment of a secret hope or dream. You may be entrusted with a considerable amount of new power and authority. Use it well and the chances are you will be given even more. Encourage younger family members to pay more attention to education and the important things in life. Instilling a sense of purpose and direction can fire them up. However, guard against throwing your weight around unnecessarily. If you are going on a date choose an outfit to wear that is likely to create the impression you want to make.

22. MONDAY. Tricky. This is a rather turbulent start to the workweek. Partners or loved ones may surprise you with an unexpected announcement of their intentions. There is little point in reacting without first thinking through the implications for yourself. Unforeseen disruptions in other areas of your life could stir up deep-seated insecurities. Again, try to contain your emotions by thinking about the possible long-term consequences for you and for them. In business matters, do not take associates into your confidence before finalizing your plans. Consider a trip to the theater or movies tonight as a means of taking your mind off worries for a while.

23. TUESDAY. Changeable. Be as precise as possible in writing a report or letter. Following a logical progression from known facts to conclusions should ensure that you leave no room for later misunderstandings. Be prepared to give a family member the benefit of the doubt when it comes to a problem with outsiders. Children, in particular, may need your support in a dispute with authority figures. New ideas are likely to spur you on to new challenges. Something that failed dismally in the past can be given a new lease on life if you tackle it from a fresh angle. Conditions do not favor signing anything that will legally bind you or your descendants.

24. WEDNESDAY. Fortunate. Contacts with business connections abroad should be smooth. Dealings with foreigners in general should also prove worthwhile. You may find yourself daydreaming about faraway places or about living abroad. By talking to someone about your dreams you may be surprised to learn that they are not as impossible as you think. A meeting today might be just the opportunity to make new contacts and market yourself. Discussions about a business merger are also favored. Studying a subject connected with the mysterious or the occult could give you special insight as you make new plans.

25. THURSDAY. Routine. Although you may feel like getting away from it all, on this Thanksgiving holiday, it will be quite difficult. You might be able to lift the midweek blahs by getting a haircut or a massage. Or you might prefer to pump some iron at the local gym, or join in an aerobics class. If you have an intellectual pursuit as a leisure interest, you may have to skip a seminar or class because of the pressure of current work. Consider buying yourself a luxury item. The pleasure you are now likely to derive from it will more than justify the expense. Libra weightwatchers can find new recipes in a magazine for food that is both delicious and healthful.

26. FRIDAY. Mixed. You can afford to relax a little while others take the reins. Do not let anyone pressure you into doing what does not appeal. Neither should you talk yourself into doing something out of a sense of duty. Spend your time thinking about the larger issues in your life, particularly your career direction. Reading a work of fact or fiction may provide the inspiration to achieve your goals. Obtaining additional academic qualification, such as proficiency in a foreign language, could give you new focus for the coming months. Even though you may sometimes find it difficult to believe, older relatives have your true interests at heart.

27. SATURDAY. Variable. Local social events of all kinds are starred. A neighborhood get-together will probably be a huge success. If you are in business, consider organizing an informal luncheon for your employees so that you all can meet in a social context. A shopping trip with a friend is also favored. The local grapevine may reveal some interesting news, but avoid idle gossip. Your words could get back to the wrong person, or they could be quoted out of context. There is a possibility of striking up a friendship with a younger person of the opposite sex; romance is unlikely, however. Beware of mistaking friendship for something more.

28. SUNDAY. Disquieting. Your weekend routine may be disrupted by the news that a close friend is leaving the area soon. Or a long-absent schoolmate may unexpectedly get in touch with you. Problems with younger people at home or away at school are likely. If you suspect they are getting into bad company, a judgmental attitude may make them even more stubborn. An attempt to curtail their movements could alienate them completely. They may have to make their own mistakes in order to learn a valuable lesson, but be ready with advice if asked for it. Guard against comfort eating as a way of coping with stress.

29. MONDAY. Confusing. This is another day when partners, both professional and romantic, may be putting the pressure on you in various ways. The best policy is to refuse to make snap decisions, which you may well regret at a later time. Unfortunately, some people already have an impression of you from hearsay or rumor; trying to persuade them otherwise could turn out to be difficult if not impossible. An alibi, or someone who can corroborate your version of events, may be needed to clear away any mixup. Guard against making snap judgments of your own or making baseless accusations in the heat of the moment.

30. TUESDAY. Fair. There is little point committing yourself to something which you are not completely sure you want to undertake. If you have reservations about someone or something, scrutinize your feelings carefully to see how they match up against the facts. Other people are apt to let you take the rap for a joint mistake. Fight for what you want without landing someone else in trouble. Later in the day you should have plenty of opportunity for relaxation, fun, and entertainment. This is a good time for participating in competitive sport. An opponent who can give you a good run for your money is sure to inspire you to try harder; you may even set a record.

December 1999

1. WEDNESDAY. Rewarding. Conditions do an about-face today, which should be a welcome relief. An ongoing disagreement can be amicably resolved by giving in a little and also accepting an apology. The easygoing side of your Libra nature is taking control. Clear the air so that you can start with a clean slate. Try to begin a dialogue with a young person who has been sullen or withdrawn, even if the lines of communication are barely open. Limit your activities to those you can do as a joint project or as part of a team. Wishful thinking can lead you astray; there is a risk of acting unreasonably unless you face the facts.

2. THURSDAY. Difficult. Guard against an accident due to carelessness while you are out and about, especially if you are in places that are unfamiliar to you. Although people at a distance may appear a little uncaring, they are unlikely to be openly hostile. Do not provoke an argument with someone you want to team up with. You cannot hurry their decision and may well suffer the consequences if you try to do so. Many Libras find it hard dealing with complaining associates, but stay out of any disagreements that have nothing to do with you. You need every ounce of the diplomacy for which Libras are so famous when listening to one person's side of a story.

3. FRIDAY. Changeable. An event from the past is apt to influence the way you react when a similar set of circumstances arises today. Remind yourself that not only is this a different time and place, but you are a changed person. As the season of goodwill approaches, try looking for the best in everyone. If you can help people showcase their talents and strong points, you are most likely to get along well and work out an important agreement. Romance may blossom from a working relationship. Business trips are starred, especially one connected with events occurring at a distance from your usual base of operations.

4. SATURDAY. Disconcerting. Staying busy with work or outside influences is a good way to put a personal dilemma out of mind for a while. Continuing to worry can result in your getting worked up for no good reason. Thinking about something entirely different may produce a flash of inspiration. There are roadblocks keeping you from finishing a project. Although you want to get it completed before the new year, this appears unlikely. Plug away as much as you can, then shelve it until you are once again able to move forward. Financing is uncertain, especially if you have just applied for a loan or a grant.

5. SUNDAY. Pleasant. This is another day where personal relationships are strongly influencing your mood and effectiveness. Cooperation is yours for the asking, although there may be some strings attached. For a single Libra looking for love, a special friendship is about to turn into a more intimate relationship. Do not sit back and wait; if you do not actively pursue romance, it could well slip through your fingers. Married Libras may find that creating a favorable impression with in-laws is difficult. Guard against letting a pet project turn out just like everybody else's; put your creativity to work.

6. MONDAY. Manageable. Flexibility gets you ahead, even as others continue to consider their options and make elaborate plans. Nothing is certain today. What seemed positive yesterday is almost sure to be reconsidered now. Although change is going on all around you, you are unlikely to notice until it affects you directly. This is a starred day for Libras interested in a new job. If you have just learned a new skill you will probably have a chance to turn it into paying work. Staying abreast of technological developments is vital. Good opportunities exist away from your usual base of operations.

7. TUESDAY. Productive. The morning hours may be peppered with distractions and interruptions. Being firm with yourself and others is likely to ensure steady progress. Guard against an ineffective person taking advantage of your good nature or your seasoned experience. If you step in, you will probably get the job done, but you are unlikely to receive many thanks and could even incur some resentment. This is a good time to enter into vigorous negotiations for goods you produce or want to buy. Hold out for what you believe is fair while remaining flexible enough to strike a bargain. Your good reputation precedes you, but it is up to you to prove that your admirers are correct.

8. WEDNESDAY. Confusing. You could be deceived into believing what someone wants you to believe, despite your better judgment. As a Libra you do not often let your instincts guide you. However, all indications are that you should do so in this circumstances. You have necessary leadership qualities, but consider being more direct and outgoing to get your message across. You have to aggressively go after what you want; nothing is going to be handed to you. The ordinary and mundane is unlikely to satisfy you. Begin to branch out in a new direction. Show that increased responsibility is not burdensome.

9. THURSDAY. Excellent. Today's lighter, brighter conditions put the emphasis on socializing. Accept a last-minute invitation to a special social occasion. You are likely to be concerned with issues of a humanitarian nature and will probably meet people who share your ideas and vision. In dealing with children, the key to success is letting them know that you trust them. If they feel they have your respect, chances are they will live up to your expectations. This is an especially starred day for imaginative ventures. Taking a gamble on your skills and talents being recognized could pay off. Do not hesitate to be a little more passionate with your loved one.

10. FRIDAY. Mixed. If you keep your wits you should be able to turn even the most difficult circumstance to your advantage. As a Libra you usually put yourself in another person's shoes. This can do much to gain their confidence and win them over as long-term allies. Information you receive through unofficial channels could prove useful. Keep your ear close to the ground; take what you hear via the grapevine seriously. You may be tempted to go to an auction, but only enter into the bidding if you have experience and expertise, or if you tag along with someone who has.

11. SATURDAY. Frustrating. Whatever you decide to do is likely to cost more than anticipated; you will probably have to go over budget just to keep up with the crowd. You may be bombarded by a forceful sales pitch that proves difficult to resist. Knowing where you stand in partnership or team activities can also be tricky. Someone is keeping you in the dark, not telling you even half of what is going on. Be extra vigilant when dealing with strangers. Do not be afraid to challenge an unfamiliar face; ask for the credentials of anyone claiming to be on official business. Talking too freely can lead to revealing secrets.

12. SUNDAY. Variable. You are apt to be your own worst enemy where money is concerned. Your craving for the good things in life can all too easily lead to unnecessary extravagance. If a large part of your hard-earned income is being depleted, chances are there is an emotional motive behind this compulsive spending. Gambling can be disastrous. Later in the day is a good time to write a letter which could have an important influence on your future. Take the time to choose your words with extra care so that you make your intentions crystal clear.

13. MONDAY. Good. You can afford to take a lighthearted attitude to what the day holds. There should be ample opportunity to mix work and pleasure; not everything needs to be repetitious drudgery. Your creative talents are beginning to receive the recognition they deserve. It is also likely that one breakthrough will lead to another, especially for Libra artists, entertainers, and creative writers. In teamwork and cooperative endeavors, experiment with something completely new and untried. If you are fashion conscious, a new designer or design can make you a trendsetter.

14. TUESDAY. Disquieting. A sense of perfectionism and a need to get everything absolutely right can be your undoing, creating problems and disruption for yourself as well as others. Although what you are trying to achieve is important, it is not the life-and-death matter you may want others to believe. A change in company or governmental policy could produce improvements faster than you anticipated. The way is clear for Libras in business to aggressively pursue merger plans. This is a starred day for signing a contract or other agreement, especially one which has long-term implications for your family's future security.

15. WEDNESDAY. Tricky. Personally take care of a job that is usually done on your behalf. Skills that are not used frequently can become rusty. Consider teaming up with a colleague who has a special talent that you need. Malfunctioning equipment may mean that you have to resort to a slower manual system, but the fault should be quickly rectified. It should not be too difficult to clear any backlog. With the festive season in full swing, it is important to budget carefully so that you do not have to scramble for funds. Concentrate on meeting your own needs rather than trying to keep up with the Joneses.

16. THURSDAY. Mixed. The day begins on a rather confusing note. You are probably not the only one to sense problems in relating to your partner, mate, or spouse. Keeping the lines of communication open and clear is unlikely to be easy, especially if you have something you are trying to hide or protect. In the long run, however, honest openness is the only way to keep a relationship viable and happy. Professional activities are starred. As a Libra you have a special knack of reaching people, affecting them in ways they cannot readily explain or understand. The manner in which you present your case can be more important than the facts of the matter.

17. FRIDAY. Fortunate. Consider ways of making your job more exciting and challenging. You may want to offer to take on work that everyone else is avoiding. Or come up with some constructive suggestions for solving a problem you have identified. Local contacts have a direct and powerful influence on choices. Keeping communication lines open ensures that you do not end up operating at cross-purposes. Do not hesitate to tackle work with an unconventional approach; there is no need to shy away from new techniques just because they are unfamiliar to you. Travel is favored provided it does not include an overnight or longer stay. You are likely to miss home comforts.

18. SATURDAY. Misleading. Combining romance and finance can lead to trouble. Even married Libras would be wise to keep separate accounts as well as a joint account. Having your own fund means you can maintain a level of financial independence. Single Libras risk losing out if you dismiss a romantic interest purely because their current earning power is not great. Look for ways to increase your own take-home pay by acquiring a new technologically advanced skill. Returning to school may well cost time and money but can be a worthwhile investment for the long term.

19. SUNDAY. Difficult. You cannot force the outcome of certain situations or bend others to your will. Time is a necessary ingredient. Patience and tolerance is indicated. Accept what others do, even though it may not measure up to the standards you have set. While attempting to bring your outstanding debts to a zero balance, continue to keep a tighter than normal rein on your budget. Extra outlays for the festive season can be particularly difficult to control. Even though a child yearns for a name-brand Christmas present, a cheaper but perfectly adequate alternative would do just as well.

20. MONDAY. Buoyant. There is just enough variety and diversity to keep you on your toes. You would be wise to keep a low profile when taking steps toward something new or different. Attracting attention to yourself is likely to raise expectations and make it more difficult for you to backpedal out of unfamiliar territory. Keep an open mind if a loved one or co-worker offers constructive criticism. The fewer people you have to answer to, the easier it is going to be. You can be especially successful with a new contact or in a job interview; express yourself with conviction.

21. TUESDAY. Disquieting. Close family members may be trying to stir up trouble at home. In-laws, in particular, are apt to be critical and demanding. If placating them is not successful, take a firm stand. Children, too, may have discovered the art of playing one parent against the other, so present a united front with your mate. As a Libra you are not known to have a jealous streak. However, a mysterious telephone call or letter to your loved one could leave you wondering and worrying. Possessiveness on your part may only make your partner feel smothered. Let the matter drop.

22. WEDNESDAY. Variable. A conflict over a point of ethical conduct is likely. Make certain that anything you say about this matter is said in private. There is little point in adding insult to injury by publicly embarrassing your opponent. Lending money to a friend can lead to difficulties, but one of your friends genuinely needs a small loan to help through a cash-flow crisis. You may find the glare of the limelight turned on you during a meeting. This is not a good time to air your differences with those who hold the power. All the signs are that you are right, but they will probably not be easily convinced.

23. THURSDAY. Rewarding. An early Christmas present is foreseen in the form of an inheritance or other windfall. However, the cash will probably not be forthcoming right away. During this season of goodwill, share your good fortune by making a donation to a worthy cause. Your ideas may be ahead of their time. This can make some people a little guarded in their reactions, wary of joining forces with you. However, eventually you should be more than able to convincingly explain your case. Libras in decision-making positions can afford to make a bold move at this time. Support from others will ensure that you are not left out on a limb.

24. FRIDAY. Disquieting. Unforeseen complications threaten to disrupt your carefully planned schedule. Family members may be too preoccupied with their own concerns to be worrying about what you regard as a priority. As a result you may feel a little unappreciated, even left out. An impromptu visit from friends can be just what you need to restore the holiday spirit. Refuse a panic request from your boss to put in some overtime during the next few days. Cramping you own timetable just to keep the boss happy would be unfair to yourself and to your loved ones.

25. SATURDAY. Merry Christmas! You should be feeling in top form on this day of good cheer and celebration. You may derive the greatest pleasure from caring for others and from simple acts of service. This can also be an important and memorable day for romance. Dreaming of a shared future together can provide the firm foundation for a lasting and permanent relationship. For Libras who are already attached, there are special opportunities for moving even closer to your spouse or partner. You could receive a gift that gently pokes fun at you. Even though your feelings may be a little hurt, playing along can prevent embarrassment.

26. SUNDAY. Enjoyable. Visit friends and acquaintances who live near you. It is a starred day to take photographs, especially natural shots of all that is going on. If a friend begins to tell a story you have heard more than once, bite your tongue and listen appreciatively just one more time. Family members can also be friends; you are likely to feel most comfortable with those who know you best. Playing a new board game can be particularly entertaining. Include children in your plans for the day; their spontaneity will more than make up for their boisterous behavior. A trip to the grocery store may be needed to cope with an impromptu party.

27. MONDAY. Satisfactory. Acquaintances in high places are willing to exert their influence on your behalf. However, do not expect complete dependability from them. You may have been a little too inward looking in the past weeks. This is a good time to renew old friendships and make new ones. At work, stick rigidly to the rules and regulations. There is little point in fretting about what other people may be thinking of you. Today's events mark a turning point in a long-term relationship. The coming year is likely to see you looking back on this day as a watershed in achieving a special ambition.

28. TUESDAY. Challenging. A project undertaken in secret can pay a special dividend to those involved. Take a long-range view of all that is developing, but do not expect immediate benefits. The more people who know what is going on, the less your chances of keeping it a secret for much longer. Although you can try to restrict access to a select group, you may require the help of an outside expert to provide technical assistance. Decisions made today, even those based largely on intuition, should be on target. A well-calculated gamble is likely to work out exactly as planned. A long lunch with a new or potential associate can shed new light on a problem.

29. WEDNESDAY. Fair. The less you say and do, the less anyone can find fault with you. A passive role suits you best while conditions remain in flux. A promise made by a higher-up cannot be relied upon; they probably are sincere but misinformed. Consider a proposal made to you without commenting one way or the other about it. Reserve judgment until you have the weekend to mull it over. A new friendship could begin at a gathering of virtual strangers. Do not hesitate to put aside all but the most personal of your plans to follow the lead of a loved one. This is a time to be a follower, and an enthusiastic one at that.

30. THURSDAY. Successful. Dress to convey the image you want others to have of you. Keep jewelry and accessories to a minimum. Accept a lunch date or evening dinner, but pay your own way. As a Libra you can often go stale if you work for too long on one thing; diversity keeps your interests at a peak. Putting aside a new project for a couple of days can give you added insight and new incentive. Conditions favor you being left to your own devices. Fulfilling your own needs, your own desire to get ahead, and your own creative impulses does not mean that you have to conflict head on with others.

31. FRIDAY. Unsettling. Truth can be stranger than fiction. Although you probably thought you knew what was going on, a friend or co-worker may put some doubts in your mind. Ask more than one person for an opinion, then weigh the responses you get. A written report may be full of half-truths. Guard against being apologetic for something that you were not personally responsible for. Mulling over the morning's events is likely to put things back in perspective for you. Although parties are likely to be going on at every other house this evening, you may prefer to welcome in the year 2000 in a relatively low-key and personal way.

AMERICA'S TOP PSYCHIC NETWORKS

"My psychics tell it like it is ... Just like I do!"

STRAIGHT TALK
LA TOYA JACKSON'S Psychic Network

USE YOUR CHECK OR CREDIT CARD AND SAVE up to TWO DOLLARS A MINUTE

1-800-994-1800 OR CALL
1-900-737-2442 $3.99 PER MIN

La Toya

MOTHER LOVE'S Love Psychics

Nationally known Film and TV Star, Author, and Talk Show Host

Is Love In Your Tarot?
Is Love In Your Stars?

USE YOUR CHECK OR CREDIT CARD AND SAVE up to TWO DOLLARS A MINUTE

1-800-218-2442 OR CALL
1-900-370-5330 $3.99 PER MIN

Spiritual Answers from Authentic Psychics

LET THE ANCIENT SPIRITS GUIDE YOU TOWARDS LOVE AND HAPPINESS. CALL NOW FOR AN AUTHENTIC NATIVE AMERICAN READING

USE YOUR CHECK OR CREDIT CARD AND SAVE up to TWO DOLLARS A MINUTE

1-800-923-3444
OR CALL
1-900-454-1156
$3.99 PER MIN

NOSTRADAMUS
His Predictions Changed the World

1-800-727-7438

ASTROLOGY & TAROT READINGS
What Does The Future Hold For You? The Answer Is In Your Stars

CHECK OR CREDIT CARD $1.89 PER MINUTE

1-800-347-7007
OR CALL
1-900-288-8329
$1.99 PER MINUTE

CANADA'S SUPER PSYCHIC
JoJo Savard

"MY PSYCHICS WILL PERSONALLY ANSWER YOUR QUESTIONS ABOUT LOVE, HAPPINESS, & SUCCESS"

USE YOUR CHECK OR CREDIT CARD AND SAVE up to TWO DOLLARS A MINUTE

1-800-748-3444
OR CALL
1-900-896-JOJO
$3.99 PER MINUTE

Past Life Readings
To know where you're going you must know where you've been
1-800-564-8668

RECEIVE A FREE CHART WITH EVERY READING

Astrology Readings
Call Now • Toll Free
1-888-873-2473

PSYCHIC CLUB
JOIN TODAY
1-888-306-CLUB (2582)

THE AMAZING PSYCHIC TWINS

LISTED IN "100 Top Psychics IN AMERICA"

Terry & Linda Jamison

1-800-728-9271

FREE TAROT CARDS
With every Reading

Tarot Card Readings
Call Now • Toll FREE
1-888-732-4733

PSYCHIC READINGS

3 MINUTES FREE

Laura Bryan Birn
Soap Opera Star

Don't wait another minute...CALL NOW!
1-800-232-0052
CELEBRITY PSYCHIC NETWORK

THE WITCHES OF SALEM NETWORK

BRIGITTE NIELSEN

HAVE FAITH AND COURAGE...
DON'T HESITATE • CALL NOW!

Use your CHECK OR CREDIT CARD and Save up to TWO DOLLARS A MINUTE

1-800-799-5959 OR CALL
1-900-370-1586 $3.99 PER MIN

2 MINUTES FREE
ALL FEATURED IN "100 TOP PSYCHICS IN AMERICA"
THE FIRST 2 MINUTES OF EVERY CALL ARE FREE

MASTER PSYCHIC
Leah Lusher
AMAZINGLY ACCURATE
CREDIT CARD or CHECK
1-800-232-0160
or call
1-900-884-1333
$3.99 PER MINUTE THEREAFTER

MASTER LOVE PSYCHIC
Voxx
WILL HELP YOU FIND TRUE LOVE
CREDIT CARD or CHECK
1-800-232-0157
or call
1-900-288-6949
$3.99 PER MINUTE THEREAFTER

MASTER PSYCHIC
Emma Faciollo
AMERICA'S MOST GIFTED PSYCHIC
CREDIT CARD or CHECK
1-800-232-0164
or call
1-900-288-6989
$3.99 PER MINUTE THEREAFTER

MASTER PSYCHIC
Imara
HER INSIGHT WILL AMAZE YOU
CREDIT CARD or CHECK
1-800-232-0173
or call
1-900-374-4334
$3.99 PER MINUTE THEREAFTER

BARBARA NORCROSS
THE PALM BEACH PSYCHIC
Psychic Advisor to the Rich and Famous

LISTED IN "100 TOP PSYCHICS IN AMERICA"

CALL NOW • TOLL FREE
1-888-393-0111

The Zodiac Group, Inc.• Boca Raton, FL 33433 • Must be 18 years or older • For Entertainment Only US PAT. 5,802,156 • PATENTS PENDING

Find Love & Happiness

The Professional Psychic Loveline

Talk live to our genuinely talented Psychics in matters of the heart. They have helped thousands of people just like you find true love, wealth and lasting happiness. Call anytime and get the answers you need from psychic who care.

NUMEROLOGY · TAROT
ASTROLOGY · CLAIRVOYANT

FREE 2 MIN!
AS LOW AS $1.93/MIN
1-800-472-9015
CREDIT CARD OR CHECK
1-900-420-6500
FIRST 2 MIN FREE $3.99/MIN. AFTER

24 HOURS. 18+. ENTERTAINMENT PURPOSES ONLY.

AMERICA'S BEST PSYCHIC SOURCE

Astrology · Clairvoyants · Tarot Numerology

Have the life you always dreamed of with amazing insights from gifted psychics

AS LOW AS $1.93/MIN
1-800-472-4966
CREDIT CARD OR CHECK
1-900-420-0033
FIRST 2 MIN FREE $3.99/MIN. AFTER

24 HOURS. 18+. ENTERTAINMENT PURPOSES ONLY.

The PSYCHIC Romance SPECIALISTS

Try our elite group of gifted Psychics specializing in your personal questions about romance, love and mysteries of your heart. Our Specialists will empower and help guide you to the true happiness you deserve.

FREE 2 MINUTES! $3.99/MIN.AFTER
1-900-740-4466
1-800-784-9758
AS LOW AS $1.93/min.
CREDIT CARD OR CHECK ONLY

24 HOURS. 18+. ENTERTAINMENT PURPOSES ONLY.

Your Loving Angel

Get Immediate Answers about

Relationships

Compatibility

Career

Money

1-800-234-9777
3.48/ min. VISA/MC/CHECKS

or try

1-900-255-2266
3.98/ min.

18+. AMER. STAR. (323) 966-4201. ENTERTAINMENT ONLY. TOUCHTONE

DISCOVER THE HIDDEN SECRETS IN YOUR LIFE!

GAIN ASTONISHING INSIGHT INTO RELATIONSHIPS • FINANCE • CAREER

LIVE 1 ON 1 PROFESSIONAL CONSULTATION WITH LEADING

ASTROLOGERS & PSYCHICS

1-900-226-6639
3.98/ MIN.

OR TRY

1-800-244-6770
3.48/ MIN. VISA/MC/CHECKS

18+. AMER. STAR. (800) 946-9889. ENTERTAINMENT ONLY. TOUCHTONE

HAVE YOU EVER NEEDED SOMEONE TO TURN TO FOR ADVICE ON LOVE, MARRIAGE, ROMANCE? LET OUR LIVE PSYCHICS BE THERE FOR YOU!

24 HOURS A DAY 7 DAYS A WEEK THEY'LL NEVER LET YOU DOWN! CALL NOW!

1-800-873-8327

OR

1-900-745-5601

The answers to your problems are only a phone call away!

Just $3.99 per min. Billed to you Visa/Mc/Amex or directly to your phone you must be 18+

ALL NEW!!! **Direct Connect**

Connect Directly with our Amazing Psychics,
No Credit Cards, No Hassles!

011-683-9121

011-678-739-53

1-473-938-4355

AMERICA'S MOST TRUSTED PSYCHIC NETWORKS

Does He Really **LOVE** Me?
Will I Ever Get **MARRIED**?
Is He **FAITHFUL**?
1-900-255-7636
$3.99 PER MINUTE
USE YOUR CREDIT CARD & SAVE 50¢ PER MINUTE
1-800-472-8769 $3.49 PER MIN.
10 MINUTES FREE!

your **Guardian ANGEL**
Knows • Protects • Guides
10 MINUTES FREE!
CALL NOW TO HEAR WHAT SHE NEEDS TO TELL YOU!
1-900-378-6277 $3.99 per min.
Use Your Credit Card & Save 50¢ Per Min.
1-800-781-7865 $3.49 per min.

SERVING YOU 24 HOURS A DAY!
Is it **TRUE LOVE**? OR IS YOUR LOVER USING YOU?
10 MIN FREE
Our PSYCHICS have ANSWERS to MARRIAGE & ROMANCE problems
1-900-378-6661 $3.99 PER MIN.
1-800-277-6661 $3.49 PER MIN.
USE YOUR CREDIT CARD & SAVE 50¢ PER MINUTE
Call NOW!

Discover the **HIDDEN SECRETS** in Your Life!
Gain insight into **HEALTH, LOVE and ROMANCE!**
20 MIN FREE
1-900-378-5959 $3.99 PER MIN.
1-800-478-6298 $3.49 PER MIN.
Use Your Credit Card & Save 50¢ Per Min.
AS SEEN ON TV
SUSAN BROWN Known as the respected "Dr. Gail Baldwin", Psychiatrist, Port Charles

6 MINUTES FREE
PAST LIFE READINGS
YOU MUST LEARN ABOUT THE PAST IN ORDER TO SAVE YOUR FUTURE
1-900-378-6161 $3.99 PER MIN.
Use Your Credit Card & Save 50¢ Per Minute
1-800-446-0798 $3.49 PER MIN.

PSYCHIC ANSWERS
Love • Health • Money
30 FREE MIN
1-900-378-5858 $3.99 PER MIN.
Use Your Credit Card & Save 50¢ Per Min.
1-800-781-7836 $3.49 PER MIN.

The **NEW MILLENNIUM**
ROMANCE LOVE MONEY
Call Now To Find Out What's In Your Future
1-900-255-7879 $3.99 Use Your Credit Card & Save 50¢ Per Min.
1-800-443-8169 $3.49 PER MIN.

DREAM INTERPRETATIONS
6 MIN FREE
1-900-378-6468 $3.99 PER MIN.
1-800-469-4864 $3.49 PER MIN.
Use Your Credit Card & Save 50¢ Per Min.

ASTROLOGY READINGS
1-800-430-2783 $3.49 PER MIN.

Get Your LUCKY NUMBERS
THE LOTTERY MASTER
Call NOW!
1-900-786-9933 $2.99 PER MIN.
Get RICH!
WIN THE LOTTERY

NOSTRADAMUS has FORECAST the FUTURE for more than **SIX CENTURIES!**
HIS PREDICTIONS CHANGED THE WORLD!
14 FREE MIN
1-900-378-6386 $3.99 PER MIN.
1-800-781-7896 $3.49 PER MIN.
Use Your Credit Card & Save 50¢ Per Min.

TAROT CARD READINGS
1-800-431-7529 $3.49 PER MIN.

Make The Most Important Call Of **YOUR LIFE!**
12 MIN FREE

ISABEL "WEEZY" SANFORD Star of "The Jeffersons"
AS SEEN ON TV
MASTER PSYCHIC READINGS
1-900-378-6225
$3.99 PER MINUTE
USE YOUR CREDIT CARD & SAVE 50¢ PER MIN.
1-800-988-6785 $3.49 PER MIN.

ANCIENT ACCURATE ANSWERS
from Authentic Psychics
LUCK - LOVE
20 MINUTES FREE
TRUE CHANGE
24 HRS LIVE! Incredible Readings
1-900-378-6262 $3.99 PER MIN.
1-800-781-7865 $3.49 PER MIN.
Use Your Credit Card & Save 50¢ Per Min.

PSYCHIC BELIEVERS NETWORK • BOCA RATON, FL • MUST BE 18 YEARS OR OLDER TO CALL • FOR ENTERTAINMENT ONLY.

MOTHER LOVE'S
Love Psychics

Nationally known Film and TV Star,
Author, and Talk Show Host

Is Love In Your Tarot?
Is Love In Your Stars?

Use Your **CHECK** or **CREDIT CARD** and
SAVE up to **TWO DOLLARS A MINUTE**

1-800-218-2442 OR CALL
1-900-773-1327 $3.99 PER MIN

AS SEEN ON TV

BARBARA NORCROSS
THE PALM BEACH PSYCHIC

Psychic Advisor to the Rich and Famous

SHE READ FOR ELVIS
PASO DEL NORTE HOTEL
El Paso Texas, June 3, 1976

Use Your **CHECK** or **CREDIT CARD** and
SAVE up to **TWO DOLLARS A MINUTE**

1-888-609-5111 OR CALL
1-900-680-2772 $3.99 PER MIN

AS SEEN ON TV

THE ZODIAC GROUP, INC. • BOCA RATON, FL • MUST BE 18 YEARS OR OLDER • FOR ENTERTAINMENT ONLY • US PAT. 5,802,156 • PATENTS PENDING

What Does Your Future Hold?

 **PSYCHIC SOURCE**
877-730-2335
WE KNOW

MC768   Toll Free Call   www.psychicsource.com

The Psychic Zone

The Ultimate LIVE 1 on ! Psychic Center
No Extra Charges - No Credit Cards - Instant Credit

011-683-2896
011-678-739-53

INT'L LD RATES APPLY

The Live Psychic Hotline

1-800-239-7685
1-800-813-4625

From $2.99/Min. Credit Cards/Checks 18+

America's #1 Psychic Service
Since 1989

CERTIFIED PSYCHIC®
American Association of Professional Psychics

Police detectives, movie stars, and government officials have consulted our psychics for years. Now it's <u>your</u> chance to speak with a genuine psychic who truly cares about you and your needs. Don't wait another moment. Call Now!

Gail Summer - Founder

American Association of Professional Psychics®
Registered with the U.S. Government. Guaranteed Authentic.

1-900-407-7065 — $3.99/min. Must be 18+
1-800-797-3343 — Save with VISA/MC $3.50/min

Private Appointments 410-750-0077   Checks by Phone Accepted

KENNY KINGSTON PSYCHIC HOTLINE

AS SEEN ON TV

THE MOST IMPORTANT PHONE CALL YOU'LL EVER MAKE

Kenny Kingston is the most sought after psychic in modern times. World famous celebrities and stars seek his guidance. Now you too can know what lies ahead. Take control of your own destiny. Talk to your own personal and confidential psychic today.

Stephanie Williams   *William Katt*   *Sharron Farrel*

Don't be afraid. Call now.

1-900-454-1829   7 days, 24 hours.
Only $3.99 per minute

Use your credit card and SAVE $1.00 per minute. Only $2.99 per minute

      1-800-498-5741

www.kennykingston.com

Must be 18 years or older • Gold Coast Media, (305) 576-1358
3050 Biscayne Blvd., Miami, FL 33137

THAN1829

RISK FREE
Emergency Readings!
Gifted Live Psychics!
Call 24 Hours!

011-678-739-62
Love specialist

1-900-255-0626
Money Specialist
First 2 Minutes FREE!

011-678-739-69
Master Specialist

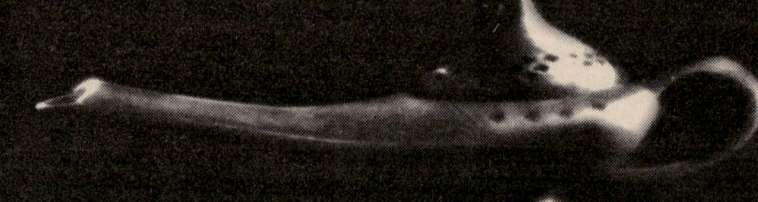

18+   011# Int'l rates   900# $3.99/min.